DEAD WOMEN TALKING

Dead Women Talking

Figures of Injustice in American Literature

BRIAN NORMAN

The Johns Hopkins University Press
Baltimore

Printed in the United States of America on acid-free paper
9 8 7 6 5 4 3 2 1

The Johns Hopkins University Press
2715 North Charles Street
Baltimore, Maryland 21218-4363
www.press.jhu.edu

Library of Congress Cataloging-in-Publication Data

Norman, Brian, 1977–
Dead women talking : figures of injustice in American literature / Brian Norman.
p. cm.
Includes bibliographical references and index.
ISBN 978-1-4214-0752-4 (hdbk. : acid-free paper) — ISBN 978-1-4214-0799-9 (electronic) — ISBN 1-4214-0752-3 (hdbk. : acid-free paper) — ISBN 1-4214-0799-X (electronic)
1. American fiction—History and criticism. 2. Women in literature. 3. Dead in literature. I. Title.
PS374.W6N67 2013
813.009′9287—dc23 2012012926

A catalog record for this book is available from the British Library.

Special discounts are available for bulk purchases of this book. For more information, please contact Special Sales at 410-516-6936 or specialsales@press.jhu.edu.

The Johns Hopkins University Press uses environmentally friendly book materials, including recycled text paper that is composed of at least 30 percent post-consumer waste, whenever possible.

CONTENTS

ACKNOWLEDGMENTS

I loved writing this book. To be sure, the labor was difficult and occasionally drudging. Still, the conversations it allowed—among colleagues and students, as well as with the texts themselves—reminded me what it means to devote one's life to literature and to the kinds of questions it allows us to ask of ourselves and the world. Some of the dead women talking in American literature do so only reluctantly. I am grateful to those colleagues who didn't follow suit and obliged me in discussions ranging from why the dead have class, whether we have the legal right to dictate what happens to our corpses, and why posthumous sex scenes are so darned weird.

As I presented various portions of the manuscript over the years at various conferences and universities, scholars and students provided the twin gifts of curiosity and skepticism. I am especially grateful to Lisa Marcus for bringing me to Pacific Lutheran University to speak about the project in its infancy; then, as the project neared its launch into the world, Robert Levine invited me to speak in his Americanist lecture series at the University of Maryland. I also received generous feedback from colleagues at my home institution of Loyola University Maryland, especially my department members and those colleagues participating in the humanities symposium run by Andrea Thomas. Conversations with Lia Purpura, Elizabeth Kennedy, Nandini Pandey, and Kaye Whitehead were also revelatory. I received crucial material support from Loyola, including a sabbatical, summer research funds, and funds for a research assistant in the form of Andrew Zaleski, a promising mind in his own right. In particular, I thank the Center for the Humanities and James Miracky, Dean of the Loyola College of Arts and Sciences.

I continue to profit from the guidance and support of so many colleagues in the field whose stirring intellects are matched by their remarkable generosity, chief among them Marianne DeKoven, and also Elizabeth Abel, Hillary Chute, Erin Goss, Joycelyn Moody, Channette Romero, Alex Socarides, Zoe Trodd, and Cheryl Wall. Leonard Cassuto delivered unfailingly spot-on advice regarding the full manuscript—I couldn't have asked for a more thoughtful and canny reader. I am so grateful to Matt McAdam at the Johns Hopkins University Press for the enthusiasm he brought to the project, as well as the whole crew at the press for their support and professionalism throughout the process, and also Jeremy D. Horsefield for his astute copyediting. I am also grateful to Gina Barreca at *Literature Interpretation Theory* for publishing a version of the chapter on Randall Kenan.

This project was cultivated in the laboratory of the humanities: the classroom. Students at Loyola University Maryland were critical to the early formation of this project, and then again at its final stages. I discovered the material anew each time my students rolled up their sleeves for the hard work of figuring out what all these dead women are up to. Their dedication and intellectual curiosity inspire hope for the humanities in the twenty-first century.

As always, I reserve the final word for my partner, Greg Nicholl, who always pushes me to think bigger. And better.

DEAD WOMEN TALKING

INTRODUCTION

Recognizing the Dead

As a general rule, dead women are rather quiet. The same goes for dead men. But in American literature, the dead talk more often than we might expect—especially women. They appear in works by such classic American writers as Edgar Allan Poe, Emily Dickinson, Henry James, and William Faulkner, as well as in more recent work by Toni Morrison, Tony Kushner, and Alice Walker, among many others. Now, it is almost old hat when dead women talk in contemporary literature and popular culture, from Alice Sebold's best-selling novel *The Lovely Bones* to the hit television dramas *Desperate Housewives* and *Drop Dead Diva*. What are we to make of all these women?

Collectively, these dead women, at least the more literary ones, constitute a tradition in which writers address pressing social issues that refuse to stay dead. When they talk, they speak not only to their own lives but also to matters of justice, history, and dearly held national ideals—whether the community welcomes it or not. Thus, writers stage encounters with that which should be past but has not passed. For instance, an American narrator encounters atrophied lines of aristocratic privilege in Poe's 1839 tale "The Fall of the House of Usher." Or, in Morrison's 1987 novel *Beloved*, a mother confronts slavery's legacy a generation after its demise. And in Kushner's *Angels in America*, Ethel Rosenberg sits at the deathbed of Roy Cohn in Reagan-era America, taunting the man who orchestrated her notorious McCarthy-era execution.

Dead women tend to talk in American literature when their experiences of death can address an issue of injustice that their communities might prematurely consign to the past. When declarations of injustice's end do not coincide with the achievement of actual justice, the resulting gaps create spaces from which these women speak. In a meditation on death and subjectivity, theorist Colin Davis asks, "Can the Dead Speak to Us?" He suggests that we are more likely to hear our own words imposed on the dead, though their traces may be found in moments of surprise, that which we can't anticipate.[1] Inside literary worlds, though, dead women need not wait for a discerning listener attentive to the indirect and unexpected, nor must they accept the passivity their deceased status entails. They can speak for themselves. In doing so, they raise questions about gender and voice, sexual violence and nonnormative sexuality, class privilege and cross-class contact, reparations for past racial injustices, and the immigrant's fraught relationship with national identity, among other pressing concerns.

Of all the examples of dead women talking in American literature, Beloved stands as the prototypical example. Long after Sethe, an escaped slave, commits the horrific act of infanticide to spare her daughter from life as chattel, Beloved returns full-grown and with an insatiable hunger. The murdered girl-child is neither mere corpse nor figure of speech. Denver, Beloved's surviving sister, describes her as a "greedy ghost,"[2] but that category, too, is insufficient. Paul D asks, "You think she sure 'nough your sister?" Denver responds, "At times. At times I think she was—more" (314). Beloved's power derives in part from her inability to be categorized. So too, her fellow dead women talking arise as unfamiliar, strange figures, often disrupting an otherwise realist mode underpinning the story. They resemble such familiar figures as ghosts, zombies, spirits, revenants, vampires, mediums, mythical figures, and even corpses, but they are more. The horror of *Beloved* is not only that the dead woman has a body and talks but that she seeks membership in and recognition by a living, present community. She is not sequestered in dead spaces such as a tomb or even the slave ship's hull. Nor is she an abstract allegory of the past or synecdoche of black suffering in general. She is not content to stay in the realm of the dead, to speak from her tombstone as in Edgar Lee Masters's popular 1915 sequence of epitaph poems in *Spoon River Anthology*, or to relive past experience as a dead watcher as in Thornton Wilder's 1938 play *Our Town*. Rather, as I will argue in chapter five, Beloved inserts herself into the community in search of something else: citizenship.

The appeal for a posthumous form of citizenship may seem more pedestrian than that of, say, a vampire in search of blood, but such a request requires that the community reconceive itself to endow such recognition. What these women seek turns out to be the inverse of what Russ Castronovo calls *necro citizenship*. "The U.S. democratic state loves its citizens as passive subjects," he argues, "unresponsive to political issues, unmoved by social stimuli, and unaroused by enduring injustices."[3] He points to Hester Prynne in Nathaniel Hawthorne's 1850 classic *The Scarlet Letter* as a sort of "walking corpse" who inhabits the public sphere of a community without its attendant rights and recognitions.[4] Castronovo is extending the concept of civil death and following such influential work as Orlando Patterson on "social death," which describes those living bodies, such as slaves, who are not enlivened by the rights doled out by the state.[5] Beloved, however, is no metaphorical corpse—she is in fact dead. Further and more importantly, what is so inexcusable to the community is that Beloved, like her counterparts, demands active participation in a community that might prefer her absence, silence, or acquiescence. As Ella explains in Morrison's novel, "But if it took flesh and came in her world, well, the shoe was on the other foot. She didn't mind a little communication between the two worlds, but this was an invasion" (302).

Generally, within modern doctrines of natural rights, to be recognized as a formal member of a political community—that is, citizenship—one must have a body. We see this in contemporary debates about legal rights of the unborn, as well as in long and varied histories of parceling citizenship rights based on the race, gender, and so forth assigned to different bodies.[6] Whether we are speaking of membership in a national community or more local forms of community, the body is the entry ticket. The bodies of dead women who talk must be recognized as one of the community's own, a fictional corollary to the legal exercise of identifying a body at the morgue. Further, their bodies are often uncanny and bear marks of past struggles and social anxieties. In *Beloved*, for instance, the community around 124 Bluestone Road encounters the strangely adult body bearing a familiar scar across her neck. Beyond that iconic example, we encounter a body allergic to the stench of the living in a novel by Ana Castillo, a young boy's body housing a woman's knowledge in a story by Randall Kenan, and a wailing and bloodied body shrouded in white in Poe's tale. On the other hand, even before Addie Bundren dies in Faulkner's *As I Lay Dying*, her bones are a desiccated bundle of sticks. Addie is a corpse long before the moment of her death, not to mention her posthumous monologue. In fact, as many have noted, Addie's corpse is much more active than she herself was in life.

Can, will, or should a community recognize such dead women's bids for citizenship? Many of these dead women are not terribly pleasant. Beloved is greedy and perhaps grotesque in her strange plumpness, not to mention her disturbing refrain, "I am Beloved and she is mine" (243, 248). She is in good company: Madeline Usher is off-putting with her pallid body and incoherent wail; Addie Bundren reveals a surprising depth of bitterness and sadism in her posthumous chapter; in Suzan-Lori Parks's 2003 revision of Faulkner, *Getting Mother's Body*, Willa Mae Beede really is as trashy as they say underneath her pluck and charm; one of Castillo's dead women in the 1993 novel *So Far from God* is unrepentantly misanthropic; and Sebold's adolescent protagonist is, well, adolescent. Further, some dead women are downright gossipy and mean-spirited, as we see in Kenan's and Kushner's works. But surely recognition by a community should not depend on being pleasant.

Recognizing the dead comes with its risks and rewards, for in doing so communities may become—reluctantly or not—akin to what Joseph Roach calls "cities of the dead." "Cities of the dead," Roach explains in his landmark study of death rituals in the Atlantic world, "are primarily for the living. They exist not only as artifacts, such as cemeteries and commemorative landmarks, but also as behaviors. They endure, in other words, as occasions for memory and invention."[7] For Roach, this is largely a welcome prospect: he looks to performances and sites of memory to counteract the forgetting central to modern power, especially colonial whiteness. In the American literary tradition of dead women talking, such women demand much more than commemoration on the part of the living. The invention they demand is what they were denied in life: social justice. But if we confer citizenship upon the dead, their narratives ask, might we risk becoming necro citizens ourselves, mere denizens of a present hamstrung by the past?

Dead women such as Beloved constitute a curious, uncanny kind of potential citizen. Paul D says, "She reminds me of something. Something, look like, I'm supposed to remember" (276). These women are "something," but they are also inexplicable. To describe Beloved as merely a ghost is to dismiss her. As Anne Cubilié argues about survivors who testify about atrocities, "To name a woman a 'ghost' . . . not only removes her (again) from the human but privileges her speech as that which comes from the realm of the dead or the uncanny."[8] While the women in this book may in fact be both dead and uncanny, they refuse such designation and demand a presence in their living communities. The larger narratives tend to acknowledge the uncanny or fantastical nature of these talking dead women, while also making room for them, insisting on their place in a realist world. A good example is the frame tale for James's novella *The Turn of the Screw*, which explicitly distinguishes its dead from the stuff of generic ghost stories and folk legends. Therefore, I am being as precise as possible in describing these figures as dead women talking. That is how these narratives understand them. It is odd that they are dead. It is sometimes odd that they are women. And it is definitely odd that they are talking. Making sense of them entails making sense of the systems of injustice that gave rise to each bewildering figure in the first place.

Of Ghosts, Corpses, and Their Kin

Scholars have mostly approached this topic from two angles: the corpse and the ghost. When scholars focus on the corpse, this can lead to more abstract questions about death and its representation, or what classicists call *ars moriendi*.[9] Or, as Elisabeth Bronfen illustrates in her study of dead women in Western art and literature, when scholars approach the female corpse, psychoanalysis and deconstruction have been the go-to theoretical apparatuses because they get at the intertwined structures of social power and symbolic representation. Scholars have also done terrific cultural studies of the corpse, be it real or symbolic, such as Karla FC Holloway's compelling study of the African American funeral business[10] and Michael Kammen's social history of notable reburials in America.[11]

Yet what happens when the dead become or remain animate, no longer inert, if exquisite, corpses? This often leads to the second approach: ghosts and their kin (revenants, vampires, and so on). Ghosts are plentiful in American and British literature, especially in women's writing of the late nineteenth and early twentieth centuries, when the ghost story enjoyed a resurgence, led especially by such writers as Edith Wharton, Mary Wilkins Freeman, Sarah Orne Jewett, and Elizabeth Stuart Phelps.[12] Gothic literature scholar Kathy Justice Gentile sees such ghost stories as "supernatural commentaries on gendered fin de siècle anxieties."[13] Ghost stories have long helped a nation work through all manner of anxieties about identitarian ties, be they welcome or repressed, acknowledged or buried. Literary critic Kathleen Brogan explains that the ghost story was subsequently reinvented by the modernists, who were inspired by Freudian-era psychology and its vision of an internally haunted self. Then, she argues, ghost stories became prominent in twentieth-century American ethnic literatures because they enact how shared histories are recalled and reshaped in the present. In such stories of "cultural haunting," ghosts are a trope for "acculturation and cultural transmission in a polyethnic society" so that "the bloodline family ghosts of different ethnic groups belong in fact to the same cross-cultural genre."[14]

Ghosts and corpses have proved good fodder for theories of justice, power, and inequality. Sociologist Avery Gordon argues that haunting is one of the ways that systems of oppression and exploitation make themselves known in everyday life.[15] So too, feminist and queer theorist Sharon Patricia Holland argues that literary encounters with the dead equip us to listen to the silenced and bring voice to the voiceless.[16] Such cultural studies fit well within studies of death and biopower, such as Vincent Brown's persuasive account of the "mortuary politics" of black Atlantic slavery cultures[17] and Achille Mbembé's theory of "necropolitics" and the creation of "death-worlds" among the living.[18] Such thinking has a long pedigree in critical theory, from Hegel to Foucault to Agamben. In "On the Theory of Ghosts," a draft note for *Dialectic of Enlightenment*, Max Horkheimer and Theodor Adorno argue that ghosts are more than a return of the hated, the primitive, or the repressed in the individual psyche, as in Freudian thinking. Such figures, they suggest, signal how humans have become detached from history, including through modern practices of funeral rituals and beautified corpses. "Only conscious horror of destruction," they argue, "creates the correct relationship with the dead: unity with them because we, like them, are the victims of the same conditions and the same disappointed hope."[19]

But what about when ghosts cease to be the ethereal stuff of spooks or mute cadavers and become something else—embodied, talking, and wanting more? They are closer to what feminist literary theorist Diana Fuss deems "speaking cadavers," Claire Raymond calls "posthumous voices," Mary Worthington calls "posthumous postures," Janice McLarren Caldwell calls "animated cadavers," and Lisa Perdigao and Mark Pizzato call "reanimated dead."[20] Some see the potential for agency in such women,[21] though a rush to celebrate them may overlook the troublesome fine print that death is prerequisite to achieving voice or agency. Fuss asks, "Why, and when, is a dead voice more appropriate than a live one? What does speaking through the fictional persona of a cadaver allow poets to achieve that writing in their own living voices apparently prohibits?"[22] Fuss's inquiry leads to elegies and poetic acts of apostrophe and prosopopoeia, when speakers throw their voices into the wind, personify the dead, or take on the voice of a corpse, which she finds particularly prominent in nineteenth-century lyric poetry.[23] This book builds on such work as it aims for a more comprehensive account of what happens when corpses speak for themselves in American literature, especially in more recent fiction. Fuss locates most of her voices in the tomb, while Raymond considers disembodied posthumous voices. The latter are especially close kin to ghosts and an end-run around a key mode of feminine subjection, what Worthington calls "the problem of the body."[24] In these cases, the body is a prop or an impediment. The women in my study, on the other hand, typically inhabit very real, often conspicuous bodies as they seek entrance into living communities. When such women talk, they tap into not only aesthetic and psychological ideas about uncannily beautiful female death and poetic techniques for representing dead speakers, but also concerns about political ventriloquism, inactive citizenship, posthumous legal rights, and racial blood memory.

I cover a lot of ground as I track this curiously pervasive and recurring figure in American literature. The tradition crosses eras, identities, genres, sensibilities, and movements, from the nineteenth-century gothic tale to modernist experimentation to the postmodern sublime. Too much ground, some may object. Still, I could go even further and place these talking dead in a much longer line back to mythic figures of antiquity. In that vein, one is more likely to find a posthumous voice that is not her own, without body, or somehow removed from the community of the living. For instance, prosopopoeia, a device from classical Greek rhetoric and popular among the romantic poets, can locate a voice in a corpse, but ultimately it is an act of ventriloquism: the corpse is a mask or a persona for the speaker. Or we may encounter pure voice, as in the case of Ovid's Echo, whose body, rejected by Narcissus, withers away until all that remains is a lone voice, condemned to be a mere reverberation of another's. Sometimes we encounter such women beyond the world of the living in heaven or the underworld, as in the case of H.D.'s "Eurydice," a 1916 persona poem in the voice of the mythical woman left behind in Hades by Orpheus. The best classical forebear may be Euripides's Alcestis when she goes to Hades in place of her husband, who in turn promises to not replace her. When Heracles confronts Death in order to restore Alcestis to her husband, the returned wife is initially veiled and silent, unrecognizable and unable—at least initially—to resume her place among the living. While this classical dead woman eventually talks and tentatively rejoins the community, the dead women in this project are less hesitant, and often insistent. Sometimes they are downright bold as they return with both body and voice to claim citizenship among the living. Antigone is another classical precursor because, while not dead herself, she seeks an ethical space outside her community and Creon's legal regime to honor the dead.[25] The dead women in this study, in contrast, seek a place *within* their communities and often the legal apparatus itself.

I could also trace these talking dead to classical elegiac traditions in Virgil and others, or iconic dead men in the Western tradition, such as the ghost of Hamlet's father, Dr. Frankenstein's monster, Lazarus resurrected, or even Jesus Christ after crucifixion. Or I could move outside Western traditions, perhaps to *vodun* concepts of the undead, which would lead in turn to African-derived tropes. Or I could place these women among more contemporary vampires and ghosts, the stuff of *Dracula* knockoffs, Scooby-Doo mysteries, or the *Twilight* phenomenon. Indeed, modern readers are well equipped to make sense of Anne Rice's vampires or Angela Carter's feminist reinventions of fairy tale characters, Catherine's ghost in *Wuthering Heights* in British gothic fiction, or, as an interesting limit case, the ghost-women at the end of Toni Morrison's 1998 novel *Paradise*. These female vampires or ghosts are not dead women talking per se; they are, ultimately, female vampires or ghosts. While many of these examples are interesting reinventions of familiar categories, as akin to the black Frankenstein metaphor that Elizabeth Young traces in American literature,[26] such animated dead are nonetheless recognizable, even expected, by those readers well versed in convention.

A key question remains: why women? Several of the examples I note above are men, most notably *Hamlet*'s ghost and Jesus Christ. And we can find many more in the period covered by this study, from Poe's 1838 novel *Arthur Gordon Pym*, in which the titular character escapes a mutiny by masquerading as a recently dead man, to Joe Gillis narrating his life and eventual murder in Billy Wilder's 1950 film noir *Sunset Boulevard*, to Jim Grimsley's contemporary gay coming-of-age novel *Dream Boy* featuring a possibly haunted plantation house. In fact, there are talking dead men in two of the works featured in this study, Kenan's *Let the Dead Bury Their Dead* and Kushner's *Angels in America*. Still, talking dead women maintain prominence in American literature. Even within the Kenan and Kushner examples, the dead women have a distinct status, in both narrative function and social justice concerns. In part, the question of gender points us to the oft-noted and long-studied cultural association between femininity and death. In a special issue of *Studies in the Novel* on "Death in the Novel," Diana York Blaine notes how "death and the feminine are nearly always aligned,"[27] which prompts questions about women's agency in addition to formal questions about how to narrate the unnarratable. Carolyn Dever goes one step further to observe that death and mothers in particular are intertwined.[28] Dead women have long been the subject of distinct artistic fascination, so much so that Bronfen finds that the female corpse is a long-standing object of wonder and dread in Western culture, an object to behold as its morbid beauty veers into the sublime.[29] From this backdrop, dead women come to be associated with both silence and collective histories of injustice, which is why not only their dead status but also their speech is so powerful. It is no coincidence that the two examples furthest from speech and self-awareness—Madeline Usher and James's governess—are also furthest from the social justice concerns that become central to the literary tradition as it develops.

With all these precursors and corollaries in mind, I trace a distinct American literary tradition concerned with questions of national belonging. These dead women talking in American literature do not fit—and often explicitly resist—familiar tropes of gothic, horror, and mythic modes. In the end, they seek agency not as ghosts or other tropes readily accessible in the literary imagination but rather as citizens, which is ultimately more disturbing to the communities from whom they seek recognition.

Dead Housewives, a Buzzing Fly, and Lady Lazarus

Dead women now talk routinely in contemporary popular culture. In addition to Mary Alice Young, the dead narrator of the hit series *Desperate Housewives* (2004–2012), the talking dead appear all over prime-time television and premium cable. Prominent examples include *Six Feet Under*, a drama series about a family-run mortuary business that ran on HBO from 2001 to 2005 and that regularly featured talking cadavers in literally portrayed daydream sequences; *Pushing Daisies* (2008–2009), a short-lived but high-budget network comedy series in which a pie baker can bring the dead back to life, including his sidekick lover Charlotte "Chuck" Charles; and *Drop Dead Diva* (2009–present), a feel-good show on the Lifetime network about a shallow model who dies and comes back in the body of an overweight lawyer. Horror films, of course, have long featured reanimated dead. In *The Others*, a particularly artful example from 2001, the matriarch played by Nicole Kidman struggles to protect her children by ridding her British manor of ghosts only to find in the end that she is the ghost haunting another family. Beyond the horror genre, Hollywood has long provided milquetoast examples, such as the 1992 screwball comedy *Death Becomes Her* featuring Meryl Streep and Goldie Hawn trying desperately to retain their beauty as their corpses fall apart, literally. And one can't forget the 1987 romantic comedy *Mannequin* about a mall employee's romance with the eponymous mannequin played by Kim Cattrall, who turns out to be an ancient Egyptian woman who now helps the affable hero design attention-grabbing window displays.

There are, of course, plenty of examples of dead men talking, including in some of the above examples. In fact, they create some weird moments in American popular culture, such as Natalie Cole's posthumous duet with her father Nat King Cole for the hit song "Unforgettable," which she performed at the 1992 Grammy Awards accompanied by film of her father projected on a giant screen. In a strange reprisal, Janet Jackson danced with her recently deceased brother Michael at the 2009 MTV Video Music Awards. Likewise, Elton John teamed up with a deceased Humphrey Bogart, James Cagney, and Louis Armstrong to peddle Diet Coke in a 1991 commercial. Soon advertisers used technology to exhume departed celebrities to hock all sorts of wares, such as John Wayne in a 1996 Coors beer advertisement and Fred Astaire's bizarre posthumous endorsement of Dirt Devil in 1997. Perhaps the most uncanny example is Nike's 2010 "ghost dad" commercial featuring the voice of the deceased father of Tiger Woods scolding his son in the wake of a highly public sex scandal. As the black-and-white camera pans in, the adult son looks straight into the lens and we become the disappointed father reprimanding the philandering son while, Nike hopes, also implicitly forgiving him. Yet we are of course *not* the father of Tiger Woods. Therefore, we also feel uneasy overhearing this private moment, an unease that becomes doubly uncanny given the way Nike employs a dead man as the voice of a nation's moral authority.

Such posthumous product testimonials prompt discussions, not to mention legal quandaries, about the rights of the dead,[30] especially when the gigs seem out of step with or beneath rightful legacies. The fictional examples, on the other hand, play with gendered scripts as the dead women interrupt otherwise conventional genres such as heterosexual romances. They may nudge living communities to diagnose their own social ills, be it the stultifying boredom of a shiny suburban existence in *Desperate Housewives* or, if we push it, the ahistorical and inhuman plasticity of 1980s consumer culture in *Mannequin*. Of course, these examples rarely venture into even the shallow end of justice issues. And it is probably not fair to expect as much from popular culture enterprises. Nonetheless, in disrupting otherwise normative scripts—however mildly or meekly—they join a long line of literary sisters whose narratives more often than not *do* plunge into the deep end of justice concerns.

With that in mind, I turn to two of the more noted users of posthumous voice in American poetry: Dickinson and Plath. Admittedly, this is a familiar pairing in scholarship on women writers, one that nonetheless provides a good entrance into my pursuits. Dickinson's dead speakers don't tend to raise justice concerns directly, focusing instead on more metaphysical questions. Still, they make room for such possibilities by linking female speech and death. In one of Dickinson's more famous poems, "I heard a Fly buzz" (591),[31] a speaker narrates the moment following her own death:

> I heard a Fly buzz—when I died—
> The Stillness in the Room
> Was like the Stillness in the Air—
> Between the Heaves of Storm—

At this transitory moment of death, the speaker becomes active. She is the subject in a short, declarative clause, "I heard a Fly buzz," which is linked synchronously with an equally concise subordinate clause, "when I died." The poem emerges out of silence, which is metonymically linked with that which is living, that which is before. Sensation and speech become possible in the liminal moment "when I died." The first line houses the simultaneous event of her death and perception, in this case hearing a fly buzz. In death, the speaker attains hypersensitivity, able to hear and appreciate not only a fly buzz but also absence. She stands ready to document the moment of salvation in the future, "when the King / be witnessed—in the Room." Her agency lies in contradistinction to the surrounding stillness, which emanates all the way into the cosmos.

In Dickinson's poem, the moment of death and voice are inextricably linked. In death, the speaker attains powerful agency, both legally binding and spiritually adept, so that "I willed my Keepsakes—Signed away / What portions of me be / Assignable." "The King" may hold an enduring religious and communal power, but in this ephemeral moment all agency and certitude belong to the speaker, juxtaposed to the fly's "uncertain stumbling Buzz." As the measly insect becomes the focal point of a scenario typically rife with inflated imagery and divine revelation, Dickinson gently lampoons poetic conventions of the deathbed while maintaining a serious aim: imagining posthumous speech and the possibilities it affords. In this treatment of death arises what literary critic Alexandra Socarides terms Dickinson's "poetics of interruption."[32] The signature dashes, disjointed syntax, and bedeviling capitalization, along with the notorious variations in Dickinson's fascicles, create an exhilarating feeling of excess, newness, and posthumous ability to defy convention, even within otherwise elegiac terrain.

The very idea of a posthumous speaker is odd because, as Blaine notes, death is an inherently indescribable experience. Those who experience it by definition cannot be around to narrate it. Further, if death is necessarily a secondhand account, Sarah Webster Goodwin and Elisabeth Bronfen argue, "every representation of death is a misrepresentation."[33] The trope of a dead speaker attempts to solve this paradox. In a corpse's self-representation lies power—at least within the realm of the poem. As such, Claire Raymond places Dickinson in a tradition of "feminine self-elegies" that break a paternal line because a speaking female corpse is no longer available as "an object to be mourned." As a result, Raymond argues, "the trope of a disembodied posthumous feminine voice reveals the blind spot of the paternal metaphor's alliance of woman and death, of femininity and silence."[34] Fuss, on the other hand, deals with the leftover body and tends to find speaking cadavers in tombs. Dickinson's poem fits neither approach: the speaker resides where she dies, in the same kind of room from which Dickinson herself often perched. Helen Vendler suggests that the poem does not move chronologically, so that after the announcement of the speaker's death in the opening line, the poem enacts the death throes of the soon-to-be corpse in the kinesthetic "Heaves of Storm—." In the end, she argues, "the voice is speaking posthumously, positioned nowhere."[35] Nonetheless, the scene of utterance is the speaker's room, neither a tomb nor a disembodied cosmos. It may be a private or domestic space, but it is still in the geography of the living.

The Dickinson poem, not to mention all the popular culture examples, may seem a curious place to begin a book on a literary tradition that stages confrontations with the past for social justice aims. Nonetheless, Dickinson's posthumous speaker is something of a prototype for later dead women who will take the opportunity to speak more directly to unjust systems hemming them in or leading to their deaths. Some will go so far as to demand justice, whether posthumously for themselves or for those who remain living. What they perceive and utter upon their deaths is not incidental, unlike a (seemingly) trivial buzzing fly. So too, their posthumous appearances will resonate with feelings of injustice, from Madeline Usher's bloodied and torn fingers from having clawed out of her tomb, to the suffocating smells and cramped quarters from which Beloved emerges, reminiscent of the Middle Passage.

And yet, perhaps the stillness that greets Dickinson's speaker *does* resonate with justice concerns. Raymond argues that women writers are often drawn to death because it offers a liberating disembodiment, or "homelessness," within a culture that treats women's living bodies as tombs, spaces of stasis.[36] Dickinson's speaker is removed from the social world, entombed in a stillness broken only by the event of her death and her corollary coming into voice. The legal discourse with which she parses her life points to a breach, as subtle as it is powerful. As the speaker "Signed away / What portions of me be / Assignable," she exercises legal power in the domain of the living and, by nineteenth-century custom, the male.

There is a catch: the power afforded by posthumous speech entails a loss of individual identity because to will "Keepsakes" is to forsake that which is private, personal. The speaker passes on her worldly specificity as she passes on to a more permanent death—silence. The act of willing brings her closer to the end of the poem when she will no longer exhibit the power of perception or speech: "And then the Windows failed—and then / I could not see to see—." Bronfen and Goodwin note that "the possibility of misreading the body as corpse is a nightmare fantasy,"[37] as typified in the recurring fear of being buried alive. Dickinson's talking dead woman tiptoes that line between life and death, but her utterances need not be terrifying. When there is no longer an "I" to speak and see, there is no more poem. Therefore, to read the poem is to testify to the agency afforded by the speaker's death, the willfulness the event grants her, even if temporarily. Further, the buzzing fly is a conspicuously genderless intermediary between the speaker and the hypergendered figure of "The King."

The legacy of Dickinson's death-speaking "I" comes to fruition nearly a century later when dead women talking begin to cohere into a literary tradition. We can see this in Plath's poetry, well known for its artful death poses and necrophilic sensibilities, as well as its resonance with the feminist movement of the time. The best example is the 1965 poem "Lady Lazarus," in which the speaker chronicles her life's work of spectacle suicide, only to return for another go of it so that "one year in every ten / I manage it—." As a figure of resurrection, she is

A sort of walking miracle, my skin
Bright as a Nazi lampshade,
My right foot
A paperweight,
My face a featureless, fine
Jew linen.

Like in her signature poem "Daddy" from the same period, Plath draws on the ultimate twentieth-century images of powerlessness: Nazi concentration camps and the mass extermination of Jewish bodies. Though critics debate whether Plath earns such metaphors, within the poem it is clear that the speaker finds kinship in, perhaps even embraces, the silent Jewish corpse as it becomes art object and commodity—a human-skin lampshade, a paperweight, and all manner of grotesque fiber art. So too, the speaking "I" makes art out of her own suicides, as well as the conspicuous body that enables her act.

Plath attempts to wrest empowerment from abjection. Her speaker does not wait for death, for Dickinson's buzzing Fly to greet her. Instead, she takes control of her own mortal body and captivates "you" who join the "peanut-crunching crowd" ogling her "big strip tease." As we become members of a carnival audience, she becomes a living and speaking corpse performing for her public:

Peel off the napkin
O my enemy.
Do I terrify?—
. . . Soon, soon the flesh
The grave cave ate will be
At home on me.

The grave is typically an endpoint of death rituals. As a final resting place, it is out of the community's sight and far from the hearth in the twentieth century. A funeral may be related in kind to a public event such as a carnival, but "Lady Lazarus" describes an inverse affair. The people do not travel to the grave site; rather, she brings the grave to them. She meets her audience on uncanny terrain where the womb and the tomb intermingle. After all, as Freud postulates, the earthly womb is the familiar home to which everyone eventually returns, as the homely and the unhomely converge.[38] Plath's talking and ever-returning dead woman is unsettling as her dead flesh becomes both as disposable and removable as a napkin and as familiar and enduring as home. Her death ritual terrifies and thrills, rather than comforts and nurtures. Her uncanny body is central to her power over the audience; she is not a mere disembodied voice haunting the living.

As a dead woman talking, Plath's speaker taunts and titillates her public, acting as her own carnival barker. Plath protests the fate of women held up as objects to behold, not intellects to heed. In this way, she seeks to escape a culture that renders women's bodies things, powerless and vulnerable. The poem ends,

> Ash, ash—
> You poke and stir.
> Flesh, bone, there is nothing there—
> . . . Out of the ash
> I rise with my red hair
> And I eat men like air.

While these final lines add a layer to her Holocaust imagery, Plath also draws on mythic tropes of feminine violence and empowerment, from the phoenix rising from its own ashes to Medusa and her gorgon terror.[39] In the ghastly smokestacks and the destruction of the body lies the speaker's retribution and ascension into another kind of body, the oxygen-seeking flame as hungry as it is powerful—a power fueled by the hunger itself.

Bronfen and Goodwin write, "To give a voice to the corpse, to represent the body, is in a sense to return it to life; the voice represents not so much the dead as the once living, juxtaposed with the needs of the as yet living."[40] Plath's speaker and her fellow dead women talking literalize what it means to give voice to a corpse. The suicidal, death-seeking speaker is a particularly powerful version because she maintains posthumous ownership of her body, as well as her voice. Bronfen and Goodwin argue, "Just as woman *is* the body, she is also the body's caretaker, the nurse, the layer-out of the corpse."[41] Plath's necrophilic speaker, however, refuses the roles doled out to her body. She embraces her ability to disturb in the way her contaminated body does not seek purification through social customs such as funerals. Instead, she ritualizes her own death, daring the living community to participate.

Across the ensuing eleven chapters, each centered on an exemplary text, I focus on dead women who, like in the Dickinson and Plath examples, speak for themselves. Thus, I join scholars who in some way praise such women's "art of being dead," to use Diana Fuss's phrase. Fuss notes that the poems in which dead women speak "often resemble epitaphs" so that their "speech survives the finitude of writing" or rejects the silent body that "simply disappears, completely buried under layers of cultural indifference."[42] She finds that "corpse poems" take a social turn in the twentieth century in two ways: "the first group humbles those corpses that have been culturally canonized, while the second group elevates those corpses that have been culturally debased," both of which "aim to correct a social injustice."[43] So too, I consider posthumous vocal acts that speak in the register of the social more so than the personal or the abstract. In addition, I focus on the failures and successes of living communities to recognize the dead and their strange appeals for justice. To do so, I turn to the realm of narrative, which further puts the voices of dead women in the context of their communities. Cultural theorist Laura Tanner has noticed the tendency to bring the dead back to life in contemporary popular culture but worries that animating corpses in the fictional realm merely replaces material bodies with symbolic representation.[44] The dead women in my study, however, insist upon the materiality of their bodies and their role as active citizens. Are their communities ready, they ask, to recognize them as such?

The Emergence of a Tradition

This book surveys the evolution of dead women talking into a full-fledged American literary tradition by the later twentieth century. Their forebears begin to emerge in the nineteenth century in crevices between realist and romantic or gothic modes. In these fissures, the ordinary and the super-ordinary meet, often in collisions so that characters themselves are unsure of the rules of their newly shaken worlds. This provokes crises of belief and cognizance, which in turn create fertile terrain for social change, whether welcome or not. By the early twentieth century, Alan Friedman finds, "posthumous existence, and mock versions of it, became a leitmotif of modernist writing: numerous protagonists die early, and then get on, more or less badly, with their lives."[45] Lisa Perdigao extends this arc to identify a shift from entombment to exhumation in the progression to postmodern literature,[46] though my study demonstrates that dead women have been talking in American literature well before it was fashionable in a postmodern moment. By the later twentieth century, the trope is almost commonplace, prone to intertextual play, and the dead women are able to interact in the story as much as any other character, living or dead. These women become more and more central to postmodern and contemporary American literature's toolkit for accessing the past, and also for creating new futures. Even though dead women can now talk without their literary worlds being turned upside down, their appearances and utterances still hold the power to create crises of community, namely, whether and how to make room in the living community for the dead, and the knowledge they bring from another world. These women speak the unspeakable and help us to imagine the heretofore unimaginable.

My method throughout the book is primarily text driven—I take my cues from the literature itself. In terms of scholarly apparatus, I engage debates on death and citizenship in American literature and culture. I turn to contexts and theoretical frames as the literary example warrants. For instance, I consult legal theorists on posthumous rights in tort law to address the question of whether and why the dead have class status in my discussion of Henry James's *The Turn of the Screw*. Meanwhile, Sianne Ngai's affect theory and the self-help aisles help me get at the way Ethel Rosenberg is so brilliantly annoying in *Angels in America*, whereas genre criticism proves most useful to answer the question of whether a dead girl can be the protagonist of a coming-of-age novel in Sebold's *The Lovely Bones*. Or, to discuss Beloved's allure, I draw on literary critic Elaine Scarry's *On Beauty and Being Just*, legal theorist Martha Nussbaum's *From Disgust to Humanity*, and disability studies scholar Susan Schweik's *The Ugly Laws* to get at the question of which bodies are worthy of citizenship in Morrison's community. While my apparatus varies by chapter, my argument remains consistent: these dead women seek posthumous citizenship, which renders them neither ghosts nor corpses nor mere testaments to victimization. Rather, they are figures of potential justice—if the community welcomes them.

The first two chapters concern progenitors who slowly, hesitantly, and unsurely start to talk—or at least stand there or wail inarticulately. We see this most clearly in Poe's mid-nineteenth-century account of "The Fall of the House of Usher" and James's proto-modernist novella *The Turn of the Screw*. These tales each draw directly from the gothic trough and the ghost story. But Poe and James shuttle such elements into decidedly realist terrain, often explicitly distinguishing their accounts from the stuff of ghosts, vampires, and dark-and-stormy-nights. After all, as Freud explains, the uncanny is the stuff of realism, not magic and fairy tales, because in the realm of the fantastical one *expects* severed hands to move, wooden dolls to come to life, and the dead to talk. By rearranging realist worlds, we confront the buried or unexpected. In these instances, we encounter aristocratic privilege in a reputedly populist country in Poe's nationalist parable, or the unwelcome possibility of class ascent and ensuing cross-class friction in an American expatriate's novella set in a British country estate.

While Poe and James stage potentially fatal encounters with another's past, chapters three through five concern stories that return to pasts from which characters cannot fully break, even if they want to. For instance, in Faulkner's *As I Lay Dying* Addie Bundren seeks posthumous autonomy *away* from her immediate community. The novel chronicles the grotesque escapades of a rural family on a nine-day quest to lug their dead mother's body to Jefferson to bury her among her blood family. In the middle of the narrative, and long after Addie dies, she narrates a beautiful, revealing, and beguiling chapter. Where Addie locates her trauma is the biggest surprise: motherhood and the loss of her virginity, which violate her prized aloneness. While Addie wishes to leave her community, by the later twentieth century, the absence of dead women from the present community becomes a problem. In her famous 1975 essay "Looking for Zora," for example, Alice Walker locates and marks the grave of Zora Neale Hurston, thereby reviving a lost black woman writer's legacy for a new generation. Walker turns full-throated to social justice issues in another essay from around that same time, "Only Justice Can Stop a Curse," in which she inhabits the voice of an anonymous, long-dead woman delivering an ancient curse. Walker provides a model for how the living can respond to the dead: work for justice in the present to put an end to the suffering, violation, and degradation that is the legacy of these dead women. Walker's exhumation of history, including its devastating absences, sets the ground for Morrison's signature return in *Beloved* to America's most haunting past: what she thinks of as the graveyard of slavery, which is "formidable and pathless" (xvii). In the ensuing neo-slave narrative, Sethe, like Morrison's contemporary nation, can't break from this unthinkable past. The past, or what Morrison more suggestively calls *rememory*, is embodied in the bewitching and needy figure of Beloved, who eventually enters the community not as a ghost but as a strange body wanting citizenship in the present.

After Walker and Morrison, writers begin to employ necrophilic tropes of burial, graves, and desiring the dead in order to not only mend broken lines of genealogy but also create new models of kinship. The contemporary world must do right by its long-gone women of unjust pasts, as we see in Kushner's postmodern play *Angels in America*, in which Ethel Rosenberg sits at the deathbed of Roy Cohn, the McCarthy sidekick who orchestrated her execution. As Ethel taunts Roy and wonders if she can forgive him, she fits in among the angels who want to sue God for abandonment, a housewife on Valium who hangs out in Antarctica, the strangely animate mother in a Mormon diorama, and an AIDS patient who is an unwilling prophet. Kushner shows that if the living are to make room for the dead, they must learn how to listen to them. We see this also in *Let the Dead Bury Their Dead*, the 1992 short story cycle by black gay Southern writer Randall Kenan in which the dead are quite at home in the small North Carolina town of Tims Creek. Yet the history they bring with them—from catty gossip to higher-stakes stories of racial violence and treason—may not always be welcome in the pedestrian present. By bringing the fantastic into the realm of the real, Kenan and Kushner use talking dead women to construct genealogies that do not fall along cemented lines of blood, ideology, or identity—in other words, multicultural citizenship.

The final chapters also feature themes of burial, trauma, and returns to earlier eras, but for another end: healing. This can lead to large-scale critiques of injustice, such as in Ana Castillo's 1993 Chicana Catholic novel *So Far from God*, in which death is rarely a finite event, but rather a new state of being. In this world, which I deem *telenovela realism*, a character can be described as "is died" and remain an active, welcome member of the community. In the novel, each of four sisters suffers horribly, including not only early death but also rape, familial abandonment, political abduction, and radiation poisoning within a privatized military industrial complex. As such, their posthumous healing carries social justice implications on a global level. The challenge Castillo poses is how to create a viable alternative public able to recognize the lives, dignity, and voices of the disappeared. Alice Sebold's 2002 novel *The Lovely Bones*, on the other hand, imagines a different kind of healing. The narrator is Susie Salmon, a dead girl who is brutally raped and murdered before the story begins. While Sebold sets up the story within classic crime novel conventions, the dead narrator ultimately turns away from that genre's expectations of vengeance or nabbing the bad guy and opts instead for a coming-of-age novel. When Susie temporarily inhabits an acquaintance's body late in the narrative, she sleeps with her teenage crush to consummate her cut-short teen dreams. This may be, I argue, an unexpected form of justice, even if it seems childish or suburban. This teaches us not to impose a predetermined vision of social justice on any of these women.

By the twenty-first century, dead women talking constitute enough of a recognizable literary tradition that writers can consciously enter it and claim it as their own. The best example is acclaimed playwright Suzan-Lori Parks's 2003 novel *Getting Mother's Body*, which reinvents Faulkner's tale for one that features a civil rights–era rural black family seeking not to inter their dead matriarch, but rather to exhume her. Willa Mae Beede begins the story dead and, unlike her counterpart Addie Bundren, she talks throughout. In fact, she mostly sings the blues. Though Willa Mae dies traumatically from a self-induced abortion, her story allows the rest of the characters to find personal hope and redemption amid their lives of poverty and desperation. So too, Parks draws on the tradition of dead women talking to facilitate a larger confrontation with the nation's recent past as readers confront the mundane realities of Jim Crow from their post–civil rights vantage. In this way, the climactic embrace of the mother's corpse works against forced amnesia in the post–civil rights, post-racial present.

In all, the literary tradition of dead women talking includes some of American literature's most important writers and celebrated texts. The fact that it has been largely unnoticed may be because it crosses periods, identity-based traditions, generic conventions, and other widely recognized ways of organizing literary history. While the earliest examples are best understood as a trope that draws on nineteenth-century gothic and ghost story models, the tradition emerges as such in the later twentieth century and comes to include magical realist tales, nonfiction meditations on history, fantastic stage plays, and middlebrow novels. *Beloved* represents the full flowering of that tradition. She is in turn kin to Addie Bundren, who stands as both icon and outlier in that she wishes to leave her community in death, rather than seek posthumous recognition among the living. But that right to privacy, too, is a form of posthumous recognition. If by the early twenty-first century dead women talking constitute a fully emerged literary tradition, that tradition runs the risk of losing its uncanny abilities to provoke unexpected confrontations with the past. In fact, the posthumous narrator of *The Lovely Bones* seems something of a gimmick, signaling perhaps a new phase in an era when we come to expect the dead to talk, at least in fictional terrain.

By the end of this study, we should find it odd when dead women *don't* talk. I conclude by turning to a counterexample of what happens when the dead remain resolutely, stubbornly quiet: Maxine Hong Kingston's 1975 mythic tale of the "No Name Woman," which opens her famous *The Woman Warrior: Memoirs of a Girlhood among Ghosts*. Kingston meditates on the silence of the corpse, as well as its unspeakability on the part of the living, to underscore unanswered social justice questions around sexual shame, ethnic heritage, immigration, and clashes between tradition and change. From there, I turn to larger cultural questions of what we expect of corpses today by way of Mary Roach's plucky journalistic adventure *Stiff: The Curious Lives of Human Cadavers*. Like the literature in which dead women talk (or don't), Roach raises basic philosophical issues about death, what it means to have a body, and our obligations to the dead. When she asks for guidance on what to do when she herself inevitably achieves corpsehood, the cadavers just sit there, mute and rotting. Ultimately, I argue that Kingston, Roach, and Addie Bundren may have it right: to demand that dead women talk may be a violation of their posthumous integrity and right to silence.

I return to my opening question: what are we to make of all these talking dead women? At the outset, I shall say that they accept the task of addressing those injustices a living community might prematurely consign to the grave. While these women occupy the centers of their narratives, ultimately it is the job of the living to seek justice, for dead women need only talk when the living abdicate that responsibility. To fully seek justice requires that we confront not only these women's stories, often horrid and unjust in their own right, but more importantly the nation's past. In due course, these women prompt us to explore the prospects for achieving a world in which dead women need not talk.

1

Dead Woman Wailing

Edgar Allan Poe's "The Fall of the House of Usher"

When we look in the darkened corridors of American literature, we find dead women talking. They emerge from the cellars, catacombs, garrets, and forgotten wings of what Wahneema Lubiano calls the house that race built.[1] When they thrust themselves into well-lit parlors, they evoke matters long buried or scuttled away, though sometimes they seem unconscious or even unwilling participants in their own stories. We encounter a formative example in Madeline Usher, the famously entombed sister of Edgar Allan Poe's 1839 gothic tale "The Fall of the House of Usher." Poe's writing notably teems with cadavers, expiring bodies, necrophiliacs, smooth-talking maniacs, and other alluring figures of death and irrationality. Madeline typifies his signature death-of-a-beautiful-woman theme, but with a twist in that she returns—with a voice. Poe's tale begins in a quasi-realist mode with a narrator who recounts in precise, albeit elliptical, prose his unsettling visit to the grand home of an old acquaintance, Roderick Usher. By the end of the short tale, Madeline is at the threshold of her brother's studio shrouded in white, covered in blood, and moaning inarticulately. She is grotesque and doesn't belong in this world, so much so that the entire House of Usher crumbles upon her return to the realm of the living and her terminal embrace of her twin brother.

It is unclear whether Madeline has a story of injustice to tell, though such designs can be projected onto her given that her voice stops short of speech, inviting ventriloquist possibilities. Speech belongs solely to the two men of the tale, Roderick and the unnamed narrator. Their exchange sets in motion a fundamental American tension: the new possibilities of cross-class encounters and mobility taking root in Jacksonian America on the one hand, and on the other the maintenance of lineage, patrimony, and aristocratic power extending the line from the nation's colonial past and connecting it to British terrain. When Madeline escapes from her tomb and inserts herself into the studio, she not only signals the decay of blood-borne privilege on American soil but also troubles national claims to new democratic structures free from Old World residue. That being said, the sister's inchoate wailings are as illegible—and ultimately unnarratable—as Poe's politics. Madeline Usher is not a mad woman in the attic with a feminist or belated anticolonialist tale to tell, but rather a wailing corpse from the basement who prompts us to fear and possibly examine, if not go so far as to protest, what else lies underneath the foundations on which not only the House of Usher but the nation itself is built.

Crumbling Bodies, Crumbling Aristocracy

Critics have returned to Poe's notorious skepticism toward the idea of a national literature to suggest that his gothic experiments harbor sophisticated meditations on race, power, and populism in antebellum America. In *The American Face of Poe*, Shawn Rosenheim and Stephen Rachman position Poe "in a syncopated relation to American culture, at once both in and out of step," a "Janus-faced" figure whose irresolution convenes "literary issues and broader aspects of a democratic mass culture."[2] This includes the role of race, especially slavery and black-white relations, in Poe's portrayals of broken, mad, servile, and living dead citizens.[3] Poe's engagement with the national project also entails questions of class and social mobility. Poe is no populist, though, but is instead, as Terence Whalen and others argue, a fitful commercial writer as skeptical of the literary marketplace as he is of nationalism.[4]

While she is central to my concerns, Madeline is not the principal character in Poe's story of the fate of aristocratic privilege and descent in America. That role belongs to Roderick. With a "morbid acuteness of the senses,"[5] Roderick suffers from a malady that is both physical and mental. Stimulus from the world is in and of itself oppressive and insufferable. Following Poe's penchant for the hyper-real rather than the fantastical, Roderick is not so much detached from experience but rather overly attached. Encounters with the world threaten his bodily integrity. Whereas Poe the Southerner engaged the volatile marketplace of literary publishing,[6] the Ushers remain cordoned off from the nation and national time. It is not even clear in which country the House of Usher resides, leading Poe scholars such as Jeffrey Savoye to attempt to pinpoint a specific European locale by sifting the evidence of Old World origins: an ancient family history, a castle dating back to "remote feudal times" (329), words such as "tarn" and "peasantry," and so on.[7] When the narrator enters Usher, he brings with him an encounter with the worldly, the present, and, I argue, the American—all that is perturbing to Roderick's body.

Roderick's body, the mansion, and his line are, of course, one in the same, locked in a metonymic embrace. Roderick comes from an "ancient family," the narrator reports, and "I had learned, too, the very remarkable fact, that the stem of the Usher race all time-honored as it was, had put forth, at no period, any enduring branch; in other words, that the entire family lay in the direct line of descent, and had always, with very trifling and very temporary variation, so lain" (318). This early passage alerts us to oft-noted themes of incest and familial secrecy in the image of a family tree that is all trunk and no branches. The description also cues matters of aristocracy, history, and postcolonialist vitality in a land perceived to have no history. Reneé Bergland goes so far as to describe the indigenous person as the uncanny ghost of colonial America.[8] But there are no indigenous Americans in Usher's fictive world, save for what Leon Jackson calls the "indianation" of Poe himself by his critics.[9] This stands in contrast to other tales in which Poe examines the relationship between native American and Native American identity, including especially in "Loss of Breath," "The Journal of Julius Rodman," *The Narrative of Arthur Gordon Pym*, and "The Man That Was Used Up: A Tale of the Late Bugaboo and Kickapoo Campaign." Of the latter, published around the same time as "The Fall of the House of Usher," Jackson writes, "America, Poe suggests, has failed to come to terms with its own bugaboo: the eradication of the Natives on which its progress is predicated."[10] Usher, on the other hand, features only the frail twins who are relics of a past age, as well as a conspicuously rootless narrator and the occasional valet or physician who populate Usher's peripheries.

Usher is an outpost of the Old World crumbling under its own "excessive antiquity" and "discoloration of ages" (319). The tale invites not only a psychological reading, as many critics adopt, but also one attuned to the surrounding nation from which the Usher house is curiously unmoored. Its fate is symptomatic of what happens when denizens of an old world order attempt an extended errand into the wilderness, to use Perry Miller's famous formulation of the American experiment. The purebred Usher strain, deliberately cultivated over a "long lapse of centuries," cannot survive transplant in alien soil. So Usher turns inward, cloistered and apart. "It was this deficiency, perhaps," the narrator ruminates, "of collateral issue, and the consequent undeviating transmission, from sire to son, of the patrimony with the name, which had, at length, so identified the two as to merge the original title of the estate in the quaint and equivocal appellation of the 'House of Usher'" (319). The anglophilic ring of "House of Usher," along with such lofty words as "sire" and "patrimony," connotes bloodlines, status, nobility, and a connection to the new nation's colonial past not readily shed. Further, the "equivocal appellation" does more than merge man, house, and line; it also distinguishes the nameless narrator who lacks status markers and the extensive pedigree of Roderick and Madeline which long predates the American nation. In fact, it is the peasantry who author the curious appellation, those statusless inhabitants of the landscape in which the Ushers atrophy. The collapse of Usher marks the demise of what Duncan Faherty calls "the collapse of patrician privilege and power" in an era of Jacksonian populism. "Instead of functioning as a site of cultural order," he argues, "the pseudoaristrocratic house of Usher fails to extend any issue beyond the boundaries of its own unstable foundation," thereby rendering the Ushers obsolete.[11]

In the March 22, 1845, issue of the *Broadway Journal,* Poe weighs in on the prospects of a wholly native-born national identity in his satiric essay "National Nomenclature." He mischievously excerpts the New-York Historical Society's committee report on "a proper name for the country," be it America, Columbia, or Appalachia, so long as "all bring to it a hearty love of country, a deep sense of our great want as a people, and a warm admiration of those beautiful Indian names which are passing from our hills and waters with every successive year."[12] In response, Poe muses, "We give our vote for Apalachia [*sic*]—first because it is distinctive; America is not, and can never be made so." The remaining reasons merit quoting at length because they are equally witty and resonate with the curious appellation "House of Usher." Poe wryly votes for "Apalachia,"

> secondly, because it is indigenous, springing from the country itself, or from one of its most magnificent and distinctive features—thirdly, because in employing it, we do honor to the Aborigines, whom, hitherto, we have at all points unmercifully despoiled, assassinated, and dishonored—fourthly, because in itself it is musical, and of sufficient length to have dignity and force—fifthly

> and lastly, because it is the suggestion of the most deservedly eminent among all the pioneers of American literature. It is but just that Mr. Irving should name the land, for which in Letter he first established a name.[13]

Poe subtly lampoons the tenets of the committee's work as well as literary nationalism while also raising many of the themes of "Usher" along the way: the conflation of name, race, and territory; sentient land; disappearing bodies (be it Madeline or Native Americans); the bodily experience of artistry; and the prospect of status and prestige in a new nation. Poe speaks uncharacteristically in the register of injustice when he chronicles abuses toward indigenous peoples. But this is sublimated when Poe reserves the explicit designation of justice for the prospect of honoring Washington Irving as literary "pioneer." The name "Apalachia" may spring from the land itself, in direct contrast to the crumbling and disappearing House of Usher, but it is still uttered from the lips of a founding white writer, not the absent Aborigine whom the name ostensibly seeks to honor.

In "Usher," patrimony is a crumbling male body, a body that is wan, pallid, sickly . . . and also feminine and foreign to the narrator's eye. Roderick's face is so off-putting that "I could not, even with effort, connect its arabesque expression with any idea of simple humanity" (321). Arabesque is a conspicuous descriptor here, even if it is a word closely associated with Poe and his aesthetics, as announced in the title of the larger collection, *Tales of the Grotesque and Arabesque*. As a description of a face it is odd—no shape repeats to form an ornate geometric pattern. "Arabesque" refers instead to its other layers of meaning: feminine (linguistically), eastern (regionally), strangely mixed (figuratively), and a beautifully strained position (as in ballet). The narrator further describes Roderick through various conceits of otherness, including a "nose of a delicate Hebrew model, but with a breadth of nostril unusual in similar formations" (321). As an enduring racial symbol, the Jewish nose, along with his arabesque expression and predilection for the fine arts, marks Roderick as bewilderingly alien, if not also alluring and highly cultivated. Juxtaposed to the presumably healthy male American narrator, Roderick is sickly, feminine, and foreign. He is dangerously close to becoming what Karen Weekes and others describe as Poe's feminine ideal: an ailing woman whose beauty grows as her skin pales, cheeks redden, and body convulses against her will, especially at the moment of death, or, more gloriously, as a revived corpse.[14]

Madeline suffers from the same disease as Roderick, but at a faster clip. Further, she wastes away from the story itself. Shortly after arrival, the narrator reports, "I learned that the glimpse I had obtained of her person would thus probably be the last I should obtain—that the lady, at least while living, would be seen by me no more" (324). The foreshadowing of Madeline's return is obvious here. What is less obvious is Poe's use of the word "person," which underscores Madeline's physicality, the body itself on display and set off from the realm of speech. Further, while stopping short of an unfounded feminist reading, I would note that the patrimonial frame of the Usher line excises women from history, not unlike Madeline's curious non-presence in the story and also the proprietary status embedded in the "of" in her own appellation, "the lady Madeline of Usher" (335). While Madeline's body exits the above-ground floors, she remains very much present throughout the tale, returning first by way of a wail and then by way of a body that is either a corpse or a soon-to-be corpse. In the interval, she goes "unmentioned" (324) until Roderick announces that "the lady Madeline was no more" (328), creating a space of deliberate silence from which she will emerge.

Madeline's return, or, to be more precise, the return of her body, to the narrated realm is among the more famous gothic scenes in American literature. She appears draped in white, simultaneously bridal, virginal, and funereal, and streaked with blood, a vision rich with imagery of incest, menstruation, birth, death, violence, and genealogy. The ensuing embrace between Madeline and Roderick is one of congress in sex, death, and quasi-marriage, all of which lead to the same end: a non-procreative coupling, which is to say the fall of the House of Usher. While it is unclear whether Madeline enters the scene a living woman expiring or dead woman wailing, it *is* clear how Roderick leaves it: "a corpse, and a victim to the terrors he had anticipated" (335). Roderick ends the scene in the same state as Madeline—a body.

Less noted in this scene is the relationship between voices, especially the role of transcription. Whereas Madeline moans inarticulately, Roderick "shrieked out his syllables" (335). Whereas Madeline's wailing and scratching are heard at first only by hyperacute Roderick, the narrator is able *from the beginning* to hear and pass along Roderick's words. What precedes the death embrace is a contest over who controls the narrative space. "For a moment," the narrator recounts, "she remained trembling and reeling to and fro up on the threshold, then, with a low moaning cry" (335). At this moment, the rising action and climax merge with rather inflated sexual imagery, visual, auditory, kinesthetic, symbolic, and otherwise. More important is the role of voice: Roderick operates in the high register of the shriek, Madeline in the lower register of the moan. But only one is legible. Madeline remains primarily in the visual realm, as body.

While Madeline's body fully reenters the realm of narration at the end of the tale, her own words do not. Earlier Poe writes, "'Her decease,' [Roderick] said, with a bitterness which I can never forget, 'would leave him (him the hopeless and the frail) the last of the ancient race of Ushers'" (323). Here Poe disconnects voice and body in a subtle yet telling mistranscription. Oddly, Roderick speaks in the third person about the prospect of the end of the House of Usher. While the dialogue is delivered in quotation, the narrator in fact throws his own voice into Roderick's body. His ventriloquist move stands in stark contrast to his treatment of Madeline, whose utterances the narrator cannot or will not transcribe, let alone decipher. Further, Poe's wordplay with decease/disease renders the sister's death both pathological and tantamount to the end of an entire hereditary line, not just her own life. Madeline's body is not her own, but rather a vessel she inhabits temporarily on behalf of the Usher tribe. Perhaps she only has claim to her body posthumously because it no longer carries the capacity to further the Usher bloodline. Still, this posthumous body is as speechless in death as it was in life.

Uncanny Wailings

We cannot know for certain what story Madeline has to tell. She is less an early example of a dead woman talking than a more incoherent and troubling figure: a dead woman wailing—or, given the ambiguity surrounding her status upon first entering her tomb, a *possibly* dead woman wailing. This renders her doubly uncanny. In general, the uncanny marks the return of the repressed, what is familiar and known but should remain secret or buried. "But the uncanny is not simply an experience of strangeness or alienation," Nicolas Royle explains. "More specifically, it is a commingling of the familiar and unfamiliar."[15] The effect is a peculiar feeling, a dread that Sigmund Freud describes as "that species of the frightening that goes back to what was once well known and had long been familiar" and is now on public display, well beyond the private home where it is meant to be kept out of sight.[16] (Less frequent is the inverse, when the public goes domestic.) Freud's examples tend toward twins and doubles, madness, spastic bodies, and uncontrolled sexuality, all of which come together in some way in the figure of Madeline and, to some extent, Roderick. Madeline is uncanny from many angles, from Roderick's doppelgänger-lover, to a walking corpse, then to a speaking cadaver returned from the tomb, and finally to a virginal bride with a voracious, deathly embrace. "To many people," Freud notes, "the acme of the uncanny is represented by anything to do with death, dead bodies, revenants, spirits and ghosts."[17] The narrator's reaction upon first viewing Madeline is a textbook response: "I regarded her with an utter astonishment not unmingled with dread" (323).

It is not clear whether it is entirely accurate to call Madeline a dead woman talking (or, wailing). First, her status as dead is not certain. Is she a returned and talking corpse or buried prematurely? Most interpretations of the tale follow Roderick and conclude that Madeline was entombed prematurely, a victim of her male counterpart. But why trust Roderick on this and choose the rational and explicable over the extraordinary, supernatural, or unnatural possibilities that Poe deliberately cultivates? The ambiguity surrounding Madeline's status as *possibly* dead creates what Ernst Jentsch, from whom Freud draws, terms *intellectual uncertainty*.[18] This uncertainty is the creative engine behind what makes the story so interesting in the first place. The narrator himself describes the deposit of Madeline's body in the basement vault as a "temporary entombment" (329), presumably in advance of a final resting place in the family burial ground. This is before the narrator knows that she will return, at which point he describes "her violent and *now final* death-agonies" (335, emphasis mine). Critic Desirée Henderson suggests that the Usher story, along with Poe's other premature burial tales, responds to nineteenth-century burial practices when death happened more frequently in hospital than home, which led to "increasing alienation between the living and dead." She argues that Poe captures the resultant "opposing trends, the sensational and the sentimental, which alternately depicted death as horrific, violent, and senseless or as beautiful, peaceful, and meaningful."[19] Moreover, the Usher house itself becomes uncanny feminine territory complete with womblike imagery of the basement tomb. From this angle, when Madeline claws her way out, it is unclear if her return marks a birth or a death.

While the question of Madeline's status as dead or alive is most central to the plot, in a way it is also not clear that Madeline is a woman. It may be more appropriate to think of her as a doppelgänger of Roderick, a cipher of Poe's imagination, or a cultural monster, what critic Joan Dayan calls a "phantasm caught in the craw of civilization."[20] Madeline is not just a sisterly mirror of

Roderick, but almost interchangeable, an echo or distillation of the original. When the narrator glances at pre-entombed Madeline, his vision immediately goes back to Roderick: "When a door, at length, closed upon her, my glance sought instinctively and eagerly the countenance of the brother" (323). The brother quickly regains the center of the narrative vision, reclaiming the space left by Madeline's absence. Madeline's living body is scant on display; as a possible cadaver, however, she thrusts herself into the focal point of the narrative. Some critics look for the potential power in Poe's idealized heroines able to wrest life from death, from Madeline to Eleonora, Morella, and Ligeia. On the other hand, some go so far as to argue that ultimately there are no women in Poe's fiction, leading one feminist critic to contend that Poe's female characters are merely ciphers, "means to a (male) end," whether ill-fated creatures in an androcentric universe or placeholders, "*tabula rasas*," "pasteboard props for the purposes of the narrator's emotional excesses."[21] In Freudian thinking, the uncanny becomes associated with the feminine body, especially the womb, the ultimate place of origins. It is both life-giving and a grave-like dark space with no air. In the end, Freud argues, any instance of the uncanny, any feeling that "'I know this place. I've been here before,' this place can be interpreted as representing the mother's genitals or her womb."[22] For Dayan, Poe's work brims with figures of "radical dehumanization," be they living dead or humans turned to animal or angel. Madeline is all three and one more: "a brute and bloodied thing, the frenziedly iterated '*it*' of her brother Roderick."[23]

Finally and perhaps most importantly, it is not clear that Madeline is talking. In other words, is her wailing and moaning a form of speech? Before Madeline emerges, the narrator hears an "unnatural shriek," which he takes to be that of a dragon arising inexplicably from Roderick's recitation of the tale of Ethelred. When Madeline's body appears, the narrator locates the sound as her voice, audible but unspeakable. In the end, the narrator recounts only Roderick's words. As the soil envelops the House of Usher, likewise the narrator entombs Madeline's legible voice, never to be retrieved. What might we glean from her uncanny wailings? Or, failing that, what might her equally uncanny body have to say?

For Freud, the uncanny is the cornerstone of an aesthetics of anxiety, a state in which the stark lines that govern our world become permeable and the unthinkable becomes thinkable. In Poe's story, the breached lines are between not only life and death, siblings and lovers, public and domestic, but also the new American nation and the Old World. Poe cuts off the House of Usher from national time and portrays the inhabitants as frail, decaying relics. When we meet the Ushers in the present, they are anachronisms, instances of what I elsewhere call the "historical uncanny."[24] The historical uncanny is a disquieting feeling that the past is not passed. It arises when temporal boundaries are breached, such as when the primitive erupts into modern settings in Freud's progress narrative of civilization.[25] The historical uncanny can be provoked by not-so-welcome reminders that what we consign to a bygone era—in this case, caste and blood-borne privilege—remains alive (and wailing!) today, signs of an era to which we resist returning and yet are ineluctably drawn. This stretches the concept of the uncanny beyond the realm of the individual psyche so that it enters the domain of public, national memory. Whereas Roderick's body, lineage, and the mansion are one in the same, Madeline's twin body both recalls the Usher line and marks the end of it for the narrator to chronicle.

In addition to a dead woman wailing and wandering about the house, there are numerous earlier uncanny moments of seeing life where it is not, ought not, or no longer is. For instance, the narrator twice describes the house itself as having "vacant eye-like windows" (317, 318) and then observes that Madeline's corpse in the coffin has a face of a "tenant" (329). The inverse of the uncanny is also uncanny, as when the narrator does not see life where it is or ought to be, such as in Roderick's "cadaverous of complexion" and the "ghostly pallor of the skin" (321). In these breaches arise what many critics frame as the problem of pervasive sentience in Poe's use of organicism, a belief system that sees "sentience in all vegetable things" (327). In this gothic story, life also extends into the inorganic realm, including the house itself, so that Roderick's disintegration is linked to the descent of his external world into disorder.[26] In the end, there is no place for the Usher House in the canny world of national time and democratic masses. Dayan considers Poe's figures of privilege brought low by incapacity, madness, and perversities to become "emancipated, or rather ejected, from the circle of citizenry," thereby becoming kin to the "civil dead," those deemed dead in the legal sphere, such as the slave denied citizen status by blood or the felon denied property rights by common law.[27] For Dayan, the Ushers are relics of a mythic time when "blood conferred an unpolluted, legitimate pedigree,"[28] though Poe also inverts racial and caste lines so that the Ushers, not the slave or the felon, are in jeopardy of civil and corporeal death. They are victims of a bloodline with no future in the real time of Jacksonian America. In this way, not only is Madeline a possibly dead woman wailing, but Roderick has been a dead man sitting all along.

The gothic mode is apt terrain for such uncanny encounters between the nation and its mythic or repressed past, a region between the fantastic and the realistic. The uncanny dwells primarily in the latter. "An uncanny effect often arises when the boundary between fantasy and reality is blurred," Freud explains, "when we are faced with the reality of something that we have until now considered imaginary, when a symbol takes on the full function and significance of what it symbolizes, and so forth."[29] The dead returning is a common theme in fairy tales, he notes, but in realist narrative we expect the dead to stay dead, cordoned off from the living in all but memory.[30] That is why it is important that Madeline is no mere symbol, but a mobile, wailing, living corpse. When her wailing could be explained away as the wind or an overactive imagination reading a knightly romance, she is not yet a figure of the uncanny. It is only when she appears as a body and emerges from the tomb onto an above-ground level, the level of realism, that she becomes a full-fledged figure of the uncanny. She now harbors the power to disrupt—and perhaps dismantle—the world.

The Ushers are a curious kind of uncanny foreigners: white ones. In *Gothic America*, Teresa Goddu suggests that Poe is engaged in a project of imagining "perfect whiteness," one that is not specific to the South, but as a national identity, one that belongs at the head of the American literary tradition.[31] This makes good on Toni Morrison's influential discussion of American Africanism in *Playing in the Dark* in which she, too, places Poe at the head of an American literary imagination of whiteness. In this way, Madeline may be an unexpected example of what Leonard Cassuto calls the *racial grotesque*, the liminal subject of American race relations in which "one group tries to objectify the other, but even as they do so, they admit that they see these 'objects' as human all the time."[32] Poe is particularly ripe for such twin pulls given his "oscillations on race between rational certainty and fearful anxiety."[33] Cassuto points to such black figures as the deceitful rebellious slaves in *The Narrative of Arthur Gordon Pym*, the dutiful ex-slave of "The Gold Bug," and the murderous orangutan of "Murders in the Rue Morgue." Madeline is also tugged in competing directions of "human" and "not human," which falls along the lines of dead versus not-dead, as much as perfectly white versus marred, or present American versus not of this time.[34] Further, the Ushers are also early examples of what Americanist critic Amy Kaplan conceives as the domestic foreigner, which she finds at the center of U.S. notions of citizenship and forged at its domestic frontiers.[35] "At these borders," Kaplan argues, "foreign relations do not take place outside the boundaries of America, but instead constitute American nationality."[36] Usher is a peculiar domestic frontier because from it we look not outward and forward, but eastward and backward toward British origins embodied in the Usher bloodline.

Madeline's appearance at the threshold of her brother's studio just before Usher crumbles may be what happens when American literary nationalism collides with gothic figures of uncanny otherness, as speechless as they are inassimilable into the national narrative. In *Dislocating Race and Nation*, Robert Levine reconsiders American literary nationalism and its moves to emphasize British or German blood ties in contradistinction to French, Spanish, African, and Native American heritage. Levine seeks out interracial episodes that disrupt such racial conventions and uncover the tenuousness of imagining a nation based on white imperialism.[37] I suggest that the meeting between the unnamed narrator and the Ushers is such an interracial encounter, one in which the crumbling aristocracy plays foil to the American narrator who will emerge from the rubble able to tell the story of his nation: from whence it came . . . and from which it escaped.

Encountering Other Pasts

As a moaning cadaver who erupts into the terrain of the present, the living, and the narrated, Madeline offers—insists upon—a confrontation with the past. But ultimately it is untenable to argue that Poe's tale has directly political designs, let alone to position Madeline as a voice of injustice, as is more often the case in twentieth-century American literature and beyond. Even famed New Critics Cleanth Brooks and Robert Penn Warren threw up their hands and insisted on the tale's artful elusiveness. "Does the story have a meaning," they ask, "or is the horror essentially meaningless, horror aroused for its own sake?"[38] We do well to go back to the opening of the story, well before the dead woman wails. On approach, the narrator asks, "What was it—I paused to think—what was it that so unnerved me in the contemplation of the House of Usher?" (317). The source of the horror, like Madeline's untranscribed alien wailing, is ineffable. There is a deliberate hesitance, a circuitous quality in the prose, which captures the narrator's intellectual uncertainty in the ratiocination of chronicling with precision a potentially irrational response to a potentially unnatural atmosphere. The narrator is well aware of his role in wresting reason from irrationality, leading to critical debates about the narrator's faculties, deciding between what Philip Martin calls a "non-imaginative narrator"[39] and what Ronald Bieganowski calls a "self-consuming narrator."[40] Scott Peeples examines the constructedness of the prose to detect in the loping, repetitive, labyrinthine, clause-heavy, adjective-riddled syntax a "motionlessness . . . reflecting the morbid scene it describes."[41] Still, there is no evidence to suggest that the narrator's bloodline, unlike the Usher's, is entwined with Old Europe and therefore in jeopardy.

While the Ushers meet their demise, what of the narrator's fate as a citizen of the surrounding nation? He may be a prime candidate for what American literary critic Russ Castronovo calls a necro citizen, the civilly dead subject content to acquiesce and loath to instigate social change. In his study of "half-living corpses" in the American political imagination, Castronovo considers the somnambulist of Poe's 1844 story "Mesmeric Revelation" and the corpse of the women's rights advocate Zenobia in Nathaniel Hawthorne's 1852 tale *The Blithedale Romance*. While Poe notoriously frames the death of a beautiful woman as supremely poetical, Castronovo insists that dead women, and corpses more generally, are central *political* objects, too. "Public womanhood deadens citizenship," he argues, because we bring the bodily and the private into a public space that values neither. When Zenobia's bloated, decayed body is retrieved from the river and readied for public display, Castronovo writes, "her dead body bears the eloquent memory of discord in a community that was supposed to have none." He continues, "The dead speak: the question is whether the living will hear a story about the ways in which belonging, incorporation, and other processes of democratic community produce social corpses."[42] Of course, Castronovo operates on a metaphorical level: Zenobia's corpse doesn't speak and the good citizen is only a figurative corpse. Madeline, on the other hand, is quite literally a wailing corpse, one who seems uninterested in propagating docile citizenship.

What would it entail for us to listen to Madeline Usher? First, there is a core problem: because she wails, rather than speaks, we cannot easily follow a decree to listen. The American narrator fails at this task, though he is the sole person to survive the story and, in his capacity of transcribing the events, our only means of hearing Madeline. When Madeline appears at the threshold, it is Roderick who shrieks while Madeline moans. The palpable sexual imagery notwithstanding, there is a gendered reversal in Roderick's high-pitched yelps and Madeline's guttural sounds. Yet Roderick alone retains the privilege of transcribed speech. Ultimately, this story is not about the Ushers, or even the House of Usher. It is about the narrator and his community, the one who records—but stops short of transcribing—Madeline's wailing. We don't end with the death embrace between the twins when at least one begins the scene alive and both certainly end as corpses. Rather, we end where we began: with the narrator's words and the story recalled. He flees from the mansion only to look back and gaze at the red, gashed moon. He then witnesses another death embrace, "the deep and dank tarn at my feet closed sullenly and silently over the fragments of the 'House of Usher'" (336). Note the silence of the earth, in contrast to the voice of the narrator and the never-legible wailing of Madeline. Gillian Brown suggests that Poe tells a story about "the end of a line, the degeneration and extinction of the Ushers," while the repetitive, elliptical telling of the story provides a form of endless regeneration in art, if not nature.[43] Thus, the narrator preserves and propagates the story of the House of Usher beyond the existence of the eponymous bloodline or structure, not unlike the science of preserving a corpse beyond the body's life span or the transmission of individual habit in the propagation of a species resisting extinction.

For some, Madeline intrudes upon not only a living and narrated realm, but a decidedly masculine space, thwarting a bid for a homosocial means of transmission of the Usher line.[44] This transmission carries Madeline's wails and moans, ever in search of a narrator to make them legible. Though Madeline remains inarticulate and forever inscrutable, she stands at the head of an American literary tradition that proliferates with dead women who *do* talk. The challenge, their communities will find, is to learn to listen.

2

Dead Woman Dictating

Henry James's *The Turn of the Screw*

"The Fall of the House of Usher" tells the story of crumbling aristocracy and its uncanny posthumous return. Thus, Poe helps us consider whether class status can travel across oceans, nations, and generations. A corollary question is, must it? In fiction, the dead don't necessarily mind their stations, sometimes going so far as to make bids for class ascent. That is the dread undergirding *The Turn of the Screw*, Henry James's signature ghost story. In the tale, a governess protects her two young charges from intruders, whom she determines to be her predecessor and a valet, each of whom died under unclear circumstances. Of course, James is no economic populist, preferring the finery of the elite to the coarse cloth of the masses in his position as an American expatriate in Britain. Still, this story is ambiguous in its meditation on cross-class contact in the guise of a ghost story. The initial moment of horror in *The Turn of the Screw* is not exactly when the governess first sees what she will come to identify as a ghost. Rather, the scene reaches its peak when she recognizes him by means of a class marker: *he has no hat*. As she describes the bareheaded invader to Mrs. Grose, the head housekeeper, the governess adds, "He's tall, active, erect . . . but never—no, never!—a gentleman." The governess is certain of one thing about this stranger: he doesn't belong in the posh clothes he wears so defiantly. "They're smart," she reports, "but they're not his own."[1] At the governess's prodding, Mrs. Grose surmises they are alone with Peter Quint, the dead valet. The shock has less to do with the prospect of the dead returning and more to do with the specter of class ascent, or perhaps even inversion. Her terror is that Quint is "in charge."

The question of whether the governess's visions are real has fueled debate for generations, and it is a central trope in the Victorian ghost story.[2] What is never in question is the social rank of the ghosts. Marxist critic Bruce Robbins argues that the story is "systematic, indeed almost obsessive, in its confusion of ghosts and servants."[3] He continues, "The master turns his subordinates into ghosts" in a story willing "to consider the ghosts less as supernatural phenomena than as social phenomena."[4] Still, it is worth pausing to insist on their deceased status and thereby consider the prospect of class mobility in death, especially in a society so intricately organized around class roles as a nineteenth-century British estate. In a meditation on Balzac's *Colonel Chabert*, another novel of death and intrusive return, critical theorist Cathy Caruth contemplates the legal aspects of what she calls "the claims of the dead." Property law, she suggests, preserves historical memory, such as when Holocaust survivors seek restitution of not only their lost property but their property rights. Caruth frames this as "the drama of the legal struggle to come alive before the law," which a ghost story can literalize.[5] In James's story, we see the inverse: the actual dead attempting to shed their class statuses to seek rights and privileges to which they never held legal claim in life. The current governess, I argue, follows suit.

Rigor Mortis

In America, posthumous class mobility is more exception than rule. In fact, class status is largely immutable in death. Let me back up to offer two representative examples, the first fictional, the second legal. In *The Others*, a taut psychological horror film starring Nicole Kidman, a mother tries in vain to protect her children from unseen ghosts who seem to mean them harm. She is helped by three servants who appear midway through the film, quick to indulge the mistress's attempts to protect her children's vulnerable skin from the daylight to which they are fatally allergic. With its quiet artistry, *The Others* earns a place in a very small circle of smart horror films. The film also directly evokes James's novella in terms of theme, mood, setting, and plot, save for the ending twist when we learn with certainty that the mother, her children, and the servants are all ghosts haunting the manor's present-day occupants. What is more striking to me is why the servants remain as such, obeisant to the mother's every command. Why not cast off their inferior stations? When we first learn that the servants are ghosts—the ultimate figures who don't respect their places (or lack thereof) among the living—the revelation raises more questions about the absurdity of posthumous class than it answers plot-based questions about who is haunting whom. These dead have a severe case of rigor mortis: they may move physically, but their class won't budge.

Posthumous obedience to class is not confined to the stuff of ghost stories. In fact, it is so commonplace that it is embedded in legal structures, especially tort law. A good example is the September 11th Victim Compensation Fund, a typical, if high-profile and high-stakes, example of how tort law deals with compensable damages. The fund was established by Congress[6] and overseen by Kenneth Feinberg, who decided the dollar amount each family received based in large part on a victim's projected future earnings over the course of a full lifetime. In such a structure, there is no provision for class mobility—neither upward nor downward. America's core narrative may be based on rags-to-riches stories and schoolroom assurances that anyone who works hard enough and plays by the rules can rise to the top, but tort law, rightly or wrongly, belies that prized national story. The economic status of the victim at the moment of death becomes her legally recognized class after death. So, the families of those who worked in well-paid positions merit compensation at significantly higher amounts than families of those who worked as janitors, clerks, or Port Authority employees. It is worth nothing that there are alternate models to compensate victims in a more egalitarian manner, such as some insurance schemes with set schedules for various damages—say, $50,000 for a lost index finger, more for a severed hand, much more for a lost life. But that system is more the exception, the Feinberg fund the rule. Further, most worker's compensation payments are also prorated based on wages. Lo the person who dies or becomes permanently disabled while a member of a class to which she prefers not to belong. The rigor mortis of class status dictates that it will be binding.

Recognizing class posthumously not only is a linchpin of tort law but is also at the core of how the nation understands its commitments to its citizens. Tort law, as legal scholar Arthur Ripstein explains, "predicates liability on responsibility,"[7] which means that restitution is typically paid by the agent deemed to have caused the harm. This falls under the concept of corrective justice, which legal theorist Jules Coleman describes as "the principle that one has a duty to repair the wrongful losses for which one is responsible."[8] The Feinberg fund is an interesting outlier because the government paid without being found at fault, using funds collected from a variety of sources, both voluntarily and by seizure, while participants in the fund had to agree not to pursue legal claims.[9] The government may have paid out of what Coleman calls "correlativity,"[10] not out of direct responsibility but because the nation decides it has an interest in doing so. To make victims whole, to use the parlance of tort law, class becomes legally sacrosanct in death.

Outside of tort claims, the law tends to be rather slippery regarding posthumous rights, and it becomes more ambivalent the longer a person is dead. In a study of dilemmas triggered by death, British legal theorist Daniel Sperling proposes that we recognize certain "posthumous interests." He explains, "It is difficult to regard the newly-dead only as a mere corpse, a decaying organic matter, a mere 'thing.' The dead retain their value after death and are distinguishable one from another due to specific characteristics representing the persons they were."[11] Ultimately he suggests *human subject* as a legally recognized category that includes the perished who are no longer legally persons, and therefore no longer bearers of rights, but whose interests still merit protection.[12] Sperling is concerned pragmatically with the newly dead—what to do with the corpse, how to divvy up an estate for warring heirs, whether health professionals must uphold medical privacy, and so forth.

The literary realm, in contrast, often concerns the not-so-newly dead. These dead can stick around or return, often demanding recognition in the world of the living after many years or even generations have passed. Property law, more so than tort law, thinks in longer timelines when it approaches cross-generational succession through the concept of "mortmain" (*dead hand*), which imposes a statute of limitations on how long the dead can control property. Enshrined as a rule against perpetuity, *mortmain* is most commonly invoked in such matters as wills, estates, and trusts, the typical mechanisms by which the dead speak before the law to pass property on to the next generation. A person may put whatever restrictions she likes on the property, but generally those restrictions remain in place only until the death of the last individual alive at the creation of the interest plus up to twenty-one years. The rule ensures that the deceased property owner, the "dead hand," can't rule the living from the grave in perpetuity. Legal historians are tracking how the dead hand has grown stronger since the late nineteenth century, from eroded estate taxes to extended copyright time spans. According to Lawrence Friedman, this "raises the question of the legal fate of dynastic, long-term arrangements" and, by extension, the endurance of systems of class inequality.[13] Out of all this context *The Turn of the Screw* considers the legally unthinkable: posthumous class ascent.

James's Classy Dead

The Turn of the Screw considers the possibility that class status is not a legal fact that can replicate itself across generations, but rather mere social custom.

The residents of Bly are very concerned with keeping everyone in place: servants remain servants, masters grow up to be masters, and the dead stay dead. But Quint and the former governess, Miss Jessel, don't cooperate. This sets in motion the driving question of who is in charge of whom. The current governess considers a particularly terrifying possibility regarding her charges. "They're not mine—they're not ours," she asserts. "They're his and they're hers!" (207). This follows another equally terrifying possibility. "I was under the spell" of the children, she considers, and "I perfectly knew I was" (168). In turn, the governess declares proprietary control over "my children" (168), and then all of Bly as she cuts off all communication with the outside world. In doing so, she asserts a power above her station yet also obediently follows the derelict uncle's singular injunction: "That she should never trouble him—but never, never: neither appeal nor complain nor write about anything only meet all questions herself, receive all moneys from his solicitor, take the whole thing over and let him alone" (151). Thus, the governess finds herself "strangely at the helm" (156) of both Bly and the narrative itself as our sole first-person witness.

The problem of who is in charge of whom highlights an even more important question about succession: who reproduces the next generation's masters? James's tale of class transgression relies on two key factors, one plot based and one built into the structure of late nineteenth-century British culture. First, the children, Miles and Flora, are orphans. Their grandparents are killed in India,[14] two years after the death of their military father (there is no mention of the mother), after which they are left to the care of the bachelor uncle, who in turn removes himself from Bly. As charges, they are free radicals, able to bond with whoever commandeers the estate. Second, servants perform the labor of a manor, including tending the property and rearing the children. Such a family structure has built-in intimate and prolonged cross-class contact, which creates the possibility of cross-generational disruption in the absence of a rightful master and the presence of servants prone to class disobedience.

Quint is the ultimate figure of class transgression, in life as in death. We learn that he was "too free" as a servant, and Mrs. Grose accuses him of "spoiling" Miles, the young master-in-training. The governess responds possessively, "Too free with *my* boy?" to which Mrs. Grose clarifies, "Too free with every one!" (177). In part the assertion that Quint is "too free" lends credence to theories of Quint's sexual depravity, or queer readings of cross-class homosociality. It also marks Quint as another free radical set loose in the field of

Bly to disrupt the social order. Mrs. Grose is most concerned with Quint's freedom in terms of his disobedience to class roles, which she is quick to enforce for servants and young masters alike. For instance, she reports admonishing Miles, "*she* liked to see young gentleman not forget their station." The governess presses further, "You reminded him that Quint was only a base menial" (189). If the governess is now "strangely at the helm" of Bly, she learns to her horror that this "base menial" also once commandeered Bly. Mrs. Grose reports, "'So he had everything to say. Yes!'—she let me have it—'even about *them*'" (178). Not only does the specter wear a hat signifying a station to which he has no rightful claim, but he apparently wielded the actual power at Bly. His posthumous class ascent, then, merely restores the illicit authority he held in life.

Quint may intrude where he does not belong, but he is hampered by the fact that he ultimately lacks voice. In other words, he is not a dead man talking. His silence is what convinces the governess that even though the vision is hideous—"hideous just because it *was* human" (196)—he is not like her. "It was the dead silence of our long gaze at such close quarters," the governess recounts, "that gave the whole horror, huge as it was, its only note of the unnatural. . . . I can't express what followed it save by saying that the silence itself—which was indeed in a manner an attestation of my strength—became the element into which I saw the figure disappear" (196). Silence is the realm of the dead and the unnatural in the governess's way of ordering her universe. It differentiates her from the specter. The two exist on wholly different sensory registers—the governess sees, Quint is not heard.

While Quint is curiously silent in death, Miss Jessel manages a posthumous voice of sorts. First, she writes. At one point she appears at the bottom of the stairs composing a letter. The scene reverberates with James's overall theme of failed communication, signified by blank pages, screens, and letters written but unread or unsent, coupled with the frame tale's concern with handwriting, authorship, and authority. More troubling is the possibility that Miss Jessel is a dead woman dictating. In a scene at the estate's lake, when Flora denies seeing Miss Jessel and instead expresses horror at the very thought, the governess professes, "Of course I've lost you: I've interfered, and you've seen, under *her* dictation" (241). The governess describes Flora as "an old, old woman" (239) and concludes, "The wretched child had spoken exactly as if she had got from some outside source each of her stabbing little words" (240). While the prospect of Miss Jessel dictating from beyond the grave is disturbing enough, I should also note an alternate explanation: the governess has a history of ventriloquism as our narrator. For instance, she reports, "When Mrs. Grose finally got up she kept the child's hand, so that the two were still before me; and the singular reticence of our communication was even more marked in the frank look she addressed me. 'I'll be hanged,' it said, 'if *I'll* speak!'" (236). Mrs. Grose in fact never utters the words. Instead, akin to the ventriloquism of Poe's narrator, the governess is dictating her unspoken words and placing them in quotation marks.

If Flora is under the dictation of her former governess, the high-born child is brought low. Upon Flora's denial, the governess regards the girl clinging to Mrs. Grose and "her incomparable childish beauty had suddenly failed, had quite vanished. I've said it already—she was literally, she was hideously hard; she had turned common and almost ugly" (240). Flora takes on the shape of a commoner, which the governess sees in both aesthetic and corporal terms—she is "hideously hard." Hard is a curious term, except insofar as the governess is concerned with distinctions between the material living and the noncorporeal, be they demons like Quint and Miss Jessel or cherubs like Miles and Flora. The concreteness of the commoner is central to how the governess orders the world. She consigns Flora to the same contemptuous status as Mrs. Grose, a simpleton "exempt" from seeing the visions (239), presumably by station. Further, the governess sees Flora, like Miss Jessel, as a fallen woman, a "chit" (243) who talks like "a vulgarly pert little girl in the street" (240). Whereas it is the governess who comes to Bly from Harley Street, she inverts the class hierarchy and projects contempt upon the children of the upper class. Eventually, she sneers that Flora is just a little brat who "resents, for all the world like some high little personage, the imputation on her truthfulness" (243) from the likes of a mere governess.

The governess's class contempt fuels her disdain for cross-class transgressions. This is most evident in her response to the rumored sexual liaison between Quint and Miss Jessel, which may have resulted in an unspoken pregnancy. The governess inquires,

> "In spite of their difference—?"
>
> "Oh of their rank, their condition"—she brought it woefully out. "*She* was a lady."
>
> I turned it over; I again saw. "Yes—she was a lady."
>
> "And he so dreadfully below," said Mrs. Grose. (185)

In the insistence that Miss Jessel is a lady, we see again that one's station is primarily a matter of social custom—moral postures, manners, and in this case, sexual purity. Class transgressions have an equalizing effect. When the governess first sees Quint, she reports that they are locked in a "straight mutual stare" (165), even though he is atop a phallic turret in an unused wing while she is exposed below in the grassy courtyard. Their horizontal relationship is literalized at his next sighting. He stands directly outside a window, cut off from the waist down, almost as if the governess is looking in a mirror (169). Cross-class contact is dreadful not just because it flaunts social custom or even sexual mores, but also because it carries the possibility of class contagion, if not inversion. The governess is well aware of the danger, such as when she imagines what Flora would report to the uncle were he to return: "she'll make me out to him the lowest creature—!" (244).

The question of who possesses whom—or what—at Bly works on the level of the ghost story, in its possibilities of demonic possession, the sexual story, in its prospects of consummation, and also the novel's more legalistic concerns with class status and its propagation. In his 1908 preface, James himself famously insists, "Peter Quint and Miss Jessel are not 'ghosts' at all, as we now know the ghost, but goblins, elves, imps, demons as loosely constructed as those of the old trials for witchcraft" (41). At the technical level, this is an important assertion because, as we saw at Usher and in Freud's conception of the uncanny, ghost stories must venture into the realm of the real, whereas fairy tales are content to dwell in the realm of the fantastic. As far as Quint and Miss Jessel are concerned, they want to be not only in the realm of the real and among the living, but also in charge of them. Perhaps the governess has it right the first time: they are best described as intruders, not ghosts, claiming titles not their own. The frame tale flags the suggestive slipperiness of that term. A female audience member asks of Douglas, "What's your title?" to which he responds, "I haven't one." The unnamed narrator interjects, "'Oh *I* have!' I said. But Douglas, without heeding me, had begun to read with a fine clearness that was like a rendering to the ear of the beauty of the author's hand" (151). As many have noted, the multivalent word *title* signals authority on two counts, at least: one who has claim to either social status or the story.

To return to Freidman's legal history *Dead Hands*, he detects in the late nineteenth century the beginning of an expansion in property law to account for changing family structures that include not only bloodline descent but also what he calls "family of affection and dependence."[15] This upsets, he explains, long-standing principles of how to pass down property and power. Further, power is portable, as we see in the case of Douglas reciting the story of Bly from a title not his own, be it that of the unnamed narrator's station or the governess's manuscript. So too, Quint the "base menial" and one unnamed governess in a line of governesses jockey for the authority to call Bly their own. Equal in terror to the possibility that the dead are in charge at Bly is the specter of base menials atop its hierarchy. And, in James's world, the two may be one and the same.

Low Woman Brewing

In claiming title to this story, the governess becomes a low woman brewing. She draws on such witch imagery as she imagines herself a storyteller for Mrs. Grose. "I had made of her a receptacle of lurid things," she muses, "but there was an odd recognition of my superiority. . . . She offered her mind to my disclosures as, had I wished to mix a witch's broth and proposed it with assurance, she would have held out a large clean sauce pan" (203). As the governess mixes her witch's broth, we, like Mrs. Grose, receive her every theory and detail. However, we harbor the skepticism someone in Mrs. Grose's station apparently lacks. That is, we purposefully reside in that uncanny terrain between fantasy and evidence-based realism.

The story's realism comes primarily from our ability, or lack thereof, to place characters in their rightful places. "Recall," Bruce Robbins argues in *The Servant's Hand*, "how far the text goes not only to show that evil is defined in class terms but also to remind us that the governess herself is a servant."[16] In fact, the governess positions herself as a collective voice for her station. When she first recounts being charmed by her charges, she cites the utter boringness of the typical life of a governess and declares, "I call the sisterhood to witness!" (168). That may be so, but the problem is that, like Quint and Jessel, the current governess does not mind her station. Critic John Carlos Rowe further argues, "The governess fears those ghosts of Peter Quint and Miss Jessel in the same sense that she struggles with Mrs. Grose for authority: all are servants, despite the different authority they are respectively granted by their master."[17] Further, when the governess attempts to confirm her sighting of Quint to Mrs. Grose, she equivocates between the living and dead servants: "I saw him as I see you" (173).

Victorian scholar Eve Lynch examines the association between servants and ghosts. "Like the ghost," she explains, "the servant was *in* the home but not *of* it, occupying a position tied to the workings of the house itself." She continues, "The cook and the maid seemed to go with the house—and sometimes did, being 'inherited' by succeeding families—furnishing the home with a ghostly agency that moved the tables and chairs, emptied the grates and chamber pots, and disappeared around corners and through passages to the 'other side' of the green baize door."[18] The ghost story genre becomes a prime vehicle to bring social concerns about class into private, bourgeois spaces. In turn, some of the most exciting new work on *The Turn of the Screw* connects it to the big social questions of the day, such as Jean Lee Cole's discussion of the emaciated photos of Cubans during the Spanish-American War that appeared in *Collier's* adjacent to James's serialized novel about a governess seeing ghosts.[19] In a similar way, the servant-filled household necessarily harbors radical adjacencies in a domestic setting. A governess is an intermediary in the intricate social order; she interacts daily and intimately with the upper-class children, but she is a servant nonetheless. In the case of Bly, the servant has been delegated total dominion—which she found so horrifying about Quint and which she herself aims to maintain.

The governess takes great pains to distinguish herself from the likes of Quint, a "base menial." To do so, she writes herself into familial relationships with her charges, especially in the implied seduction plot with Miles, the ultimate class transgression. The governess describes a dinner with Miles: "We continued silent while the maid was with us—as silent, it whimsically occurred to me, as some young couple who, on their wedding-journey, at the inn, feel shy in the presence of the waiter" (252). Critics have had much to say about this conspicuous comparison. In addition to the overt sexual implications, it is important to notice the move to distinguish herself from fellow servants by writing herself into a legal, familial bond with the young master-in-training. Indeed, she has little choice. As Miles becomes a man, the governess admits, "I found it simple, in my ignorance, my confusion, and perhaps my conceit, to assume that I could deal with a boy whose education for the world was all on the point of beginning" (162). The bid for a horizontal relationship is necessary because a woman of her station no longer has anything to teach a young gentleman.

Even for a tale so concerned with the intricacies of station, it is curious how far James goes to connect the governess to the dead servants. In addition to the persistent description of Miss Jessel as her predecessor, the governess, as many critics note, repeatedly retraces the paths and positions of the spectral intruders. She occupies the precise spots and poses of the first sightings of Quint on the turret and outside the window, as well as the second sighting of Miss Jessel at the bottom of the stairs. Sometimes the intruders reciprocate, such as when Miss Jessel "rose erect on the spot my friend and I had lately quitted, and there wasn't in all the long reach of her desire an inch of her evil that fell short" (238). The governess and the intruders share not only positions but also their spectral effects. When Quint appears to the governess through the hall window, the governess subsequently appears as such to Mrs. Grose. The governess reports, "I gave her something of the shock that I had received. She turned white, and this made me ask myself if I had blanched as much. . . . I wondered why *she* should be scared" (170). Once the governess herself raises the question of whether she is alive, James gives us plenty of fodder to feed this nagging thought. For instance, after the third encounter with Quint, the governess recounts, "The moment was so prolonged that it would have taken but little more to make me doubt if even *I* were in life" (196). Or, upon meeting Miss Jessel for the third time, the governess recounts, "I had the extraordinary chill of a feeling that it was I who was the intruder" (221).

We should consider the possibility the governess herself raises. In fact, we have little evidence that the new governess, unnamed and allegedly the conjurer of the tale, exists in the realm of the real, the external, the verifiable, the living. James impishly sprinkles other, nefarious possibilities around the text. A particularly overt example is when Mrs. Grose exclaims, "You're white as a sheet" (171). Other examples are more subtle, such as when the governess sits for a solitary dinner: "I was conscious of a mortal coldness and felt as if I should never be warm again" (242). Again on the way to church with Mrs. Grose and the two charges, the governess departs company to remain outside, alone among the graves where "I only sat there on my tomb" (219). The suggestively slippery "my" is representative of James's precise ambiguity around matters of title, death, and speech.

The final scene, which takes place in Miles's bedroom, offers plenty of fodder for any number of interpretations, including the distinct possibility that the governess herself is a dead woman seeking possession of the living. The governess recounts, "I caught for the very first time a small faint quaver of consenting consciousness—it made me drop on my knees beside the bed and seize once more the chance of possessing him" (228). *Possessing* is yet another deliciously multivalent word fueling James's story. It can refer to the governess's zealous commitment to protect her charges from the intruders, as well as to the consummation of her wedding night fantasy. It also carries associations of property, ownership, and title. And of course it conjures images of demonic possession, not unlike Miss Jessel's possible dictation of Flora. Finally, it fits within an overall portrait of the governess as possessive, even at the most literal level, such as her propensity to embrace those around her. In fact, the governess grasps Mrs. Grose repeatedly, often described in terms of clutching and seizing. A good example is when the governess declares she has no intention of answering the school's charges against Miles. Mrs. Grose says, "Would you mind, Miss, if I used the freedom—," to which the governess interjects, " 'To kiss me? No!' I took the good creature in my arms and after we had embraced like sisters felt still more fortified and indignant" (162).[20] The governess projects her possessive desires onto Mrs. Grose, whom she describes as a creature, in an embrace that prefigures her terminal embrace of Miles. This is also one of many instances when the governess speaks on behalf of Mrs. Grose, inserts an idea with certainty into a space of silence, a broken sentence, or a half utterance.

I need not press too hard on the possibility that the governess herself is a dead woman talking, though the evidence is not insignificant. My argument ultimately does not rest on whether the governess merely occupies the space left by a dead woman—"my vile predecessor" (221)—or if she herself is a dead woman talking. Either way, the governess asserts the kind of freedom available to Bly's servants in death and employs it among the living. Thus, James sets in motion anxieties about class hierarchy and its potential slippages in cross-generational transmission. Bly becomes an exercise in how the past can propagate itself in the present and into the future.

A Visitable Past

It is helpful to think of Bly in terms of what James describes in his 1908 preface as a "visitable past." If the past is visitable by the living, then surely the present is just as visitable by the dead. And they may return not as ghosts but as intruders seeking recognition on their own terms. "We are divided of course," James elaborates, "between liking to feel the past strange and liking to feel it familiar" (32). As James seeks a perfect balance between the two pulls, he aims for the uncanny and the squirming delight it affords a reader. James plucks the governess from Harley Street in London and drops her at a country estate in Essex. So too, American-born James wrote the tale from geographic displacement as an expatriate far from the streets of lower Manhattan, writing in London shortly before moving to Lamb House in Rye.[21] Bly relies on a rigid class structure so that the servants may successfully rear the next generation's masters and mistresses. If this manor were to crumble, so too would historical memory and the class system it propagates, as intricate as it is long-standing.

James famously casts us asea by presenting the very thing we are reading as an unnamed narrator's manuscript "from an exact transcript of my own made much later" (148) of Douglas's oral recitation of a manuscript written in a beautiful hand by the unnamed governess, which she gave to her current charge recounting what she could recall of her terrifying experiences with her past charges. Thus, the story is a hall of mirrors. Passages double back and reflect one another, leaving no external perch from which to orient ourselves. Such layering, combined with James's deliberate ambiguity, silences, elisions, and clashes between supernatural and scientific modes,[22] compels Peter Beidler to dub it a "chameleon text," able to take on whatever color one wishes to see in it,[23] hence the perpetual debate—as heated as it is unresolvable—whether or not the ghosts are real, and therefore whether or not the governess is a mad woman, a saintly protector, or perhaps a proto-Freudian totem of sexuality or consciousness. Each generation of scholars must comment on the sheer volume of criticism, often wittily describing the tedium of wading through it all. On this I demur to Martha Banta, who quipped in 1972 that she might "drive past the front gates of Bly out of the desire to offer the world of Jamesian criticism the gift of the absence of yet another look at 'The Turn of the Screw.' "[24] She enters, though, to make an important point: James knew his market, and "people wanted ghosts; taken straight or explained scientifically, but not necessarily 'explained away.' " She adds, "James had respect for the effect he could obtain by dramatizing the dead in confrontation with the living; he did not feel the need to apologize whenever he decided to use real ghosts."[25]

The rabbit-hole debate between the ghost camp and the mad woman camp obscures another question: not *whether* we see ghosts, but rather how we recognize *anyone* in the realm of the living. *The Turn of the Screw* has little interest in contributing yet more stock characters to the crowd of dead wandering about the ghost story tradition. Critics have traced how James incorporated contemporary spiritual beliefs and accounts of ghost sightings and demonic possessions into his realist tales,[26] while other critics have placed Quint, Jessel, and the governess among their more literary predecessors.[27] James's ghosts, like most of the dead women in this study, are striking because they do not perceive themselves as distinct from the living. They are as active in the daily life of Bly as anyone else in the story—more so in the case of the absent uncle. So too, as critic Jennifer Bann discovers in British literature, "in the supernatural fiction of the later nineteenth century, death began to bring freedom: shackles, silence, and regret were cast aside, and ghosts became active figures empowered rather than constrained by their deaths."[28] James is coy about the category to which Quint, Jessel, or anyone at Bly belongs. We see this in one of the more substantive changes to the New York edition from its original publication in *Collier's Weekly*. In discussing whether the governess should write the Uncle, the governess originally chides, "By writing to him that I have the honor to inform him that they see the dead come back?" In the New York edition, she retorts, "By writing to him that his house is poisoned and his little nephew and niece mad?"[29]

In all, this tale of intrusion hinges on a desire to be among one's own kind. This desire is especially keen in Miles, the young master-in-training. Walking to church arm in arm, the governess broaches the subject of why Miles was kicked out of school and whether he shall return. "I want my own sort!" he avows. The discussion is overtly about age and gender, as well as social station. It could also be about sexual kinship. The category *sort* works on all levels because it is as ambiguous in its meaning as Miles is in the vehemence of its delivery. The word is more multivalent still: Miles could also be asserting his desire to be among the living as he converses with the governess in the church graveyard. In all cases, Miles wants to be among his own kind. Which persons belong to which station is precisely the question driving the ghost story.

The Turn of the Screw is a notoriously slippery story that has delighted generations of readers and maddened more than a few along the way. Matters of justice are implicitly at stake in terms of how—or whether—we dole out class privilege and police inherited stations. At a time in the late nineteenth century when scientific knowledge was displacing supernatural belief in the popular imagination, property law was extending the power of the dead hand so that class privilege and power could continue into the next generation. Nonetheless, in the legal domain, as Friedman reminds, "the brutal fact remains: the dead are definitely dead. The dead 'control' beyond the grave only insofar as living people let them do so. In the long run, the dead run nothing" (183).

Property and tort law may devise all sorts of measures to keep the dead in their place, but fiction has no such strictures. If the novella's meaning is fundamentally ambiguous, so too are its politics. James taps into the trope of dead women talking and heads to Bly to raise questions about the justice or injustice of the creation of an American society purportedly interested more in merit and self-made men than in blue blood and title. Quint, Jessel, and perhaps the governess show us that when the dead visit the present, they need not follow their inherited class status. Must we, James asks, recognize these intruders as masters?

3

Dead Woman Rotting

William Faulkner's *As I Lay Dying*

Beloved stands as the most iconic dead woman talking in American literature, with Madeline Usher and James's dead servants as her key progenitors. Her most fully realized predecessor, though, is Addie Bundren, the mother in William Faulkner's 1930 modernist masterpiece *As I Lay Dying*. The novel chronicles Addie's death and her family's nine-day quest to cart her corpse through the summer sun to fulfill her last request: to be buried in Jefferson, the land of her blood kin. Two-thirds into the novel, and well after her death, Addie takes over the narrative for one strange, revealing chapter. While Poe and James wrap ambiguity around their talking dead, it is clear that when Addie takes over the narrative voice she is no ghost, nor any other stock gothic figure. Nor is she explicable by literary metaphors of the symbolically dead or legal metaphors of the civilly dead. Rather, she is simply and strikingly a dead woman, lying in a box, talking.

Formally, *As I Lay Dying* is a composite picture. When pieced together, the internal monologues of multiple narrators constitute something of a cubist vision of collective reality. The resulting portrait of life in the rural South is as morbid and harrowing as it is hilarious, from a toothless farmer who hasn't worked an honest day in his life (sweating could be fatal, he contends), to a doctor hoisted uphill by a mule and a winch because of his girth, to a broken leg set in concrete and baked in the July sun. When Addie speaks amid the cacophony, it comes as a shock—which is saying something for a Faulkner novel. Not only is it strange that she speaks in the first place, but she upends the narrative with tabloid-worthy revelations. Misanthropy! Sadism! Adultery! Blasphemy! Yet her speech is plainspoken and direct. Further, she prompts a realignment of the narrative pieces into a new composite picture, one able to account for a woman who is no longer the silent, suffering maternal figure holding together a family of not-quite-right characters.

By endowing Addie with a posthumous voice, however, Faulkner thwarts her own vision of posthumous justice: to separate herself from the Bundrens. Addie seeks to restore her original, uninterrupted self, which she understands as a return of the void that Anse Bundren and each subsequent child penetrated as she became a wife and then a mother. In short, she wants the aloneness that is her due. In contrast, Faulkner eventually grants Addie dignity by what remains curiously unnarrated: her actual burial, the ostensible point of the whole plot. At the end of the novel, when her body leaves not just the family home but the realm of narration altogether, she is her own again, no longer communal property. "On the bright side," contemporary Southern writer Nanci Kincaid quips, "at least she's single again."[1] This is no small point. Addie desires an autonomy that gets at questions of posthumous claims to the self and to the body. Who has claim to Addie's person, and who gets to say so? Such queries broach the matters of posthumous legal standing that I explored in Poe and James, as well as the bioethics approaches to the rights of the dying that I shall explore later in this chapter. Addie represents the outer limits of such claims because her body is close to a corpse while her quest for autonomy is just as lively and dependent on her present community as any other dead woman talking in American literature.

Addie's Word Problem

Strange, opaque, and unsettling voices abound in Faulkner's fiction, from Benjy the idiot narrator who opens *The Sound and the Fury*, to the maddening layers of competing narratives by Rosa Coldfield, Quentin Compson, and others in *Absalom, Absalom!* Still, Addie may be the most enigmatic in Faulkner's oeuvre, and not only because she doesn't get around to narrating her life until after it has ended. In American culture, we are trained to link voice to liberation, and silence to subjection. Women's liberation rhetoric and the feminist literary criticism that followed prized finding a voice of one's own. So too, during the height of AIDS activism, gay liberation equated silence with death. While living, Addie is nearly voiceless, save for the stern command "You, Cash!" twice repeated. As such, the fact that Addie speaks at all—however delayed or disquieting—may seem some kind of justice. Or, the fact that she speaks so little could underscore the voicelessness afforded Southern women, especially those in material poverty. Kincaid takes the latter tack in her elliptical meditation on this most elliptical novel. "Although this is clearly Addie's story," she declares, "men narrate fifty-one of the fifty-nine chapters. Women speak only eight; Addie, only one. Her voice, like her life, is surrounded by, perhaps buried beneath, the lives and voices of men."[2] And so the critical conversation goes: why and to what end Addie speaks. The fact that her body rots outside for nine days in the Deep South seems only to add insult to injury. Every vulture circling overhead, even when chased off by her grief-stricken son, is a testament to her abjection and degradation.

Even if voice allows entrance into the symbolic economy of liberation, there is a hitch. For Addie, words are intrusions, even when the voice is her own. "When [Cash] was born," she declares, "I knew that motherhood was invented by someone who had to have a word for it because the ones that had the children didn't care whether there was a word for it or not."[3] Words swap experience for lies; convert doers into the done-to; introduce dishonesty between body, experience, and utterance. Addie's semiotic theory is as homespun as it is complex and devastating. The result is not a silent nihilism, but rather a full-throated meditation on the violence of language, whose hypocrisy and patriarchy can only destroy a woman like Addie. She continues, "I knew that it had been, not that my aloneness had to be violated over and over each day, but that it had never been violated until Cash came" (172). It is motherhood, not sex itself, that ravages her aloneness, that robs her unified self and distributes portions of her into the bloodstreams of her progeny. Words like *motherhood* are tricky, needy, voluminous things. Addie asserts, "I knew that that word was like the others: just a shape to fill a lack" (172). Repeated throughout the monologue, the phrase "I knew" acts as surveyor flag, or perhaps gravestone, to mark the blank spaces covered over by a turf of words. Thus, Addie indicates moments of bodily cognition before words posed as the wooden dummy of experience.

Forced to trade in the economy of words, Addie's speech takes the form of a confessional. She articulates what had been unknown or undisclosed, whether out of shame, modesty, embarrassment, or even secret pride. She begins, "In the afternoon when school was out and the last one had left with his little dirty snuffling nose, instead of going home I would go down the hill to the spring where I could be quiet and hate them" (169). Addie's confession is as forthright as it is unexpected. While she cultivates her delicious hatred in quiet privacy, she asserts her existence through bodily interaction. This leads to one of the most shocking revelations: "I would look forward to the times when they faulted, so I could whip them" (170). This sadistic exchange was free to happen in the bright light of day, publicly sanctioned as the professional duty of a schoolteacher. "When the switch fell," she explains, "I could feel it upon my flesh; when it welted and ridged it was my blood that ran, and I would think with each blow of the switch: Now you are aware of me!" (170). Addie asserts her subjectivity via corporeal, rather than linguistic, exchange. The recipient's own body testifies to Addie's material presence in the community. So too, after death her rotting corpse offends the sensibilities of those around her—the scent lingering in nostrils akin to the welt rising on skin. Such bodily connections enact a morbid form of shared citizenship.

Addie's revelations are surprising in part because they depart so thrillingly from the maternal image cultivated by the other narrators, not to mention ingrained in Southern conventions of womanhood. Yet her misanthropy results from dutifully following her father's notorious lesson: "the reason for living was to get ready to stay dead a long time" (169). This yields a peculiar animus toward all that is living, including herself. "I would hate my father for having ever planted me" (170), she declares. So why live at all? "I believed that the reason was the duty to the alive," Addie maintains, "to the terrible blood, the red bitter flood boiling through the land" (174). She honors this duty through adultery with the local preacher, leading to her boldest confession: "I would think of sin as I would think of the clothes we both wore in the world's face, of the circumspection necessary because he was he and I was I; the sin the more utter and terrible since he was the instrument ordained by God who created the sin, to sanctify that sin He had created" (174). The bodily performance of sin is Addie's duty, not the confession of it. Indeed, the use of the word "utter" is conspicuous as it signals the degree of transgression by way of its speakability, or rather, its unspeakability.

The question of voice has driven debate about Addie in particular and the novel in general. Early feminist critics tended to see Addie as the logical endpoint of patriarchal orders, a silenced woman who only comes to voice when death allows her to openly break from her role as dutiful wife and mother.[4] Nonfeminist approaches often reach similar ends because a fully realized character in Faulkner's aesthetic requires voice, especially in a novel constituted by the words of characters who don't know they are narrators.[5] Others laud Addie's break from maternal expectations, what Diana York Blaine calls "myths of motherhood,"[6] so that she defies the suffocating, male-driven social order in which she finds herself voiceless. Her posthumous chapter is crucial to readers who look for resistance, for alternatives to the kinds of predicaments faced by the daughter Dewey Dell. Minrose Gwin, for example, considers the tomb in which patriarchy seals a mother like Addie, but she suggests that an alternative voice may be available inside the coffin,[7] or what John Liman playfully positions as "No-Man's-Land" given that it is the only place in the novel free of men.[8]

There is a much-noted irony, even a paradox, in focusing on Addie's voice: her refutation of language necessarily comes in the form of words. Silence may initially seem a way to solve this conundrum, but it, too, becomes a tool of duplicity and patriarchy when understood as the absence of voice. For when Whitfield the offending preacher narrates the chapter following Addie's, he decides that her deathbed silence is proof that he need not deliver his own confession to the cuckolded husband. The preacher has already confessed to God, so who is Anse to think he also deserves to hear it? Equating voice and subjectivity is ultimately a dead end. Addie seeks instead a non-word-based form of recognition. She represents her pre-violated self through a blank space in the text. "The shape of my body where I used to be a virgin," Addie declares, "is in the shape of a   and I couldn't think *Anse*, couldn't remember *Anse*" (173). Given her adversarial relationship to words, Addie must make room in the narrative for her prelapsarian unified self through a non-word, a space that shoves, crowds, and displaces the words around it in the narrative.

In turn, Addie's coffin, more so than her body, provides the skeleton of that space, makes it legible and public. It appears in a chapter narrated by Tull, the neighbor:

> They had laid her in it reversed. Cash made it clock-shape, like this 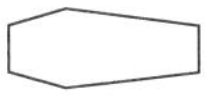 with every joint and seam beveled and scrubbed with the plane, tight as a drum and neat as a sewing basket, and they had laid her in it head to foot so it wouldn't crush her dress. It was her wedding dress and it had a flare-out bottom, and they had her head to foot so the dress could spread out, and they had made her a veil out of a mosquito bar so the auger holes in her face wouldn't show. (88)

Tull is the straight man in Faulkner's grotesque joke. In his description of the pitiful sight of the desecrated corpse-bride stuffed into a perfectly geometric shape, Addie achieves the public recognition she sought while living. "Now you are aware of me!"

Addie's Body Odor Problem

While Addie's core complaint is with words, Tull's description demonstrates that she is defined in the external community more by her material presence than by her voice. Even in the process of dying, her eyes have near-telekinetic power to push Dr. Peabody out of the room in which she lays dying—a not inconsiderable feat given his much-noted girth. Yet Addie's corpse has a rotten time in the novel. First, it desiccates for ten days before being pronounced dead; then it is laid head to foot in the coffin and Vardaman bores out the eyes when putting air holes in the coffin; then the coffin topples in the disastrous attempt to ford the river, which leaves two mules dead and the mother's corpse swimming like a fish. Not to mention the inevitable effects of the Southern summer climate, which creates a stench that draws more and more vultures. The rotting corpse offends the olfactory sensibilities of any unfortunate citizen on the makeshift funeral path.

Is Addie her body? Or, is the corpse Addie? Vardaman, at least, distinguishes between the self and the corpse: "I was there. I saw when it did not be her. I saw" (66–67). Further, Addie seems separable from her body's social station given that it is interchangeable with the new Mrs. Bundren, acquired at novel's end. Postmodern rhetorician Erin Edwards detects a "necropoetics" operating in the novel to distinguish thought from that which we see. "Before Addie's death," she argues, "the novel insists on the boundary between external, visible form and subjective inwardness only to demonstrate continually its breachability; after her death, this boundary is eroded altogether."[9] For the more discursive minded, the capacity for thought is what separates us from the status of a cadaver. As a dead woman inexplicably talking, however, Addie would seem to belie that distinction. For the more materialist minded, on the other hand, we are enlivened when our bodies are inscribed by state power and ideologies, a body-based version of citizenship to which I will return at chapter's end. As Addie becomes more and more of a corporeal presence, she is less seen than felt or otherwise sensed—a weighty burden, an intolerable smell, a decomposing problem.

The novel famously treats death as an indefinite process, not a discrete event, including in the title itself. When Peabody finally arrives, he observes blithely, "Addie's been dead ten days" (43). Dewey Dell reprises the contention: "It took her ten days to die; maybe she don't know it is yet" (59). Addie's condition is also likened to brute animals that nonetheless have the capacity to think and emote, such as when Tull notes Vardaman's fish "hiding into the dust like it was ashamed of being dead" (31). The trope continues when Dewey Dell describes Anse upon Addie's death: "his hands are halfclosed on either side of his plate, his head bowed a little, his awry hair standing into the lamplight. He looks like right after the maul hits the steer and it no longer alive and don't yet know that it is dead" (61). This unflattering description gets at the way body and cognition are not necessarily linked in this universe, not even at the moment of death.

Addie's lingering death leads to a legendary meditation on the nature of bodies, being, and the passage of time by Darl, "the one folks say is queer, lazy" (24). Darl imagines the rain outside on the coffin while he and his brother Jewel lie awake inside. "And when you are emptied for sleep," he muses, "what are you. And when you are emptied for sleep, you are not. And when you are filled with sleep, you never were" (80). Here, the sleeping body, not unlike a corpse, doesn't know it is. It is an emptied sack, a body without cognition. Darl revises the Cartesian maxim *I think, therefore I am* to include the variables of time and kin. He concludes his philosophical proof, "And since sleep is is-not and rain and wind are *was*, it is not. Yet the wagon *is*, because when the wagon is *was* Addie Bundren will not be. And Jewel *is*, so Addie Bundren must be. And then I must be, or I could not empty myself for sleep in a strange room. And so if I am not emptied yet, I am *is*" (81). Addie is *was* insofar as she is her corpse. Yet she is *is* insofar as her flesh lives on in her children, which poses a high-level math problem to which I will return. For now, it is important to note that Darl's grammatical thought experiment creates the possibility of recognizing the presence of the passed by putting the past tense in the present. Now Addie is *was*.

The theme of death and its central conceit, the corpse, pervade Faulkner's corpus. For some, Addie's body—and the gruesome plot twists it enables—is another instance of the Southern grotesque, which colors Faulkner's overall gothic portrayal of gender. Critic Gabrielle Schwab, for instance, considers the carnivalesque funeral procession and suggests that Addie's "phantasmatic body" is the logical endpoint of the symbolic mother in a "necrophilic male economy."[10] For others, the gruesome funeral parade is about proper and improper burial. The nine-day march may delay the work of grief long enough to address unfinished business before the corpse is buried once and for all. Lisa Perdigao, for instance, suggests that Addie problematizes the widespread modernist trope of entombment because neither the other fifteen narrators nor the coffin itself can contain her dead body.[11] Jessica Baldanzi and Kyle Schlabach further note that we are public witness to that which is usually private: bodily decomposition. "The stench of the decaying body," they argue, "serves as metaphor for the family's unspoken histories that have been pushed aside but stubbornly refuse burial." The outrage prompted by improper burial, they contend, be it Addie's fictional procession or the bodies dumped in the forest in a 2002 Georgia crematory scandal, signals "the mechanisms employed by the living to construct and remember our national past that are threatened with dissolution by such harrowing events."[12]

The prospect of improper burial leads to cultural and legal matters of who is in charge of the bodies of the dead. In chapter two's discussion of *The Turn of the Screw*, I noted that the law is generally unsettled around the question of posthumous rights. Legal scholars and public policy experts debate how and when to limit the power of the "dead hand" to dictate property lest the dead control us from the grave in perpetuity. Yet the time horizon for burial is short as far as legal questions go, even if nine days seems rather long for a summer funeral procession. Generally, we presume that the deceased has the right to dictate the parameters of her own burial, leaving only the question of, as legal historian Ray Madoff puts it, "determining who among the living was responsible for internment."[13] We accommodate such routine requests as a particular coffin, certain funeral songs, the color of dress in which to be buried, the location of ashes, or which body parts go to medical research. However, it may be surprising to note, as Madoff explains, that "American law has an uneasy relationship with control over the body. The foundational principle is that people do not own their bodies and thus have no enforceable rights to control their bodies after death."[14] In fact, until the nineteenth century when bodies became commodities for medical research and other pursuits, the dead retained no property interest in their corpses. English common law initially governed by the principle *corpus nullius in bonus*, or the body belongs to no one.[15]

To whom does a corpse belong? Or, who answers to Addie's corpse? Without a constitutionally protected property interest, the to-be-dead citizen must turn to piecemeal local and state statutes to control what happens to one's body when the inevitable happens. This duty tends to fall to the next of kin in what is called the "right of sepulcher," the right to choose and control final disposition of a dead human body—funeral arrangements, cremation or burial, and so on. As colorful options become more widespread and plentiful, Madoff contends that the question has become, "Can people make legally enforceable decisions about whether their body is buried or cremated, dissected for scientific study, harvested for organ transplants, or plasticized for display in traveling exhibits?"[16] Think baseball legend Ted Williams's cryonically preserved body and the family squabbles surrounding it, a modern twist on Jeremy Bentham's hay-stuffed body famously on display at the University College London since 1850. What happens to the body rests on the civic status of the living, especially survivors committed to following through on the wishes of their departed kin, the aggrieved who may sue for pain and suffering if a beloved corpse is mishandled, local law officers enforcing standards of proper care and disposal of bodies, and judges who decide which wishes of the once-alive are proper or enforceable. Skirmishes arise when the wishes of the dead are silent, unclear, contradictory, or in some way not reliable, so that the law must referee between competing claims of the living.

What of Addie's request to be buried in Jefferson? Generally, we attempt to honor the wishes of the dead because we deem them sacrosanct, if not necessarily legally enforceable. And it appears that the Bundrens are committed to honoring Addie's wish, even if Anse is dishonest when he repeatedly says he doesn't "begrudge" her the trouble. The reasons for honoring Addie's request may have more to do with the desires of the living: Dewey Dell needs an abortion in town, Cash wants some new tools, Vardaman craves a banana or toy train like the town boys, and Anse covets some new teeth and a new Mrs. Bundren. In both law and practice, the duty to fulfill the wishes of the dead falls to next of kin, starting with the closest.

It is a good thing for Addie that the Bundren clan is in charge of her body because the larger community is horrified by the desecrated and decomposing corpse paraded around for all to see (and smell). At one stop they are all but run out of town because, as Moseley reports, "it had been dead eight days, Albert said. . . . It must have been like a piece of rotten cheese coming into an ant-hill" (203). Addie's last wish comes into direct conflict with communal standards of proper care and disposal, leading the townsfolk to accuse the Bundrens of endangering local health. They cast the Bundrens as outsiders, perhaps even noncitizens: "in that ramshackle wagon that Albert said folks were scared would fall all to pieces before they could get it out of town, with that home-made box and another fellow with a broken leg lying on a quilt on top of it, and the father and a little boy on the seat and the marshal trying to make them get out of town" (203–4). In part, Faulkner employs the curious outsider to paint an external picture of the grotesque spectacle, fueling the wicked humor of the novel. The passage, especially the presence of the marshal, also signals the skirmish between competing interests of the living and their civic ability to decide where and how a corpse resides.

Addie's ordeal is, of course, fictional, so a legal framework may seem odd for Faulkner's modernist experiment. Nonetheless, the stories we tell about corpses reflect not only our capacity to recognize posthumous rights but also how we perceive any body—be it living or dead, rural or urban, male or female, smelly or not—as a container of our natural rights. In *Private Bodies, Public Texts*, cultural critic Karla FC Holloway considers how bioethics approaches questions of bodily ownership and asks, "When do the voices of the dying matter?"[17] She notes how high-profile deaths of the vulnerable and voiceless become "relentlessly public narratives"[18] written by others and circulated widely—Terri Schiavo in her right-to-die case that teleported her image to the U.S. Senate floor, the black men in the notorious Tuskegee syphilis study, those euthanized in the LifeCare ward of Memorial Medical Center in New Orleans in the aftermath of Hurricane Katrina. Their bodies became spectacular displays with little recourse to how they would narrate their own experience of dying (and living). Holloway finds Toni Morrison's concept of "unspeakable things unspoken" useful, "knowing that the dead no longer have their voices and that what they would, or might, say is spoken by others whose own identities matter as they speak for the dead."[19] This seems a perfect description of Faulkner's multi-narrator account.

Except that Addie's body differs from a legal cadaver in an important way: it talks. So too, Madoff notes wryly, "Certainly a body after death is very different from a living human being. It is no longer capable of actions or thoughts; unless treated, it quickly decomposes."[20] How are we to incorporate the voices of the dead—the is *was*—into our composite picture and our obligations to them? Perhaps her decomposition in itself is a form of legible speech, a nonword assertion of Addie's presence.

Addie's Math Problem

While Addie's decomposition provokes crises in communal standards and civil order, it also enacts how she experienced life as a wife and mother. Addie goes so far as to quantify the degree to which she became less Addie and more Bundren with each child. Upon the birth of Darl, her second child, Addie asserts, "It was not that I could think of myself as no longer unvirgin, because I was three now" (173). Maternal duty requires the negation of self, a central caveat in Addie's mathematics of motherhood. "I gave Anse the children," she declares. "I did not ask for them. I did not even ask him for what he could have given me: not-Anse. That was my duty to him, to not ask that, and that duty I fulfilled" (174).

Addie's math problem requires some advanced algebra in the case of Jewel, the bastard child from the affair with Whitfield. "I gave Anse Dewey Dell to negative Jewel," Addie explains. "Then I gave him Vardaman to replace the child I had robbed him of. And now he has three children that are his and not mine" (176). In other words,

$$1 + 1 + (1 - 1) + 1 = 3$$

or

$$1 + 1 + \qquad\qquad + 1 = 3$$

The mathematics of motherhood does not bode well for any woman, not just Addie. Dewey Dell, the lone daughter, is either a negation represented by a negative integer or a blank space with no coffin to cordon off the lack Addie finds so valuable. Yet Addie in some ways escapes her own math problem: she is simply not part of the equation. Generally, literary critics tend to agree that Addie rejects the logic of motherhood. Yet by her own logic, as she distributes herself to her progeny, she fulfills her obligations to Anse in the numerical contract of motherhood. Critic Marc Hewson bucks critical consensus to contend that Addie is, in a way, an ideal mother in that she teaches her children, especially male ones, "how to combat the oppressive and ultimately negative philosophy of patriarchy in the book."[21] Still, I find it hard to position Addie as an anti-patriarchy freedom fighter seeking the liberation of the next generation. In fact, she'd like nothing more than to rid herself of them. For when she solves her math problem, she concludes, "And then I could get ready to die" (176). If Addie's struggle is to exert dominion over her own body, the mathematics of motherhood thwarts that quest. Her unified *one* becomes a strange distributive property able to replicate itself. She is no longer a solitary integer, but rather a finite quantity.

As a quantified entity, the children seem to consume their mother—literally in the case of Vardaman. In his famous one-line chapter, "My mother is a fish" (84), the young son concocts a private symbolic system to understand death. He finds equivalence between his mother's new corpse and that of the fish he inexplicably catches in the pond—which is why he is so horrified when the Bundrens eat the fish for supper. Yet the symbolic cannibalism corresponds with Addie's mathematical logic. As Addie swims in the bloodstreams of her offspring, her unified self becomes a dispersed and limited entity. Vardaman struggles to figure out a symbolic system in which both his mother can be a fish and Jewel's can be a horse. This poses a conundrum:

> "Then what is your ma, Darl?" I said.
>
> "I haven't got ere one," Darl said. "Because if I had one, it is *was*. And if it is was, it cant be *is*. Can it?"

Vardaman joins the grammatical wordplay:

> I am. Darl is my brother.
>
> "But you *are*, Darl," I said.
>
> "I know it," Darl said. "That's why I am not *is*. *Are* is too many for one woman to foal." (101)

This exchange squares Darl's is/was cosmology with Addie's math problem. The children's presence does not mark the way Addie will live on after her death, an all too saccharine view of genealogy. Rather, their presence testifies to the horrifying theft of personhood that happens when one becomes more, when *is* becomes *are*, when a woman becomes an unvirgin and then a mother. Or when a woman becomes a mere symbol in a patriarchal order, be it a fish, a horse, or a cow. Faulkner's animal symbols signify the possibility of adulterous descent—even if Darl gets it wrong. He suggests that Jewel and Vardaman can have different mothers, rather than fathers. Yet that symbolic economy, too, threatens to rob Addie of her personhood, swapping the material fact of matrilineal descent for patrimony.

Addie's Declaration of Independence

If we imagine Addie's path toward subjectivity through either voice or bodily ownership, there is an intractable problem because she only comes to either upon her death. This conflicts with how we understand citizenship in the modern nation-state. Intellectual historian Ed Cohen explains that modern citizenship dictates that to access one's rights within the political community, one must first have claim to a (human) body. This equation between rights and the living body, Cohen demonstrates, anchors France's Declaration of the Rights of Man, whose first article asserts, "Men are born and remain free and equal in rights."[22] The focus on birth, Cohen contends, ties the nation's obligations to the living bodies of its subjects, which requires the state to maintain the conditions of natal equality and become invested in the health of its subjects' bodies. The U.S. Declaration of Independence, written thirteen years earlier, formulates its self-evident truths slightly differently: "That all men are created equal; that they are endowed by their Creator with certain unalienable Rights, that among these are Life, Liberty, and the pursuit of Happiness." Cohen argues that the focus on creation, while still linking rights to bodies, colors the natural rights claim. "This is an abstract nature," he asserts, "not a living one."[23] Yet the caveat that to have rights one must have a *living* body poses a problem for Addie and all the disenfranchised of history who cannot, do not, or will not come to voice during their lifetimes.

The speaking cadavers of American literature, I have suggested so far in this book, seek what we may call posthumous citizenship: recognition as full members of the present political community. Addie's petition corresponds most to the version of citizenship in the U.S. Declaration in that she asserts her right to dissolve ties and declare her independence from the Bundrens. The slack in the line tying natural rights and the bodies that carry them—the abstraction Cohen finds so troubling in the U.S. Declaration—allows for the kind of posthumous citizenship Addie seeks. Cohen suggests that the U.S. Declaration is in line with the concept of *habeas corpus* in English law, which, as its literal translation suggests—"you may have the body"—poses the body as something a subject possesses, separable from the person who owns it and for which it stands metonymically.

Addie's chapter is the most extreme writ of habeas corpus in the American literary tradition. She formulates her request as revenge for the trick of words like *motherhood*: "And when Darl was born I asked Anse to promise to take me back to Jefferson when I died, because I knew that father had been right, even when he couldn't have known he was right anymore than I could have known I was wrong" (173). The "I knew" again marks a space of bodily knowledge unhooked (at least temporarily) from cognition and speech. Addie's body, including in its corpse form, is a material bulwark against the tricky way words swap experience for lies. Her posthumous writ of habeas corpus petitions for the return of her body from the Bundren's jurisdiction: their home, their lineage, and ultimately the narrated realm itself.

Addie wants—declares—her independence, both posthumous and corporeal. This independence takes the shape of what Holloway calls "private personhood," the freedom to select our identities in a liberal conception of autonomous selfhood in the vein of John Stuart Mill. Such freedom, Holloway argues, is curtailed by social narratives that adhere to minority bodies, which "begin with a compromised relationship to privacy," both its presumption and the legal protection of it.[24] Holloway cites as a prime example Henrietta Lacks, the black Baltimore housewife who died of ovarian cancer in 1951, but not before her cancer tissue was harvested with neither her nor her family's knowledge. The cells proved remarkably vital and able to reproduce themselves like no other, leading to what Rebecca Skloot dubs *The Immortal Life of Henrietta Lacks*. For Holloway, this is not just a case study of medical ethics or laboratory protocol for human subjects, but an invasion on the level of narrative. The ensuing cell line—named HeLa—developed a life of its own, personified in a way that stood in for, and eventually displaced, the real Henrietta Lacks, who suffered greatly and perished as a result of the same vigorousness that scientists now find so valuable in her cell line.[25] As her private body became a public text, Lacks became part of a story against her will. Addie's wish, on the other hand, is to recede from the public text after the spectacle of her dying and macabre funeral procession. Her claim to (posthumous) personhood rests on a specific manifestation of individual privacy: the right to be left alone.

In the end, Addie's sovereignty over her own burial, more so than her voice, is where her full expression of civic personhood lies. The sole mention to that event is in a sidelong reference buried in a long sentence opening the final chapter. "So when we stopped there to borrow the shovels," Cash narrates, "we heard the graphophone playing in the house, and so when we got done with the shovels pa says, 'I reckon I better take them back'" (258). The sentence readies us for resolution on Anse's terms: his willful participation in a borrowers' economy after spending the novel allegedly "not wanting to be beholden" to anyone. Cash neglects the communal scene of interment and the labor of burial, opting instead to note the tools of digging and their rightful ownership. The Bundren clan shifts their attention to the transactions that turn the shovel and graphophone owner into the new Mrs. Bundren. Addie's burial falls away to nearly unmentioned status, with the passage "when we got done with the shovels" being an oblique reference at best. On first glance, this curious disinterest may seem an affront, one more cruel testament to the depravity of the Bundrens and why they are unfit for modern society. Or it may signal the success of the grief work that is the function of any funeral, even one as drawn out and unconventional as Addie's. But for Addie, the omission achieves justice on her terms: the restoration of her aloneness. She finally achieves her right to (posthumous) private personhood when she recedes from the public, narrated realm.

I have argued elsewhere that the Bundrens are an example of the historical uncanny as they move into an urban, technology-ridden space, thereby pitting them as relics of an earlier age who inexplicably exist in the present nation.[26] In a special death issue of the *Faulkner Journal*, John T. Matthews suggests that Faulkner's fiction "dedicates itself to the endlessly unrewarding task of recollecting what too many wish to leave unrecalled, to interrogate the forgetting that enables all remembering."[27] His prime examples are the lynched black bodies in the novels *Sanctuary* and *Light in August*, but the point holds well beyond black morbidity. Death, he contends, becomes a way for the past to trouble the nation's desire to embrace the future by way of forgetting, discarding, burying. Literary critic Tamara Slankard also argues that Addie's unembalmed corpse is a fetish that enables a "putrefying unification" among relics of the rural Old South, and it "allows the Bundrens to navigate and define the family's—and the New South's—place in the modern world."[28] Indeed, this is the function of the Southern gothic according to critic Leigh Anne Duck: to cast the South as part of the nation but apart, the residual past of modern national time.[29] In *As I Lay Dying*, the line between past and present falls along the rural/town divide within the South itself. Yet this reading would make little sense for Addie because she originally comes from town and wishes to be restored to that space. Meanwhile, the Bundrens will return with the new Mrs. Bundren to their house with no road connecting it to the surrounding community and, by extension, the nation. If anything, Addie's body stands for the terrible possibility of a modern subject sucked back into a past agrarian age. Only in death can she be restored to the nation's present in Jefferson.

I should note that, like Madeline Usher, Addie's status as a dead woman talking is up for debate. Critics disagree over not only the content of Addie's speech but also its location. Does Addie speak as a cadaver inside her coffin, perhaps one of Diana Fuss's corpse poems trapped inside this strange prose amalgam of a novel? Or does she speak from elsewhere, liberated from her body? And when exactly does Addie speak? Her soliloquy appears well after she has died in the narrative. Still, given Darl's ruminations on how time is not a forward-moving river, it could be that death liberates Addie from the physics of linear time. Darl, who we know to be skilled in the art of communicating "without the words," has yet another theory. When Vardaman reports, "She's talking to God," Darl says, "She is calling on Him to help her" (214). On the one hand, this could be a self-serving act of ventriloquism given that Darl's assertion directly precedes his attempt at ad hoc cremation of the corpse in a barn burning. (Jewel thwarts this act of mercy by rescuing the coffin from the blaze.) Still, Darl's follow-up explanation is worthwhile regardless of whether he is reporting Addie's speech or ventriloquizing her. "She wants Him to hide her away from the sight of man," he says. And later, "We must let her be quiet" (215). Like so many of his queer ideas, Darl the idiot-philosopher seems to understand justice as Addie understands it. Addie just wants to be left alone.

And that includes us. Addie reveals not only her distrust of words, her exquisite masochism toward children, and her infidelity to Anse, but also her indifference toward the reader. I might have framed this chapter not around Addie's rotting body but rather as a dead woman confessing. But this risks misperceiving Addie's voice and our relationship to it. She may reveal heretofore unspoken secrets that some of the living may wish to remain buried, but she speaks from a posture of neither repentance nor supplication. Rather, she is forthright and declarative, asking nothing of the reader. We overhear her soliloquy but can offer her nothing—which is something. We can grant her request to turn away, to restore her aloneness. To let her be quiet.

4

Dead Woman Cursing

Alice Walker's *In Search of Our Mothers' Gardens*

If Addie's dying wish is independence from the living, we do right by turning away. But more often the *absence* of women from living memory and daily life is a social justice issue. The literary tradition of dead women talking, then, holds the power to correct such injustices through a concrete means by which to commune with the dead, especially the forgotten, misremembered, or improperly buried. This power may seem exclusive to imaginative literature, but in fact the tradition extends into nonfiction terrain. A good example is Alice Walker in her notable efforts to recover and celebrate black women's literature and history. In her 1983 blockbuster collection of essays *In Search of Our Mothers' Gardens*, she employs posthumous speakers in her aim to construct new genealogies—cultural, literary, familial—or mend broken ones. Two instances are particularly relevant: Zora Neale Hurston herself in the famous 1975 essay "Looking for Zora,"[1] as well as the exhumation of the voice of a nameless cursing woman in the lesser-known 1982 essay "Only Justice Can Stop a Curse."[2] These two examples demonstrate that Walker's goal is to enter into dialogue with dead women. The result is a particularly rich model for social justice: our ability—and responsibility—to respond to those who lacked a full voice or, more crucially, a full audience in their times. Yet Walker further considers the question, what if we might not want to hear what the dead have to say? What curses might we unearth—and perhaps provoke in the process? Or, worse yet, what if our cherished dead are as uninterested in us as Addie Bundren?

"Looking for Zora" is a prime example of Walker's concern with genealogical connections, along with literature's related power to restore beauty, relevance, and *voice* to the forgotten and silenced. Voice, in this example, becomes not only figurative but also literal over the course of the essay. Walker famously marks the grave of a neglected Harlem Renaissance writer and trained anthropologist, thereby exhuming the legacy of a literary foremother for a new generation. For Walker, Hurston's unmarked grave not only signifies her near obscurity but also stands as a synecdoche of the marginalized status of black women writers and black women in America more generally. "I am used to the haphazard cemetery-keeping that is traditional in most Southern black communities," Walker declares, "but this neglect is staggering" (104).

"Looking for Zora" is Walker's most famous essay, and its influence is widespread. Originally published in *Ms. Magazine*, it is a signal text of feminist recovery projects, joining such other standards as Adrienne Rich's 1971 essay "When We Dead Awaken: Writing as Re-vision." Drawing on archival research, word-of-mouth knowledge, and a tale that she is Hurston's niece (a "useful lie," she calls it), Walker sets out to find Hurston's grave in an overgrown cemetery south of Eatonville, Florida, the all-black incorporated town where Hurston grew up. In resuscitating Hurston in a post–civil rights era, Walker also contributed to and helped popularize widespread feminist efforts to rescue, rediscover, and revalue other women writers who had been marginalized, misunderstood, or forgotten. During this time, literary history served as a key feminist site to confront past injustices and also to create usable and just pasts, thereby claiming what feminist critic Teresa Washington calls "blood-ink kin."[3] For Walker, this is no mere academic or political endeavor; it is a sort of pilgrimage and a familial homecoming. The stakes are high and the genealogical connections profound. Walker insists, "As far as I'm concerned, she *is* my aunt—and that of all black people as well" (102).

Calling the Dead

Walker does not simply recover Hurston's archive—she raises her from the dead. Walker chronicles a doomed search for Hurston's grave while accompanied by Rosalee, a reluctant local guide who is none too excited about the prospect of snakes in the abandoned field. Exasperated, Walker recounts:

> "Zora," I yell, as loud as I can (causing Rosalee to jump). "Are you out there?"
> "If she is, I sho hope she don't answer you. If she do, I'm gone."
> "Zora!" I call again. "I'm here. Are you?"
> "If she is," grumbles Rosalee, "I hope she'll keep it to herself." (105)

This moment of levity is also deeply serious. Walker creates a welcoming feeling of intimacy between the essayist and her foremother while also underscoring the severity of Hurston's neglect and therefore the hopelessness of the quest. Walker calls out a few more times, at one point chiding, "I hope you don't think I'm going to stand out here all day" (105).

At this point, the conversation is entirely one-sided, with the essayist merely inviting the dead woman to speak. And she does . . . in a way. Walker spots a strangely large insect who guides her to a sunken spot in the ground. To be sure, Hurston never has a direct voice in the essay outside the excerpts of her writing. If Hurston were to talk in this nonfiction piece, Walker would strain credibility and tip the delicate balance of humor and pathos. Instead, she endows Hurston with a different kind of voice, one connected to the universe and the natural world. As we read the essay, Walker coaches us on how to listen to dead women, to open ourselves to alternative means of communication, such as a conspicuous insect. This corresponds to the way Walker had to augment the traditional archive with her own means of piecing together Hurston's story from scraps, clues, half remembrances, competing stories, and, just as important, the unsaid.

Cheryl Wall, an expert on Hurston and black women writers, describes this scene as a "spiritual reunion" between Walker and her literary foremother. "In the essays," she clarifies, "these encounters are understood to be psychic rather than physical. They are Walker's way of coming to terms with her dead: black and white, writers and workers, artistic ancestors and close kin."[4] While I concur with Wall's lucid reading of Walker's overall aim, in a way Walker *does* seek a physical encounter with Hurston. Walker seeks to enter into a dialogue with Hurston, not to ventriloquize her. The essay goes out of its way to distinguish this moment from mere prosopopoeia. Walker is not throwing her voice into the wind and adopting the persona of Hurston. Instead, the autobiographical essay earnestly if also playfully positions Walker as hearing from Hurston herself, a sort of intimate ghost story.

Even before this strange encounter, the story is swaddled in the uncanny, bringing Hurston into the realm of other dead women talking in American literature. For instance, Walker recounts, "Eatonville has lived for such a long time in my imagination that I can hardly believe it will be found existing in its own right" (94). At this point for Walker, Eatonville and Hurston are pure story, what Hurston herself might call "crayon enlargements of life."[5] They are separate from the present, which is to say the known, the real, the canny. Hurston's commitment to black culture and indifferent attitude toward integration are throwbacks or curiosities inconsistent with contemporary national narratives. But they make sense in Eatonville. Over the course of the essay, Walker seeks to transport Hurston, as well as Eatonville, from the timeless, mythical realm of the half-forgotten into historical time and official national memory.[6]

Walker's quest to mark Hurston's grave evokes scenes of burial and grave marking throughout an African American literary tradition in which proper mourning is often not possible, such as in slavery, many lynchings, and the early Jim Crow era when black undertakers were rare.[7] The gravestone is most directly evocative of Sethe's sacrificial offering of a carved headstone for her murdered daughter in *Beloved* and, by extension, the "sixty million and more" for which Beloved stands. Sethe has no other means to pay the engraver than her own body, which only allows her the single word, half-remembered from the opening of a funeral sermon. Like Sethe, Walker desires a proper headstone but lacks the monetary means. "I realize I must honor the dead," Walker reports, "but between the dead great and the living starving, there is no choice" (107). She purchases a modest headstone and engraving, instead positioning the essay itself as the grand monument honoring Hurston's legacy.

The essay genre is uniquely well suited to Walker's project because its penchant for interpellation of others' words and voices, often through quotation, allows the essayistic "I" to enter into direction conversation with Hurston's own words, as well as those of other writers and thinkers now gone. In turn, the essay's formal ability to give voice *in the present* points to a uniquely literary means of imagining social justice for wronged figures from the past. As such, this is not just a story of mourning and proper burial. In her inspired study *Passed On: African American Mourning Stories*, Karla FC Holloway chronicles Hurston's literary portraits of death, especially her own mother's in her 1942 autobiography *Dust Tracks on a Road*, and notes, "Tragically, Zora Hurston's dramatic literary historicizing could not be put to use for the moment when the veil descended on her own life."[8] She turns to Walker's account, along with biographer Robert Hemenway's, as key sources of the story of neglect and misunderstanding that surround Hurston's death. But for Walker, our duty to Hurston is not to belatedly eulogize her or otherwise mourn her properly, nor even to provide a proper reburial, as we will see in the penultimate chapter on *Getting Mother's Body*. Instead, to celebrate her, Walker brings Hurston back to life in the present. That is, she brings Hurston into the realm of dead women talking.

The Beauty of Curses

Like "Looking for Zora," Walker's less-studied essay "Only Justice Can Stop a Curse" also features a sort of dead woman talking and deals in themes of burial and exhumation. Walker unearths a curse from another era so that a current readership confronts a wronged figure from the past. Walker then embeds it within an essay that ends in her own voice addressing a contemporary readership, first in the socialist feminist magazine *Mother Jones*[9] and then in the womanist collection *In Search of Our Mothers' Gardens*. The essay turns full-throated to issues of historical injustice on a grander scale than the one marking Hurston's grave. Along the way, Walker provides one model for how the living can *respond* to the stories of dead women talking and the injustices about which they speak.

"Only Justice Can Stop a Curse" opens with an invocation, or a "curse-prayer," by a nameless speaker. She reports, "I have been sorely tried by my enemies and have been blasphemed and lied against" (338). This direct address to a "Man God" sets in motion a rhetorical situation in which the reader overhears an apostrophic address between a generic subject of oppression and a patriarchal deity who has yet to intervene. The speaker swiftly chronicles her abuses in a rather generic register—a disrespected home, ill-treated children, and so on—for one brief paragraph. In contrast, she reserves the remaining three-fourths of her space to describe with razor-sharp, excruciating detail her vision of revenge. Among her wishes for her enemies, she asks "that the South wind shall scorch their bodies and make them wither and shall not be tempered by them" (338). She also sows a vision of death and decline by way of cross-generational calamity so that "the children who may come shall be weak of mind and paralyzed of limb and that they themselves shall curse [their fathers and mothers] in their turn for ever turning the breath of life into their bodies" (339).

The speaker's enmity shows no bounds as she methodically roots out and excavates any space for potential mercy or forgiveness. And then she fills it with retribution. The curse is exquisite in its design, an act of impressive creativity. It requires feats of imagination to ask that the natural elements turn against her enemies, as well as every last possible source of comfort, camaraderie, or survival. She seeks ancestors turned to enemy, family to stranger, friend to foe, and body to broken vessel ending only in extinction. Thus, the curse-prayer is a bewitching example of what Wall in another context calls "the will to adorn."[10] As a grand vision of destruction, it is terrifying in its ruthless adornment.

But the essay does not end in this sublime vision of obliteration. The curse-prayer opens an essay in which Walker enters into a cross-generational dialogue between herself, the speaker of the curse-prayer, and again Hurston, who collected it during her ethnographic activities in the 1920s and published it in 1935 in *Mules and Men*.[11] "And by then," Walker underscores, "it was already old" (339). Walker's voice is distinct from that of the speaker of the curse-prayer. "I am sure it was a woman who first prayed this curse," she opines. "And I see her—black, yellow, brown or red, '*aboriginal*' as the Ancients are called in South Africa and Australia and other lands invaded, expropriated, and occupied by whites" (340). Walker portrays the speaker of the curse not as herself but rather as a more synthesized figure of oppression, pure alterity.

In the dialogue between Walker and the speaker of the curse-prayer emerges a crucial split: the essayist chooses justice over vengeance. To be sure, Walker recognizes—revels in—the horrifying beauty and utility of the curse-prayer, probing the allure of the siren song of grand reckoning, which seems so possible in a nuclear age. "However," Walker writes, "just as the sun shines on the godly and ungodly alike, so does nuclear radiation. And with this knowledge it becomes increasingly difficult to embrace the thought of extinction purely for the assumed satisfaction of—from the grave—achieving revenge" (341). The essayist rejects pure revenge because it can only result in death for all. In making this break, Walker opts instead for a much more difficult task: to imagine justice. The act of chronicling injustice, as urgent and warranted as it is, is insufficient. To stop there would be a failure of the imagination.

Nonetheless, Walker's essay is woefully thin in its image of what justice looks like. It is more out of balance than the original curse-prayer's lopsided attention to the details of revenge over abuses. Instead, Walker ends abruptly with another apostrophic address, this one to her reader. Walker declares, "Let me tell you: I intend to protect my home." She turns to another prayer, this time sans curse, and insists that "only justice to every living thing (and everything is alive) will save humankind" (342). It is up to the reader, not the essayist, to figure out what justice looks like, let alone how to achieve it. The stakes are high, Walker reminds us, and our responsibilities lie with the speaker of the curse-prayer because, as Walker repeats in the concluding line,

"*Only justice can stop a curse*" (342). We must inhabit the unfinished role of the essayist to listen and respond to this dead woman talking.

This time, the dead woman talking *is* an example of prosopopoeia. Walker begins the essay by directly adopting the voice of the once-collected curse-prayer. The curse likely came to Hurston from Marie Leveau, a freeborn woman of color and famed voodoo practitioner in nineteenth-century New Orleans[12] who is a key figure in *Mules and Men*.[13] However, Walker cites only Hurston and conspicuously does not identify the origins of the curse, leaving the speaker without a particular body. Because the curse-prayer has no identified author in the essay, it is ever in search of an author to utter it, or transcribe it. As such, the curse-prayer is pure voice in search of a body. Hurston the ethnologist serves merely as a medium for the voice, as does Walker two generations later.

The curse is a pervasive, long-standing folk form, but it has been little studied as a literary genre in its own right. A curse can be a verbal act, a written document, or a material artifact, such as a voodoo doll, all of which may have differing functions. In print culture, we find the curse as a motif in medieval texts,[14] in Anglo-Saxon legal documents,[15] in magic rituals in ancient Syria,[16] in the Book of Job,[17] in Ovidian curse-poems and ancient curse tablets,[18] and as a staple in contemporary literature. Regarding curse tablets of ancient Rome and Greece, classicist Daniel Ogden suggests that "writing may have been attributed with some magical power of its own: initially the very act of writing a name, of 'freezing' it permanently in lead, could in itself have been considered a way of tying it down by comparison with the transience of uttering it."[19] Anthony Thiselton, on the other hand, questions the assertion that ancient minds placed such power in words themselves, pointing instead to the speaker and social conventions for the curse's power.[20] Either way, as a written genre, the curse retains an oral quality, bringing it into the realm of oral literature or what some scholars call *orature*.[21] As such, scholars Brenda Danet and Bryna Bogoch study what happens when an oral form enters print culture so that "curses are both a type of oral residue and evidence of growing awareness of the performative potential of writing."[22]

Walker's inclusion of the curse, as well as Hurston's act of transcription that preceded it, draws on the interplay between verbal utterance and written document. The original curse seems to exist outside of historical time, and the curser becomes anonymous in print circulation. The act of transcription and interpellation brings the curse and curser into the present in Walker's historically minded essay. Still, its condemnation of injustice seems to exist outside of historical time; it is ever adaptable for the current ventriloquist's aims. As its medium, the essayist adapts the curse-prayer for the current moment, be it the threat of nuclear annihilation at the tail end of the Cold War, post-sixties consciousness movements of people of color, or latter-day eugenicists (Walker cites physicist William Shockley's senatorial campaign).

Walker's move to catalog and embody the curser goes against an ancient curse tradition in which, as Ogden explains, ancient cursers relied on ghosts or underworld powers to carry out their curses. Such cursers specifically "avoided naming themselves on their tablets, except in the cases of prayers for justice and erotic-attraction spells. This was doubtless to avoid retribution from both the living and the dead."[23] Walker, however, adopts the voice of the curser in her own body, not that of a corpse. In this act of authorial ventriloquism, Walker puts herself in danger, binding her future to the targets of the curse. The targets, on the other hand, remain unspecified, in the vein of what Danet and Bogoch call "whoever" curses.[24]

As a folk motif, the curse is closely associated with themes of retribution of the oppressed, often the last resort of a marginalized figure. In literary studies, the curse is closely associated with colonial contact in particular, thanks to the work of Stephen Greenblatt in *Learning to Curse*, which positions Caliban as an iconic colonial subject in Shakespeare's *The Tempest*. Caliban learns the language of the oppressor. And what he does with it is curse. Greenblatt argues, "Ugly, rude, savage Caliban nevertheless achieved for an instant an absolute if intolerably bitter moral victory."[25] Of course, the cursing in question is more on the level of profanity than prophecy, but the trope of Caliban's curse has enjoyed much traction.[26] A fukú curse that opens Junot Díaz's 2007 Pulitzer Prize–winning novel *The Brief and Wondrous Life of Oscar Wao*, for example, originates at the moment Christopher Columbus sets foot in the Western hemisphere. "They say it came from Africa," Díaz writes, "carried in the screams of the enslaved; that it was the death bane of the tainos, uttered just as one world perished and another began; that it was a demon drawn into Creation through the nightmare door that was cracked open in the Antilles. *Fukú americanus*, or more colloquially fukú—generally a curse or a doom or some kin; specifically the Curse and the Doom of the New World. . . . But the fukú ain't just ancient history, a ghost story from the past with no power to scare."[27]

As Díaz's tongue-in-cheek fukú to America suggests, the curse is now a common framework for understanding colonial contact and the strategies of resistance on the part of the colonized. This leads Judith Newton and Judith Stacey to laud Greenblatt for "envisioning multicultural and less unjust futures" in their essay "Learning How Not to Curse."[28] In Walker's case, I suggest that the curse as a genre helps bring about such just futures by creating urgency and, potentially, self-interest on the part of the powerful. The difference between a curse or prayer, on the one hand, and a prophecy or spell, on the other, is that the former speak in the subjunctive ("may they perish") and the latter in the declarative ("they will perish"). The former are hypothetical or aspirational, the latter inevitable. There is something one can do to avoid the subjunctive from happening in the present. That is, a curse needn't be prophecy.

As a subjunctive utterance, the curse-prayer is forever in search of its own obsolescence. Because it speaks on a mythic register, it resides outside historical time; it inhabits the ever-present now. Walker seeks to bring the curse-prayer into historical time, in turn ever seeking a readership—or citizenry—that can deliver the justice that can stop a curse. That is why Walker considers the merits of the curse-prayer in a conditional mode. She writes, "If we have any true love for the stars, planets, the rest of Creation, we must do everything we can to keep the white man away from them" (341). By insisting on the "if," Walker sets up a contract between the universe and the reader: act in the universe's interests . . . or risk eradication. The conditional statement allows for the possibility that the vision of utter annihilation is in fact one form of justice, albeit one that includes no humans. So, it becomes a matter of urgent survival to imagine an alternate form of justice, one that will include humans and end what critic Anthony Lioi elsewhere calls Walker's "cosmic loneliness."[29] And by positioning the work of justice in opposition to that of the "white man," Walker retains the curse-prayer's polarized view of the world and insists that the category of whiteness—with its arrogant assumptions of superiority and histories of atrocities—has no place in a just world. What that world looks like, though, is up to the reader.

A Call to Imagination

In "Looking for Zora," the half-forgotten foremother called out from her unmarked grave, and the essayist herself was not yet ready to respond directly. Instead, Walker leaves the scene to later mark the grave with a headstone and reflect on the experience in the safety of the essay form. But in "Only Justice Can Stop a Curse," Walker further dramatizes the unmet call, the urgent need for a response. She uses the essay form's penchant for open-ended inquiry[30] to signify the unfinished business of the curse-prayer. In doing so, Walker acts as a medium between the dead woman talking and the live reader listening. In turn, the reader must accept the responsibility of imagining justice with as much precision, ferocity, and innovation as it took to create the curse-prayer in the first place.

As a whole, *In Search of Our Mothers' Gardens* engages matters of both social justice and genealogy, two deeply intertwined concerns throughout Walker's work.[31] Wall positions the collection as exemplary of the genealogical tropes infusing twentieth-century black women's writing, including how Walker "invites readers to puzzle the issues out with her and welcomes them to share those epiphanies she achieves." Wall continues, "Indeed, I would make the case that Walker, despite her reputation as a novelist, short story writer, and poet, has done her best work in the essay, a genre that has at present little critical currency."[32] It is no surprise that Walker's essays illustrate the richness and viability of the trope of dead women talking outside fictional forms. Moreover, the effects of hearing dead women talk in nonfiction terrain may be particularly uncanny, and therefore particularly powerful. In the titular essay of *In Search of Our Mothers' Gardens*, Walker positions her work as a belated response to a long-ago call from her foremothers. She writes, "They waited for a day when the unknown thing that was in them would be made known; but guessed, somehow in their darkness, that on the day of their revelation they would be long dead" (233). In the literary tradition of dead women talking, death isn't such an insurmountable problem. Further, these women are not just talking; they are cursing and they are calling. It is up to us to hear them—and to respond.

5

Dead Woman Wanting

Toni Morrison's *Beloved*

When dead women talk in American literature, they are often met as invaders, prompting fatal encounters with a buried and perhaps unwelcome or ugly past, as we see at Usher and Bly. In other instances, the living may be the intruders upon the dead, as we see with Addie Bundren and perhaps Walker's exhumation of an age-old curse. In still other instances, as we shall see in later chapters, the dead may be welcomed, even embraced. It is not initially clear to which camp belongs *Beloved*, Toni Morrison's renowned 1987 meditation on slavery and its legacy. The novel returns to the notorious 1856 case of Margaret Garner, a fugitive slave who opted for infanticide to spare her daughter a similar life as chattel. Morrison reimagines Garner as Sethe, a used-to-be-slave woman in Reconstruction America haunted not only by the infanticide but also by memories of Sweet Home, the plantation from which she escaped. The result is one of the most iconic dead women talking in American literature: Beloved.

The long-dead daughter returns to her mother as a curious-talking, adult-bodied, terribly demanding stranger. Her body bears a telltale scar across the neck marking her as the now-grown toddler whose throat was cut in the woodshed eighteen years prior. "But what if the girl was not a girl," wonders Paul D, another ex-slave, "but something in disguise?"[1] Beloved speaks not only as the murdered daughter returned but also as the sixty million and more who did not survive the Middle Passage and to whom Morrison dedicates the book. This prompts black feminist critic Barbara Christian to assert that "the idea of the dead returned is diasporic."[2] *Beloved* is not solely a psychoanalytic drama of the return of the repressed for one escaped slave, but also an encounter with the nation's slaveholding past, including its collective memory of dehumanization and painful severing of African connections. This traumatic history is simultaneously a proud testament of survival and a source of profound shame in contemporary African American identity. Beloved prompts the community—both Sethe's Reconstruction-era community and Morrison's contemporary readership—to confront this past outside the familiar progressive march from slavery to freedom that we have come to expect in slave narratives.

The novel hinges on whether the community deems Beloved a person warranting membership in their fold or an intruder, offensive and unfit for public view. The question, I argue, becomes one of beauty and ugliness. Disability studies scholar Susan Schweik shows how such a question leads to a political verdict, with "ugliness understood as a political situation or process, not a personal misfortune or objective aesthetic judgment."[3] Schweik traces the rise of the American ugly law, a singular term for the "unsightly beggar ordinances" enacted in many late nineteenth- and early twentieth-century cities. An oft-cited ordinance passed in 1881 in Chicago, for instance, reads, "Any person who is diseased, maimed, mutilated, or in any way deformed so as to be an unsightly or disgusting object . . . shall not thereon or therein expose himself to public view."[4] To be deemed ugly, Schweik shows, was to be banished from the civic community.

Set around this time, Morrison's novel features a post-slavery community in Ohio considering its own local version of the ugly law to determine whether the perished slave is fit for public view. The aesthetic terms of the question are important because, as literary theorist Elaine Scarry so nimbly argues in *On Beauty and Being Just*, encounters with what we deem beautiful engender desires for justice, equality, fairness, and symmetry.[5] When we designate something or someone ugly, on the other hand, such a judgment leads to asymmetry, inequality, perhaps even banishment. That is why Morrison's project is risky. She returns to a collective past that may not be beautiful, and then goes one step further by giving it a woman's body. If the community deems Beloved ugly, it follows that what Beloved wants she cannot have.

Ugly Bodies and Unwelcome Citizens

Beloved is welcome in the community as a ghost, but not as a citizen. For Morrison, the ghost story is the rightful mode of the slave narrative in a post-slavery society. As Baby Suggs declares as a matter of fact, "Not a house in the country ain't packed to its rafters with some dead Negro's grief. We lucky this ghost is a baby" (6). For Morrison, post-slavery America is a time when the past is not passed. In fact, as Paul D recounts his early days after Sweet Home, "The War had been over four or five year then, but nobody black or white seemed to know it" (63). Ghost stories become the best way to tell an honest story about those lost to history because that vernacular literary form can stage encounters with what Morrison famously terms "unspeakable thoughts, unspoken" (235). This leads Sharon Patricia Holland to argue in *Raising the Dead*, "The task was both to hear the dead speak in fiction and to discover in culture and its intellectual property opportunities for not only uncovering silences but also forming inarticulate places into conversational territories."[6]

Beloved is no mere ghost story, however, though many critics describe it as such.[7] Beloved may begin the novel as a spirit haunting 124 Bluestone Road, but she becomes something else entirely when she emerges fully clothed from the water about one-fifth into the novel. For Ella, who ultimately convinces the community to rescue Sethe, this is a crucial distinction. She "didn't like the idea of past errors taking possession of the present," Morrison writes. "She didn't mind a little communication between the two worlds, but this was an invasion" (302). Whereas Holland suggests that the dead are most powerful when they speak "from the place reserved for the dead,"[8] Beloved is most powerful when she encroaches into the terrain of the living—*and presents herself as one of them*. Beloved insists, "I am not dead I am not there is a house there is what she whispered to me I am where she told me I am not dead" (252). When she takes over the narrative voice, Beloved rejects her defining status—that she is dead—and attempts instead to write herself into a realist tale of Reconstruction, not a fantastic ghost story. Therein lies the problem: there may be room in a post-slavery society for the ghosts of those who perished, but not as active participants.

Beloved enters the community not as a ghost but as a dead woman wanting. She has a body and desires with possessive ferocity. We see this in her first, terrifying speech act: "I am Beloved and she is mine" (243). As she accrues grammar and linguistic coherence, she maintains her proprietary refrain: "You are mine / You are mine / You are mine" (255, 256). Much has been said about Beloved's unslakable appetite, which eventually turns her into a grotesque figure with a distended belly evoking both pregnancy and malnourishment. Her declaration of selfhood is clear and certain, her claim to possession less so. What does she want? In a particularly persuasive reading, literary critic Trudier Harris distinguishes between ownership and possession in chattel slavery on the one hand and Sethe's claim to her own children on the other.[9] But what does it mean for Beloved to possess Sethe? At the ghost story level, Morrison is clearly drawing on the genre's tropes of demonic possession and exorcism, as many have convincingly argued.[10] As a (neo-)slave narrative, with that tradition's petitions for legal rights and humanitarian dignity, Beloved seeks something more: formal recognition in the present as a full member of her community—in a word, citizenship. Harris and others may rightly cast Beloved as a demon, an inhuman, parasitic Thing,[11] but Beloved sees herself otherwise. That is why Ella objects to Beloved not as a ghost but as a civic subject. In this way, *Beloved* is less a narrative of exorcism than of civic banishment.

Scholars of law and literature such as Cathy Caruth have written compellingly on the question of whether we can honor the claims of the dead.[12] But when Beloved returns with a body, she defies her dead status and inserts herself into the present. Thus, she recasts the question: do we honor the claims of the forgotten, especially the reviled, the unwelcome, or what the novel might think of as the diswanted? While citizenship is often understood in national terms, especially in liberal conceptions of formal status and procedural rights, Morrison's novel thinks of citizenship in more republican terms of what it means to participate in a formal community, understood not on the national level but within the black community surrounding 124 Bluestone Road.[13] The community has the power to confer citizenship on its own grounds. The conferral or denial of Beloved's citizenship depends on whether they find her beautiful or ugly.

Their initial answer: beautiful. When the thirty women of the community gather at Sethe's gate, Morrison writes, "The devil-child was clever, they thought. And beautiful. It had taken the shape of a pregnant woman, naked and smiling in the heat of the afternoon sun. Thunder-black and glistening, she stood on long straight legs, her belly big and tight. Vines of hair twisted all over her head. Jesus. Her smile was dazzling" (308). The community's aesthetic awe is as surprising as it is sure. Beloved attracts the novel's collective gaze with the deadly power of a gorgon. Many critics attribute Beloved's attraction to her symbolic association with the lost African past and the community's desire to retrieve it, even by way of the Middle Passage. For instance, Linda Krumholz describes Beloved as "the beautiful African mother, connecting the mothers and daughters of African descent to their preslavery heritage and power, and as the all-consuming devil-child."[14]

I suggest otherwise: when Beloved emerges for public view, the community sees neither Beloved the devil-child nor the African mother but rather Sethe the lost citizen. The beauty they see in Beloved is a projection of Sethe. "Beloved bending over Sethe looked the mother," Denver, Sethe's surviving daughter, reports, "Sethe the teething child" (294). This dead woman wanting has been consuming Sethe, possessing her over the course of the narrative. This makes Beloved's beauty illusory, born of a deceit. Further, Beloved disrupts narrative time, not by turning the lookers into stone but rather by conflating the community's younger and present selves, erasing the temporal distance between now and the day of the infanticide. The community is struck not so much by Beloved's beauty as that of Sethe the new mother and fugitive slave, Sethe from eighteen years ago when she first began her slow retreat from her community. Tellingly, the first time the community witnesses Beloved is also the last. She runs from the scene, disappearing through the woods as "a naked woman with fish for hair" (315), eventually vanishing even from communal lore. She is "disremembered" (323), the opposite of recognition. Further, it is Sethe who first breaks the narrative gaze away from Beloved. "Sethe feels her eyes burn," Morrison writes, "and it may have been to keep them clear that she looks up" (308). Perhaps because Sethe is not fully of the community, a socially dead ex-slave in Reconstruction America, she is able to look anew—and look away.

What makes Beloved so alluring and revolting is her body, first in its womanly beauty occupied by a toddler mind, then in its telltale scar across the neck, and finally in its naked, distended belly. We do well to take our cue from Paul D, who earlier in the novel deems Beloved unpleasant. "Beloved was shining," Morrison writes," "and Paul D didn't like it" (76). Beloved is repellent, so much so that her presence slowly pushes him from 124 Bluestone Road, first from Sethe's upstairs bed to a rocker by the stove, then to departed Baby Suggs's bed, and then finally to a pallet in the storeroom out back. Still, like the surrounding community, Paul D is at first unsure whether to honor Beloved's right to be at 124 Bluestone Road. "It was one thing to beat up a ghost," he thinks, "quite another to throw a helpless coloredgirl out in territory infected by the Klan" (79). This moment of hesitation spurs Paul D "to place her. Consult with the Negroes in town and find her her own place" (79). Where, he must ask, might Beloved belong?

The prospect of "placing" Beloved is twofold. First, it is an act of communal benevolence to secure a home for this newcomer, which also harbors the ulterior motive of expunging her from 124 Bluestone Road and thereby restoring Paul D to Sethe's bed. Second, to "place" Beloved is, at the most basic level, to recognize her. On one level, this brings up the concept of the uncanny provoked by any dead women talking: the dreadful feeling that the familiar is unfamiliar, or vice versa. Sethe frames it as "remembering something she had forgotten she knew" (73). Or as Paul D reflects, "She reminds me of something. Something, look like, I'm supposed to remember" (276). To recognize someone also has a civic dimension: citizenship as formal status, official recognition as a member of a political community. "Placing" Beloved would require the surrounding community of African Americans on the outskirts of Cincinnati, many ex-slaves themselves, to recognize Beloved, to accept her as one of their own.

Ultimately the community can't place Beloved. It may be more accurate to say that Beloved is unrecognized than it is to describe her as unwelcome. Stamp Paid asks Paul D,

> "Who is that girl? Where she come from?"
>
> "I don't know. Just shot up one day sitting on a stump."
>
> "Huh. Look like you and me the only ones outside 124 lay eyes on her." (276)

Beloved enters the community as a stranger, an alien, unknown and even unseen by most. We see Beloved's failed quest for community recognition foreshadowed in Paul D's reaction to her. Immediately following his decision to "place" her, we encounter one of the more unflattering depictions of Beloved: "No sooner did he have this thought than Beloved strangled on one of the raisins she had picked out of the bread pudding. She fell backward and off the chair and thrashed around holding her throat. Sethe knocked her on the back while Denver pried her hands away from her neck. Beloved, on her hands and knees, vomited up her food and struggled for breath" (79). We view this mundane and melodramatic scene as Paul D, removed and likely disgusted, as opposed to Sethe and Denver rushing to intervene. For Paul D, this strange and flailing girl-woman in front of him is off-putting, unrecognizable.

Beloved's body is the problem. Morrison writes, "As long as the ghost showed out from its ghostly place—shaking stuff, crying, smashing and such—Ella respected it. But if it took flesh and came in her world, well, the shoe was on the other foot" (302). As I note in Addie Bundren's chapter, with the advent of doctrines of natural rights, to be a citizen first one must have a body. Intellectual historian Ed Cohen explains, "Our legal and economic notions of individualism and individual rights . . . rest on the premise that, as embodied persons, we possess ourselves. It seems a simple-enough formula: *to be* a person means *to have* a body."[15] The body becomes the repository of the bundles of rights and obligations called *citizenship*. Of course, not all bodies are deemed equal, and polities tend to prefer, or even restrict recognition to, bodies they deem desirable, beautiful, or, as Cohen frames it, "bodies worth defending."

Is Beloved's body worthy of such recognition? Black literature scholar Carol Henderson describes Beloved as a "fleshly manifestation," which she takes to be not only Sethe's dead daughter returned but Sethe's "private pain" dismembered from herself. She argues that Beloved is "the bridge that joins personal history to communal history."[16] Yet with her body, Beloved is no mere racial abstraction, neither history's ghost nor Sethe's psychological projection. Morrison herself insists on this distinction in creating "another kind of dead which is not spiritual but flesh."[17] Indeed, as the community comes to fully comprehend what it means that "Sethe's dead daughter, the one whose throat she cut, had come back to fix her" (301), they focus on Beloved's flesh:

> "I'll be. A baby?"
> "No. Grown. The age it would have been had it lived."
> "You talking about flesh?"
> "I'm talking about flesh." (301)

Beloved's fleshly status makes her unfit for the present, ineligible for membership in the community.

By the end of the scene on the porch, as many have noted, Beloved vanishes while Sethe belatedly rejoins the community. The thirty women have reclaimed Sethe after having held her at arm's length for eighteen years, resentful of the "reckless generosity" (162) of a grand feast Baby Suggs had convened to celebrate the arrival of her grandchildren and their mother. "This free-floating repulsion was new," Baby Suggs realizes in the aftermath of that welcome feast. "It wasn't whitefolks—that much she could tell—so it must be colored ones. Her friends and neighbors were angry at her because she had overstepped, given too much, offended them by excess" (163). This is a classic Morrison theme: the ugliness at the heart of ideals we hold most dear—love, paradise, mercy, beauty, community. As Sethe finds, entrance into the community around 124 Bluestone Road requires their consent, their welcome. That is, citizenship is earned, not given. The working model of citizenship is not the liberal nation-state that confers formal status and bundles of rights and obligations, but rather a civic republic in which participation is the mark of membership. In such a model, the local community holds the power to decide who it recognizes as one of its own. Citizenship in this community is jeopardized by excess, understood in this scene in bodily terms: full-to-bursting bellies, morning-after indigestion. Yet excess is the desired outcome of wanting, as we see in Beloved's malnourished pregnant body and, for Sethe, in what Paul D describes as her too-thick love.

Sethe's body is also central to the novel, especially as a testament to her survival of a merciless whipping while pregnant. The wound heals as a large tangle of keloids, solidifying what Amy Denver first deems a beautiful chokecherry tree as she nurses the fugitive slave clinging to life on her freedom run. More than any other trope in the novel, Sethe's scarred back signals a beautiful narrative of healing, both physical and psychological, from the wounds of slavery. Her body becomes the ever-present repository of what Morrison famously terms "rememory." In a seduction scene worthy of any dime-store romance novel, Paul D initially finds the chokecherry tree alluring, tenderly tracing its branches. However, a post-coital Paul D looks anew and finds it ugly, "a revolting clump of scars." He reconsiders, "Not a tree, as she said. Maybe shaped like one, but nothing like any tree he knew because trees were inviting; things you could trust and be near; talk to if you wanted to as he frequently did since way back when he took the midday meal in the fields of Sweet Home" (25). For Paul D the captivating scar becomes a thing of ugliness, a hideous mark of a shameful past. Like Beloved, the pregnant, malnourished figure wanting yet more as she stands astride the porch, it is initially unclear what to make of Sethe's scar. In the end, Paul D returns to Sethe, bathes her body and lays his story alongside hers (321–22). On the other hand, the fleshly Beloved may be initially alluring but not enduringly beautiful. The contrast is crucial because it frames how Morrison addresses questions of justice in a post-slavery community.

On Beloved and Being Just

In *On Beauty and Being Just*, Elaine Scarry advocates for attending more, and more deliberately, to beauty in an age when it has been banished to afterthoughts and whispers in the private dens of the humanities. "Far from damaging our capacity to attend to the problems of injustice," Scarry argues, "[beauty] instead intensifies the pressure we feel to repair existing injuries."[18] Matters of beauty, she demonstrates, have long been entwined with matters of truth and justice, from Plato's ideal-loving Republic to Immanuel Kant's good-hearted beauty. Objects of beauty, she argues, instill desires for certitude and commitments to truth, preconditions for an appreciation for justice. In fact, as J. G. A. Pocock famously explains in the influential essay "The Ideal of Citizenship since Classical Times," citizenship itself is often understood in aesthetic terms of symmetry and reciprocity, as in the right to rule and be ruled.[19] Therefore, beauty and justice are necessarily analogous, and because a beautiful thing is visible whereas justice is not, it "presses on us to bring its counterpart into existence, acts as a lever in the direction of justice."[20]

But what about objects that are decidedly not beautiful? To follow Scarry's logic, ugly things would metonymically stand in for injustice as its invisible corollary. The ugly is the forsaken, that which has no automatic claim to rights, that which inspires enmity and disgust, the opposite of the fellow feeling central to citizenship. From this angle, it makes sense that Beloved is an object of injustice in search of justice. She is alluring but also grotesque. As Paul D experiences, she makes us want to recoil but nevertheless draws us in by her uncanny gravity. Scarry may be right that the beautiful are visible beacons on the path toward the intangible ideal of justice. But Morrison insists that we also attend to the grotesque talking corpses in our community, especially when they demand recognition, be it Beloved perched naked and bloated on the porch, Addie Bundren rotting loudly (and reeking) in a box, or Madeline Usher standing shrouded in white and covered in blood at the threshold.

Morrison pits Sethe's quest for healing[21] and rejoining her community against the horrific possibilities housed in the body of Beloved. Sethe and Denver initially relish Beloved, receive her as a welcome, beautiful member of their micro-community at 124 Bluestone Road, whose perimeter becomes "the edge of the world" (281, 286). Doing so gives them a sense of what Scarry describes as *aliveness*. "The moment of perceiving something beautiful confers on the perceivers the gift of life," she reasons, "and now we begin to see that the moment of perceiving beauty also confers on the object the gift of life."[22] The beautiful object moves us, renders us more as we make room for it in our worlds. "It is that we cease to stand even at the center of our own world," Scarry explains. "We willingly cede our ground to the thing that stands before us."[23]

Beloved is an interesting case because she is both alive and dead, alluring and grotesque. Morrison plays out Scarry's thought experiment to extend a "level of aliveness" to the whole world, including memory and its emblems, the ex-slave and the ancestral perished slave. Sethe and Denver willingly cede their ground to Beloved and radically decenter their worlds. The community members around 124 Bluestone Road, however, do not yield so easily. Thus diverge two political communities, 124 Bluestone Road and the surrounding black community. Sethe and Denver give Beloved life, and she in turn instills in them a desire for aliveness. But the beauty they see in Beloved is born of parasitic possession, and therefore the contract between perceiver and perceived is not just. The consequences are dangerous: bodies wasted, starving, shrinking in their feverish attempts to satiate Beloved's voracious hunger.

To recognize Beloved as beautiful is dangerous. It requires renunciation of one's own place in the community. I have used ugliness and beauty to frame how the petitioner's body is perceived by the community, the entity with the power to confer or deny citizenship in republican models of a self-determining polity. Legal scholar Martha Nussbaum opts for similar terms: disgust and humanity. In a full-throated denunciation of citing disgust to justify denying legal equality to fellow citizens, she writes, "Seeing the shape of a human being before us, we always have choices to make: will we impute full equal humanity to that shape, or something less?"[24] Nussbaum's polemic concerns sexual minority rights, yet she frames the dilemma in ways uncannily relevant to *Beloved*, especially the moment the thirty women first see the dead woman wanting on Sethe's porch. To return to Paul D's question, is Beloved a human or "something else in disguise"? If the former, her petition for full citizenship can and must be honored; if the latter, the community will instead adopt a posture of disgust, whether warranted or not. That is why the distinction is essential between ghost and dead woman talking. The latter has the shape of a human being—a body—but it is not clear whether she merits the designation *humanity*.

Nussbaum doesn't consider this particular distinction, but then again she isn't writing about ghost stories. Still, she asks, "How . . . do we ever become able to see another as human?" She answers succinctly: "Only through the exercise of imagination." Imagination turns out to be the pathway toward respect and sympathy, what Nussbaum calls the *politics of humanity*. But there is a problem with Beloved's petition: according to Nussbaum, recognition of another's humanity and therefore right to full citizenship requires "the capacity to imagine his experience" and that of anyone like him.[25] If Beloved speaks from collective experience—a point on which critics agree—it can be said that she therefore has no experience of her own for us to imagine. In this way, Beloved is a body without humanity.

The Ventriloquist's Curse

Critics place *Beloved* at the center of a black aesthetic of remembering. To resurrect Beloved and give her life, literary critic Ashraf Rushdy argues, is to employ literature's imaginative resources for the dangerous and political act of revisiting history in order to revise it.[26] This poses a problem in the Garner story: many spoke for Garner, but she never spoke for herself. In *Who Speaks for Margaret Garner?*, Mark Reinhardt sifts through all available accounts of the Garner episode, including tracking her story to her death, the least documented part of Garner's story. The Garner archive includes sermons, news stories, editorials, interviews, and abolitionist speeches. Reinhardt also identifies direct references to such literary antecedents as the roman tale of Virginius and echoes of Harriet Beecher Stowe's *Uncle Tom's Cabin*, which shaped how people told and understood Garner's story. In retelling the event, authors proffered a whole host of irreconcilable aims—abolitionist as well as proslavery arguments, appeals for conferral or denial of black citizenship, meditations on the humanity of both African slaves and white slaveholders.

What Reinhardt does *not* find is Garner's own voice. It is simply absent from the historical record. He suggests that the relative *absence* of news coverage in the Southern press beyond local Kentucky outlets might be the best place to detect the presence of Garner's voice. He explains, "The white South's need for silence reveals that in some ways Garner was among the authors of her story, a person who helped determine how her actions were understood. She did not control the means of cultural reproduction, and could not affect the ways her words were used or invented by her supporters, but, despite that, she did commit an act that could not safely be recorded in some of the culture's key venues, locales, and forms." Reinhardt concludes that Garner's agency, if not her voice, is measured in the way she "forced whites . . . to respond."[27]

To tell Garner's story in the first person is a fundamental break from the historical record. In addition, Morrison breaks conspicuously from the project of historical revision or political pamphleteering and inserts a pure fiction in the form of Beloved. Beloved herself seems aware of her tenuous status.

She insists, "I am not separate from her there is no place where I stop her face is my own and I want to be there in the place where her face is and to be looking at it too" (248). Beloved's petition for belonging depends on her association with Sethe, a figure the surrounding community members eventually recognize as one of their own. Furthermore, Sethe is also a recognizable figure in the slave narrative tradition. Beloved, on the other hand, is an invention possible only in speculative fiction. There is no antecedent in the slave narrative tradition given its commitment to first-person testimonial and the verifiable authority of the one speaking primarily from firsthand experience. Beloved is, instead, a collective proxy. Morrison writes, "Down by the stream in the back of 124 her footprints come and go, come and go. Should a child, an adult place his feet in them, they will fit. Take them out and they will disappear as though nobody ever walked there" (324). As Alan Friedman notes, Beloved speaks "only what others thought; anyone fits her footprints."[28] Beloved necessarily cannot speak in the first person of slavery—a testament to Sethe's success in largely sparing her daughter knowledge of what it means to be chattel.

In an earlier, more polemical study of the Garner archive, Reinhardt frames any attempt to retell the Garner story as an act of ventriloquism. I think of this dilemma as the *ventriloquist's curse*, a curse that extends to any literary return to a traumatic past. Even in the genre of the slave narrative, we necessarily encounter not a slave's voice, but that of an *ex*-slave, or a fugitive speaking on behalf of current slaves, from Harriet Jacobs writing in freedom from the North to Frederick Douglass on the abolitionist lecture circuit. The ventriloquist's curse arises even out of feelings of benevolence and injustice. Reinhardt suggests that we "cannot resist filling in the silences in the record" so that we speak for Garner as a sort of "conjurer's trick,"[29] including Margaret Garner's most ardent supporters, from abolitionist Lucy Stone to contemporary cultural critics well versed in the problem of silence and historical lacunae. In framing the silence at the center of Garner's historical record as ventriloquism, Reinhardt further paints the subject of slavery as a mere wooden doll of a system that rendered Garner legally voiceless. She becomes an uncanny cipher able only to transmit voices not her own. While a ventriloquist might be self-conscious about the ethics of her trade, the wooden doll itself has no capacity for such self-reflection.

General readers and critics alike have tended to think of *Beloved* as a reimagining of Margaret Garner's story. That isn't fully accurate, however. The dead infant, not the mother, lends the novel its title. The point may seem fussy, but its ramifications are crucial. Morrison's ventriloquism is manifold in that she adopts the voice of not just the mother figure and the living daughter, but the ultimate figure of voicelessness, the murdered "crawling-already?" child. The novel fragments when the narrative moves from free indirect discourse to speak in the register of the first person. First Sethe, then Denver, and then Beloved vie for the position of narrator. Reinhardt rightfully wrings his hands over the absence of Garner's voice in the historical record, but such a focus implicitly occludes the space left by the surviving daughter and, more importantly, the lost one. Out of this absence emerges the strangely speaking, uncannily embodied Beloved.

In the end, Beloved is a ventriloquist's doll, though she doesn't know it. What memories she has belong to others. Therefore, the humanity that Morrison asks the community to recognize is their own, not Beloved's. Whatever beauty we see in her belongs to us. Whatever life we see in her is our own. In this way, the ventriloquist's curse is not inexorable. We needn't muzzle the dead, but we also needn't allow them to possess us and therefore renounce our membership in the community of the living. Reinhardt does not portray Morrison as escaping the ventriloquist's curse, but rather as a supremely gifted ventriloquist. Morrison is obviously, painfully, and visibly aware of the gravity of Garner's intractable silence. Morrison ends the novel, "It was not a story to pass on. . . . It was not a story to pass on. . . . This is not a story to pass on" (274–75). In the multiple connotations of "pass on" and the switch from "it" to "this" in this much-discussed final passage, Reinhardt detects a sophistication regarding the workings of national history and voice that he doesn't find in other accounts of Garner's story, especially politically interested ones. I would add that with the character of Beloved, Morrison breaks purposefully from the (neo-)slave narrative tradition and into the terrain of the ghost story, where ventriloquism is a speculative necessity.

The trope of dead women talking has long been available to writers to confront communal pasts, even those buried, unwelcome, or inaccessible. This allows Morrison to escape the inevitable end of the historical record. No account to date has been able to fully reconcile Garner's eventual death in slavery: she passes away as a slave in the South before emancipation, likely a victim of typhoid in 1858. In fact, accounts tend to ignore that part of the historical record altogether, including Morrison's novel. "Perhaps Garner's contemporaries deemed the manner of her death unfit for a political heroine,"

Reinhardt speculates. "Her end in obscurity and amid oppression is the element of the case that was most swiftly and thoroughly forgotten."[30] With the trope of dead women talking, Morrison is able to depart from linear accounts—birth to death, slavery to freedom—that propel a nation toward consigning the past to memory and its twin, forgetting. Instead, in a novel of *rememory*, Morrison confronts the presence of the past so that we seek not the end of injustice, but rather the presence of justice. Still, Morrison asks, is there room in the present for Beloved?

Unwanted Presences and the Future

The hole in the historical record left by Garner's murdered child can only arise as something in the shape of a human, but nonetheless not human. Beloved is a dead woman wanting. And what she wants is to join the community not as a ghost, but as a subject of the present. As she asserts in her eerie phrases and half-sentences, "All of it is now it is always now" (248). If citizenship were merely for residents of the present, Beloved would be the ideal candidate because her time "is always now." But, as Sethe learns, citizens must also have a future, lest she follow Baby Suggs to her deathbed, spending her final days counting the colors around her. Further, as Denver learns when she enters civil society and the labor economy after having retreated from the schoolhouse at a young age, to have a future requires engagement with the community beyond the domestic environs. Denver becomes the new citizen, Sethe the reclaimed one, Beloved the banished one.

Beloved is a figure of the ever present, which is to say the never past. In some ways, this makes her quintessentially American. In "The Burning of Paper instead of Children," an experimental meditation on language, power, and history, feminist poet Adrienne Rich writes, "In America we have only the present tense."[31] However, a narrative of justice, or at least survival from an unjust past, requires that we speak in three registers: *was*, *is*, and *will*. Sethe was a slave; she is an ex-slave; she will remain free. On the other hand, Beloved was, and perhaps she is, but she never will be. As a pregnant body, she is mere host to a parasitical version of the future, one that cannot be.[32] Ultimately the novel deems this figure of the ever present ugly and therefore unwelcome.

Dead women talking have long staged encounters with a community's past. But Beloved is not a willing participant in this enduring American literary tradition. She does not recognize a distinction between the past and present, a distinction central to narratives of progress, survival, or healing. Black feminist scholars have found it useful to think of black identity in America through the Freudian image of an open wound, a bodily metaphor that desires, but never achieves, closure.[33] As a figure of the ever present, Beloved embodies that open wound. Further, in her "always now" status, Beloved is pure desire—both the wanter and the wanted. Yet what she wants can never be achieved if there is no future. Desire necessarily operates in the present of wanting what one does not currently have. When we achieve the object of desire, we no longer want it. Instead, we have it. Beloved can never stop wanting because she cannot speak in the language of *will*. She even resists the language of *was*, favoring instead *is*, the time of now. This tension is signaled in her very name: one who was loved, one who must be loved. In the past tense, her name testifies to a love given and perhaps received. In the present tense, however, her name speaks in the imperative—be loved—commanding, insistent, always wanting.

Dead women such as Beloved vie for the status of the beautiful, welcome citizen, even in such gurgling, wailing, insistent, needful repetitions as "I am Beloved and she is mine." The community around 124 Bluestone Road rejects Beloved on terms not unlike the ugly laws that sprang up all around post-Reconstruction America. Ultimately, *Beloved* is not a historiographic novel of Reconstruction concerned primarily with full citizenship in the nation-state, but rather with what it means to be recognized by and participate in a local public. In this, it is a fiction of community—or, more to the point, a fiction of failed community. Beloved can signify the presence of the past—an ugly one, at that—but she can never participate in a just future. The future belongs to Sethe, the beautiful citizen.

6

Dead Woman Heckling

Tony Kushner's *Angels in America*

Of all the dead women talking in American literature, perhaps the most irresistible is Ethel Rosenberg. She appears at the end of Part One of *Angels in America*, Tony Kushner's gay fantasia set in New York City during the Reagan era. Ethel is her familiar self: the Jewish mother who, along with her husband Julius, was executed for treason on June 19, 1953, thanks in small part to the zealous work of Roy Cohn, the assistant U.S. attorney, right-hand man to Senator Joseph McCarthy, and notorious closet case. This early marquee act in the McCarthy era of anti-communist hysteria earned the Rosenbergs the distinction of being the only U.S. citizens executed under the 1917 Espionage Act. In Kushner's play, set over three decades later, Ethel sits at the bedside of Roy Cohn as he dies of AIDS, though he insists on calling it liver cancer—a disease for powerful men, not homosexuals. Ethel not only talks to Roy, she heckles him. At first confusing her for a nurse, Roy quickly identifies her: "Aw fuck, Ethel." She responds, "You don't look good Roy," while Kushner instructs, "Her manner is friendly, her voice is ice-cold." The incongruity is not lost on Roy as he eventually demands, "What is this Ethel, Halloween? You trying to scare me?"[1] Throughout the play, Roy is unsure whether she is a supernatural succubus or simply a "treacherous bitch" (II.4.i), let alone why she is there.

Why *is* this dead woman—martyr of the McCarthy era, enigmatic icon of leftist politics, testament to federal excess, talisman of conspiracy theorists—hanging around Kushner's fantastical play? On the one hand, Ethel lends historical depth and realism while helping to raise fundamental questions about forgiveness, its limits, and its role in how we imagine reparative justice. On the other hand, we also need to account for Ethel's role as enigmatic heckler. When we peel away the backdrop of a cosmic standoff between arch nemeses, Ethel is rather annoying, a consistent minor key little noticed by those who look at her primarily in Roy's vile shadow. She taunts, needles, and picks as Roy hurls unglamorously toward death. If the route toward justice is not necessarily through forgiveness or reparation, might it be possible, Ethel helps us ask, to *annoy* justice into being? If so, justice for whom? And in what form?

Annoying Justice

In *Ugly Feelings*, literary theorist Sianne Ngai takes on the underexplored spectrum of negative affect, from envy to paranoia to coined terms such as stuplimity, a racialized amalgam of shock and boredom. Ugly feelings, she explains, differ from more familiar sentimentalism and sympathy in the vein of Harriet Beecher Stowe in that they "could be said to give rise to a noncathartic aesthetic: art that produces and foregrounds a failure of emotional release . . . and does so as a kind of politics."[2] Ugly feelings are ambivalent animals, reducible neither to mere *ressentiment* nor to therapeutic valor in the age-old technique of speaking bitterness. This begins to explain the beguiling effect of Ethel's simultaneously friendly and ice-cold posture. She neither raises her fist in clear defiance or revenge nor comes to terms with her executioner in a Kumbaya moment festooned with Kushner's signature exposed wires and magical accoutrements. Nor is she exactly a grand tormentor from beyond, Roy's own Jacob Marley. Ethel largely operates on a lower, more pedestrian level of needling, pestering, gloating, all while never fully certain of her own motivations.

A good example is the penultimate scene of "Part One: Millennium Approaches," which ends with the Angel of America's world-cracking descent. Roy collapses and instructs Ethel to dial 911. "It sings!" she exclaims. Then, "(Imitating dial tones) La la la . . . Huh" (I.3.v). This moment of anachronism and antagonism is amusing, unexpected, and perhaps a bit mean and irksome. And not just for Roy, who lies prostrate in agony as she fumbles with the modern telephone. When Ethel has the opportunity to exact posthumous revenge on one of history's villains, she pulls back, adopting an almost obeisant role characteristic of the sycophants, sidekicks, and servants with whom Roy surrounds himself. Yet her call to 911 is hardly a pure act of mercy, charity, or any other high ideal. She exhibits a cheerful indifference to Roy's pain, while as curious as the audience to see how the plot plays out. This gets at another of Ngai's points: ugly feelings are "conducive to producing ironic distance in a way that the grander and more prestigious passions, or even the moral emotions associated with sentimental literature, do not."[3] We tend not to fully embrace this register of feeling; in fact, we are often ambivalent about such emotions, perhaps even feel bad about feeling them. Ethel, however, seems confident in her ironic distance. She produces befuddlement more than catharsis.

Cheerful indifference is an unexpected response given her relationship to Roy, the one who moved Heaven and Earth, not to mention broke a few laws, to secure her execution. He brags, "If it wasn't for me, Joe, Ethel Rosenberg would be alive today, writing some personal-advice column for *Ms*. . . . That sweet unprepossessing woman, two kids, boo-hoo-hoo, reminded us all of our little Jewish mamas—she came this close to getting life; I pleaded till I wept to put her in the chair. Me. I did that. I would have fucking pulled the switch if they'd have let me. Why? Because I fucking hate traitors" (I.3.v). Roy is the ultimate figure of brazen injustice. He lies in relief against other characters who fret and deliberate over matters of duty, justice, and love. He eschews ethics and breaks laws with impunity, from illegal communications with the judge in the Rosenberg trial to embezzling funds from a client in the present. This record is what earns Roy the distinction of being among the more despised actors in the McCarthy theater, perhaps more so than the leading man himself. In Louis's words, "He's like the polestar of human evil, he's like the worst human being who ever lived, he isn't *human* even" (II.4.iii). Theater critic Michael Cadden deems Roy the "satanic catalyst" of the play, which builds on a long history of "pinklisting" the actual Cohn, a reverse blacklisting designed to take posthumous revenge, from the thinly veiled glee in his *New York Times* obituary to early representations of Cohn in gay theater and literature.[4]

Ethel seems a ripe figure for the moral center of the AIDS crisis, a perfect foil to Roy. In discussing the pair, critics tend to opt for a moral discourse in lieu of, or as more encompassing than, legal parameters of justice. For instance, Jonathan Freedman puts Roy in the long-standing anti-Semitic tradition of the "monstrous Jewish pervert,"[5] while Ross Posnock dubs Cohn an American Übermensch, as well as a "monstrous brat whose pugnacity was as histrionic as everything else about him."[6] However, Posnock argues, Cohn "disarms or renders irrelevant psychoanalytic explanations as well as conventional moral judgments; they become something like the intellectual equivalent of the handwringing of a feckless liberalism—well meaning but beside the point."[7] Yet by swaddling Roy in hatred, derision, and profanity, but also profound pain and vulnerability, Kushner invites us to Roy's deathbed in the posture of hospice workers as much as witnesses at a belated execution. Or, to borrow from the title of the Rosenbergs' early sympathetic biography, Kushner invites us to Roy's inquest.[8] Critics struggle with the unmerited compassion we see from Belize, the black ex–drag queen nurse who instructs Roy on the finer points of experimental AZT and double-blind tests. And perhaps we also begrudge the company Ethel provides. We would feel justified by soaring outrage on their part. Ethel, however, dips into the lower registers of feeling where she feels most at home.

The phone call moment exemplifies what is to love about Kushner's Ethel: she is smart, wronged, confident, occasionally bitchy, and, most importantly, she is right. The operator asks her name: "My name? (beat) Ethel Greenglass Rosenberg. (*Small smile*) Me? No I'm not related to Mr. Cohn. An old friend" (I.3.v). While the audience appreciates the gravity of this impossible historical meeting, Ethel prefers the minor key of sardonic irony and Cheshire-cat smile to Norma Rae's confidently raised fist. Ethel continues to show up at Roy's bedside throughout "Part Two: Perestroika" as he continues his inevitable, ungraceful decline. Roy may ask, "What are *you* looking at?" (II.1.ii), but Ethel mainly just sits there, a silent demon as far as he can tell. Roy concludes at one point, "She won't talk to me. She thinks she's some sort of a deathwatch or something" (II.1.ii). When the plot offers her opportunities for revenge and just deserts, she wraps her vengeance in exasperation, ambivalence, and perhaps even impish playfulness.

Sometimes Ethel laughs as Roy writhes in spasms of pain. But even then there is no clear indication she relishes the moment. Her laugh is as unrevealing as her tight-lipped hospitality. So too, Roy joins her at one point, suggesting a sort of camaraderie in their standoff of bristle and will. Their encounter becomes less about forgiveness and wrath, and more a high-stakes game of one-upmanship. We see this when Roy asks Ethel where she goes during the day, expecting a horror-movie explanation, such as "The cock crows, you go back to the swamp" (II.3.ii). Her explanation is much more pedestrian:

ETHEL. No. I take the 7:05 to Yonkers.

ROY. What the fuck's in Yonkers.

ETHEL. The disbarment committee hearings. You been hocking about it all week. I'll have a look-see.

ROY. They won't let you in the front door. You're a convicted and executed traitor.

ETHEL. I'll walk through a wall.
(*She starts to laugh. He joins her.*) (II.3.ii)

Their shared laugh is an eerie sound track to this posthumous sparring match. Roy's disbarment hearing evokes Ethel's own post-trial efforts and slow march toward death. Roy sits confined in his hospital bed dialing his multi-line phone as furiously as Ethel wrote her letters in Sing Sing. Whereas the real Ethel sought exoneration or, failing that, a good home for her children, this Roy has a different final goal: cull all his bullying might and cash in all his favors to slow the disbarment proceedings enough so that he can die a lawyer. When Roy shifts from seeing Ethel as a supernatural succubus to something with which he is more familiar—a traitor without citizenship rights—Ethel pivots to the fantastical as she promises to walk through a wall. Perhaps Roy's laugh marks the absurdity of their meeting, concedes the seeming power reversal, presages the inevitability of his dishonorable exit, or signals that he still has a few cards up his sleeve. Perhaps he is heckling the heckler. We cannot know—his laugh is as unrevealing as Ethel's.

Kushner's Ethel departs from earlier literary depictions, which tend to portray her as a martyr, be it as an unconventional mother figure in work by E. L. Doctorow and Robert Coover, or as a protofeminist in work by Sylvia Plath and Adrienne Rich.[9] She also belongs in another tradition: the pestering, complaining, lovingly annoying Jewish mother. Theater critic Alisa Solomon deems Kushner's Ethel a "Yiddishe momma," a go-to Jewish archetype in American literature and culture, while her affiliation with a leftist history transforms her into "My Yiddishe Commie."[10] Little work has been done in literary studies on annoying people and their kin. A welcome exception is medievalist scholar Michael Murphy's efforts to trace the classical epic figure of the taunter, often a woman, whose function is "to provoke the known hero into the kind of heroic act that the society needs at a given time."[11] Kushner scrambles these roles as the more likely hero figure taunts a reviled man, a figure whose humiliation we may in fact welcome.

While literary criticism is underequipped to address the annoyance driving Ethel and Roy's relationship, the self-help aisles teem with advice. In *Dealing with People You Can't Stand: How to Bring Out the Best in People at Their Worst*, Drs. Rick Brinkman and Rick Kirschner advise, "Sometimes the most important and useful elements of communication are hidden, not just from the listener, but from the speaker as well. Identify these to get a positive outcome."[12] The advice industry is rather unanimous in its call for reconciliation between the annoyed and annoyer. It achieves this end by removing questions of injustice and approaching interpersonal relations in a political vacuum. For instance, in *How to Deal with Annoying People*, an evangelical Christian entry in this advice genre, Bob Phillips and Kimberly Alyn turn to Jesus. "Jesus commanded that we must love our neighbors as ourselves," they note in all earnestness. But a conundrum arises: some of our neighbors are annoying. Are they, too, deserving of our love? "When my neighbor is nice to me, it is easier to love him," they opine. "But when he is impatient, angry, grumpy or aloof, loving him becomes difficult."[13] While these books tend to be as unintentionally campy as the authors are sincere, they nevertheless get at some of the serious questions Kushner poses by bringing Ethel to Roy's deathbed. The gravitational pull of reconciliation narratives counters the equally strong desire for revenge or vindication, both of which drive Kushner's hard-won multicultural humanism. Ethel's penchant for annoying silence stymies any saccharine narratives of therapeutic redemption, which we do find in other examples of dead women talking, such as Alice Sebold's *The Lovely Bones*, which I discuss in chapter nine.

While the self-help aisles are nearly unanimous in their advocacy of interpersonal reconciliation, academic treatises on annoying people reach many of the same conclusions, though usually with less clip art and more surveys. In *Complaining, Teasing, and Other Annoying Behaviors*, psychologist Robin Kowalski considers deceit and betrayal. "If victims do not seek revenge and cannot bring themselves to forgive the betrayer," she argues, "they may fall into quiet resignation."[14] While the call for interpersonal communication seems ludicrously off the mark when it comes to Ethel and Roy, it gets at Kushner's absurd humor in making them carp at each other amid scenes of gross injustice, decaying bodies, and cosmic realignments. Kowalski concludes, "Individuals who can find meaning in these annoyances, who can infuse humor into others' annoyingness and learn to forgive them, will find the behaviors less stressful and will experience significantly fewer difficulties."[15] This therapeutic approach may not be completely off the mark given how Kowalski helps us link annoyance and forgiveness. Typical philosophies of forgiveness, as I will explore in the next section, turn instead to such matters as apology, guilt, and admission of wrongdoing. Roy, however, takes maniacal pleasure in returning the favor by annoying Ethel. He exhibits an utter lack of interest in her forgiveness.

Scientific approaches to annoyingness also provide indirect light on the standoff between Ethel and Roy. "Annoyance is probably the most widely experienced and least studied of all human emotions," Joe Palca and Flora Lichtman argue in *Annoying: The Science of What Bugs Us.* "How do we know that? We don't. There is no Department of Annoying Studies or annoyingologists."[16] Nonetheless, they deliver a wry meditation that adopts the formulas of the advice book (including a companion online quiz, "Are You Annoying?"[17]), leavened by the time-honored tradition of pseudoscience. While tongue-in-cheek, the book helps us think about that elusive attribute called annoying, which Palca and Lichtman find is highly specific to an individual (i.e., pet peeves) yet bears universal requisites: unpleasant, unpredictable, and a belief that its end is imminent.[18] Their work gets at some of Kushner's questions about love, justice, and our capacity to forgive—or at least tolerate—the annoying among us. "Tolerate" is a deliberate word, for it falls low on Kushner's pecking order of virtues, somewhere between saying thank you or please and not picking one's nose in public.[19] Tolerance has the ability to bracket matters of justice enough to foster Ethel and Roy's epic yet strangely annoying confrontation.

Ethel may not be able to annoy justice into being, but Roy gets what he wants through similarly base means, namely, trickery. Roy feigns his imminent death and asks for his momma in a pathetic display of vulnerability and childhood reversion. Annoyed, Ethel insists, "I'm not your mother Roy" (II.4.ix). But she relents and grants his request for a lullaby in his state of death. "No I'm NOT!" he boasts. "I fooled you Ethel, I knew who you were all along, I can't believe you fell for that ma stuff, I just wanted to see if I could finally, finally make Ethel Rosenberg sing! I WIN!" (II.4.ix). Ethel went to the electric chair precisely because she refused to "sing," to confess to the charges of espionage. Roy's childish trickery would be yet another grand moment of injustice—if it weren't so annoying. His tactics are at least as cloying as they are malicious. Cadden argues, "Cohn's series of deathbed scenes serves as a metaphor for the collapse of the Manichean paradigms upon which he built his life and career."[20] Solomon, on the other hand, views the scene as less Hegelian dialectic than absurd Vaudeville, but to no lesser effect. "Roy's deathbed scene is a brilliant Brechtian mixture of pathos, slapstick, and moral disjunction," he argues. "Shamelessly mawkish, the scene invites us to feel sorry for Roy then jolts us out of the schmaltz, allowing us to regard our own will to embrace Roy."[21]

Ethel's lullaby for a broken, vulnerable man merely affords him one last display of malevolence and manipulation. He is a naughty child playing a dirty trick, setting off a cherry bomb in the toilet of history. Moreover, Roy uncannily reenacts a particularly grisly historical footnote in Ethel's own execution. After Ethel was delivered two jolts of electricity at her execution, a process that had killed Julius in the same chair a few moments prior, the doctors on hand were horrified to discover a heartbeat, which necessitated two more jolts.[22] Roy's childish prank is a gruesome coda. His final act of annoyance raises matters of justice unhooked from any need for regret, guilt, or even hesitation on his part. This, however, allows Ethel to ultimately control the stakes of their standoff.

Forgiving? Forget It

If we expect progression toward some higher ideal of forgiveness or reconciliation, a posthumous glasnost between the wrongly executed and the gleeful prosecutor, we will be disappointed, or at least perplexed. In her memorable final speech, Ethel divulges her initial intentions:

> I decided to come here so I could see could I forgive you. You who I have hated so terribly I have borne my hatred for you up into the heavens and made a needle-sharp little star in the sky out of it. It's the star of Ethel Rosenberg's Hatred, and it burns every year for one night only, June Nineteen. It burns acid green.
>
> I came to forgive but all I can do is take pleasure in your misery. Hoping I'd get to see you die more terrible than I did. And you are, 'cause you're dying in shit, Roy, defeated. And you could kill me, but you couldn't ever defeat me. You never won. And when you die all anyone will say is: Better he had never lived at all. (II.4.ix)

Ethel's initial anger is as beautiful and certain as it is searing and justified. Her vision is initially close kin to the righteous curse-prayer of Alice Walker's "Only Justice Can Stop a Curse." But when she encounters Roy's deteriorating body, she falls from the vaulted heights of forgiveness and righteous wrath to taunting a sick man on his deathbed. In the end, Ethel offers a petty curse, as much personal spite as cosmic justice, delivered in the third-person collective.

Can Ethel forgive Roy when she is under no obligation to do so, especially when Roy himself does not help his case? "Forgiveness can never be unambivalent," Kushner contends in a 1993 interview for the *Village Voice*. "But how else do we set ourselves free from the nightmare of history?"[23] This requires a new vision of forgiveness as we know it. Philosopher Charles Griswold contends that forgiveness requires foreswearing revenge and moderating resentment. "Forgiveness is a certain kind of ethical response to injury and the injurer," he argues. It resides in the moral and ethical domain, separable from matters of retributive justice and legal parameters of punishment.[24] It appears that Ethel fails because she does not forego her desire for vengeance, or even commit to its abatement. Instead, she remains ambivalent, such as when she delivers the verdict of Roy's disbarment trial: "I wanted the news should come from me. The panel ruled against you Roy. . . . They won, Roy. You're not a lawyer anymore" (II.4.ix). The news carries vindication, yet it is unclear if Ethel takes the delight she claims. On the one hand, the delivery is sinister and needling. However, clad in Jewish American syntax, the phrase "I wanted the news should come from me" connotes a friend delivering bad news, someone who is supportive, can soften the blow, perhaps even recognize commonality. Much the same can be said about the petty curse delivered from an acid-green star of hatred in the cosmos. Because the news comes wrapped in Ethel's ugly feelings, the disbarment seems not exactly justice, but something else, something that makes us ambivalent about our own ugly feelings.

Ethel's lullaby may be tainted because Roy wrested it under false pretenses, but her final act is not so easily dismissed. When Roy actually dies, Belize goads Louis, the secular Jew and self-professed liberal, to sing the Kaddish. As Louis stumbles with half-remembered phrases, Ethel joins, feeding him the words (II.5.iii). The posthumous duet is earnest and moving; it bears none of the tacky oddity of Natalie Cole singing with her dead father for her *Unforgettable* album or the sappiness of Patrick Swayze's dead character joining Demi Moore in the famous pottery-making scene in the popular film *Ghost*. Kushner himself has described the scene as the most moving in the whole two-part play.[25] Cadden describes it as a "queer assortment" forging "a new community based on a solidarity across both new and old lines of group identification."[26] The beautiful scene is certainly a gift of compassion for a man undeserving and unwanting of it. But is it forgiveness?

In forgiveness as we know it, the recipient of injustice must foreswear revenge while the wrongdoer also must acknowledge the harm and offer some form of contrition. In *On Apology*, psychologist Aaron Lazare identifies why people do not apologize, including the need for control of situations and emotions, moral superiority and perceived infallibility, and that "they assume the world is hostile and that relationships are inherently dangerous."[27] I do not wish to commit the gaffe of psychoanalyzing a fictional character, but rather to identify how Kushner sets in motion a narrative of forgiveness and reconciliation—and then doesn't fulfill it. Lazare considers the case of delayed apologies, which he finds prompted by old age, sickness, and impending death. In Roy's case, his deteriorating body only ups the ante, provides him one last sure bet to "win." Forgiveness is not Roy's game; "I'm sorry" is not in his vocabulary. Posnock considers the play's curious desire to nonetheless offer Roy absolution and argues, "Forgiveness likely seemed to Cohn as meaningless as believing one can escape the nightmare of politics and history."[28]

If Roy remains gleefully unrepentant until his end, does that foreclose Ethel's options? In *Before Forgiveness*, classicist David Konstan identifies models of reconciliation in which forgiveness as we know it is strikingly absent. In its modern sense, he explains, forgiveness is a bilateral process of voluntary wrongs committed and regretted so that the recipient of harm or injustice can forego vengeance, or at least commit to doing so. But why place the wrongdoer's inner sentiment at the fulcrum, thereby empowering someone like Roy? Ancient Greeks and Romans, Konstan demonstrates, developed strategies to appease anger that were not overly concerned with divining the true sentiment of the wrongdoer. Further, he explains, "they were not equally engaged . . . in seeking to discern an inward change of character as a condition for reconciliation."[29] Therefore, forgiveness of a sort may be possible irrespective of Roy's inner sentiment.

What of the inner sentiment of the forgiver? Whether or not Ethel forgives Roy remains an open question, but she is certainly not forgiving in her demeanor. She comes swaddled in taunting, annoyance, and exasperation, in addition to righteous anger. To put the question another way, can we unhook forgiveness from forgivingness? Griswold considers "imperfect forgiveness," which includes the unrepentant as well as the dead, who no longer have the capacity to change (except in literature and drama). He allows for residual negative feelings but mandates a good faith commitment to moderating resentment.[30] With her ugly feelings, Ethel fails this test. Even if Ethel delivers something like forgiveness, however reluctant, grudging, or unearned, she is by no means forgiving in her affect—which may make her more human, if not humane. Griswold also considers the case of "moral monsters," those wrongdoers deemed unforgiveable because it is no longer possible to recognize a shared humanity.[31] Roy would seem a prime candidate, yet Griswold rejects the category. To deem someone a "monster," he contends, is a failure on the part of the injured, whose capacity to forgive marks her own humanity. In any case, as something resembling forgiveness, if not forgiveness itself, perhaps the Kaddish scene is the ultimate way to annoy Roy. For what could annoy a spiteful man-child more than a mother figure who recognizes his humanity when he spent his life keeping it from public view?

Roy's body—decaying on stage before our eyes—is central to Kushner's own ambivalence. "I'm not comfortable with the fact that, to a certain degree, Roy is forgiven," Kushner explains in an interview with gay novelist Michael Cunningham. "He is actually, in the play, only forgiven when he's dead," he adds. "I think that forgiving dead people is a lot easier."[32] Ultimately, it is not Ethel but rather Roy's body that metes out revenge. As a closeted man at the center of homophobic assaults—as vile as they were systematic and unrelenting—on the rights and dignity of gay people, Roy's contraction of AIDS may seem not only ironic but also vindicating. His own body turns against him. As Roy himself says of America, "It's just no country for the infirm" (II.1.iii). We can choose to see his ghastly death as justice, but only—and here's the catch—if we are willing to embrace our own ugly feelings.

When All the Old Are Dead

Ethel is only the most literal of the dead in Kushner's play. On his deathbed, Roy tells Belize, "Nobody . . . with me now. But the dead" (II.4.i). Communing with the dead becomes an inevitable and everyday occurrence, a metaphor for forgiveness and also historical engagement made real. In the opening scene of Part One, an orthodox rabbi speaks at the funeral of Louis's grandmother. Reflecting on the great migration of Jews to America, he declares to the post-immigrant generation, "You do not live in America. No such place exists. Your clay is the clay of some Litvak shtetl, your air the air of the steppes." By the end, he reverses the reversal: "She was the last of the Mohicans, this one was. Pretty soon . . . all the old will be dead" (I.1.i). Such prospects of communing with the dead, especially the literally dead, are not necessarily welcomed. In a comic scene following the funeral, the rabbi explains why there are only two wooden pegs in the coffin: "So she can get out easier if she wants to." Louis responds, "I hope she stays put. I pretended for years that she was already dead. When they called to say she had died it was a surprise. I abandoned her" (I.1.9). Ethel, of course, doesn't "stay put." History doesn't work that way in Kushner's world.

The encounter between Ethel and Roy initially seems akin to a lopsided wrestling match between a man and an angel. That trope runs throughout the play, from Prior's bout with the Angel of America in his own hospital bed to Joe Pitt, the closeted Mormon and confidant to Roy, who fixates on the captivating boyhood image of Jacob wrestling the angel. "The angel is not human, and it holds nothing back," Joe protests, "so how could any human win, what kind of fight is that? It's not just" (I.2.ii). Even so, Prior, like Jacob, wins. Still, it is important that Ethel not be perceived as overly supernatural, be it an angel, a ghost, or a demon, so that she is no mere fantasy or pretentious lark on Kushner's part. Ethel's pedestrian ugly feelings, for one thing, bring her to the level of the human, as does the narrative frame of interpersonal forgiveness. By allowing the dead to talk to us on the level of shared humanity, Kushner equips us for our own wrestling match with history.

At first, Roy perceives Ethel as a spooky gimmick, as do most critics who describe her as a ghost without giving it too much thought. Kushner, however, conceives of her otherwise. On this, he is clear from the outset. In his list of characters for Part One, he explicitly identifies Prior 1 and Prior 2 as "the ghost of a dead Prior Walter" (10). Ethel, on the other hand, bears no description, save for the direction that she is played by the same actor playing Hannah. Further, in his brief playwright's notes, Kushner addresses how to execute the "moments of magic," which he specifies in a list that includes no reference to Ethel, nor even any scenes in which she appears (11). The notes to Part Two are even more extensive, including particularly wry and grumpy directions on the Angel's cough. (Kushner prefers Ellen McLaughlin's: "based on a cat hacking up a furball. It was sharp, simple and effectively nonhuman" [143].) But still no special mention of Ethel. The notes also single out Roy as a fiction based on a historical figure "who was all too real" (11), in Kushner's sardonic take on the standard legal disclaimer. But he makes no such move for Ethel.

Ethel stands apart from Kushner's lineup. The play has its share of dead men talking, though often only metaphorically so. There are, of course, the prior Priors, who are identified as ghosts. Prior declares himself also inhuman when he looks at his wracked, diseased body, chest covered with lesions. "That's a cancer. Nothing more," Hannah rejoins. "Nothing more human than that" (II.4.vi). Also, when Joe finally acts on his same-sex attractions, he compares himself to Lazarus and Louis to Jesus. He declares himself, "Back from the dead" (I.3.vii). And when Roy imagines himself disbarred—a career lawyer's own private version of a necro citizen—he barks, "What am I? A dead man?" (II.3.ii). Finally, several scenes after his death, Roy becomes a full-fledged dead man talking when he appears posthumously to Joe (and kisses him). This allows Kushner one last joke on history: Roy's gig in the hereafter is to defend God against the angels' charge of abandonment in a paternity suit.

Angels in America also memorably features another talking woman who is not alive: a wooden dummy mother in a diorama exhibit at the Mormon visitor center in Manhattan. She is less a dead woman talking than never alive, though she, too, imports historical depth. Harper explains, "They don't have any lines, the sister and the mother. And only his face moves. That's not really fair" (II.3.iii). The wooden dummy is a double of Harper, the Valium-addicted, agoraphobic housewife who is so removed from the world as to be quasi-dead. She confides, "His wife. His mute wife. I'm waiting for her to speak. Bet her story's not so jolly" (II.3.iii). Eventually, the Mormon mother becomes animate and leaves the diorama, motioning for Harper to follow. "I'm stuck," Harper reports. "My heart's an anchor." The Mormon mother responds, "Leave it, then. Can't carry no extra weight" (II.3.iii). This voice from the historical prairie is hardscrabble and no-nonsense. When all the old are dead, and when we join them, we best be prepared.

Ethel joins other exhumed historical figures of injustice in American literature. Of course, historical personages show up all the time in literature, from Emma Goldman in E. L. Doctorow's *Ragtime* to the titular protagonist in William Styron's *The Confessions of Nat Turner*. But it is noteworthy when such figures come back as dead. Beyond Ethel and Margaret Garner in this study, a good example is Emmett Till, the fourteen-year-old African American boy who was notoriously mutilated and murdered on August 28, 1955, for allegedly offending a white woman in the Mississippi Delta region. Till's corpse came to national prominence when his mother demanded an open casket funeral and venues such as *Jet* disseminated the image of the horribly mutilated body, sparking outrage, editorials, and widespread moral condemnation.[33] Since then, Till has been an enduring figure in African American literature, such as in Baldwin's 1964 play *Blues for Mister Charlie*, which reanimates a Till figure in a complicated flashback structure. A 1986 novel by Ishmael Reed, *Reckless Eyeballing*, goes further when the protagonist writes a play in which a Southern white woman has the corpse of a young black man literally exhumed so that he can stand trial for rape in Reed's anti-feminist lampoon.[34] In an uncanny historical echo, Till's actual corpse was indeed exhumed and autopsied in 2005 when the U.S. Department of Justice reopened the federal civil rights case, fifty years after the murder.

When the dead are exhumed from history and then talk, Kushner performs a fantastical feat without pyrotechnics and cables. He transforms historical matters of national injustice into an interpersonal skirmish, the more familiar realm of forgiveness. Thus, Kushner opens another avenue toward confronting past injustice: third-party forgiveness. "Especially where the injured party is no longer capable of responding to the offender," Griswold explains, "those intimately affected often assume they have a right to forgive or to refuse to forgive."[35] A classic, if not extreme, case is the dead. In this way, Ethel and Roy are proxy experiments in third-party forgiveness. Like Ethel, we wonder whether or not we can forgive Roy and all the injustice for which he stands as metonym in Kushner's national imaginary. Griswold considers national silence around injustice: "But in the long run, a nation—particularly a democratic one—cannot afford to pass over in uncomfortable silence matters of such grave importance. . . . The avoidance of the question of apology in a people's official narrative is the avoidance of full and public discussion of truth and responsibility."[36] Good examples include the Truth and Reconciliation process in post-apartheid South Africa, the Vietnam Veterans Memorial, and perhaps how Kushner calls up the mass neglect of AIDS patients under Reagan, which he couples with the legacy of McCarthyism. Kushner withholds Roy's capacity to repent, however, cementing him as a gloriously childish and bile-ridden body, while still offering the nation a chance at truth and responsibility. This is civic reconciliation without apology.

The wooden dummy shows us how to win this wrestling match with history, and perhaps any encounter with American literature's talking dead. She delivers a treatise on change: "God splits the skin with a jagged thumbnail from throat to belly and then plunges a huge filthy hand in." He rearranges the guts, but "it's up to you to do the stitching." The result is a changed human, "just mangled guts pretending" (II.3.vi). While the violence is striking, it is worth noting the body imagery deployed by a wooden dummy. Change is a profoundly embodied process; we alone have the guts to do it, not ghosts or angels, as well as the acting skills to pull it off. Kushner frequently describes *Angels in America* as a play about change, both the fierce urgency to do so and the horrifying difficulty. In the opening of Part Two, the oldest living Bolshevik, Aleksii Antedilluvianovich Prelapsarianov, stands amid the rubble of the cracked-open world. He announces, "The Great Question before us is: Are we doomed? The Great Question before us is: Will the past release us? The Great Question before us is: Can we Change? In Time? And we all desire that Change will come" (II.1.i). If in biology death is equivalent to stasis, so too is change necessary for life. While Roy may remain unchanged until his bitter end, the wronged are not absolved of their part of the contract of forgiveness. In Kushner's play, Ethel Rosenberg is no longer a wooden dummy of history waiting for justice to come. She is endowed with a voice and a body, complete with ugly feelings as well as capacity for change.

Love, Ethel

Ethel mainly operates on the pedestrian level of annoyance and exasperation, punctuated by bouts of righteous wrath. On occasion, though, she speaks on a more prophetic level, as in the conversation that follows the 911 phone call:

> ROY. I have all the time in the world.
> ETHEL ROSENBERG. You're immortal.
> ROY. I'm immortal. Ethel. (*He forces himself to stand*)
> I have forced my way into history. I ain't never gonna die.
> ETHEL ROSENBERG (*A little laugh, then*). History is about to crack wide open.
> Millennium approaches. (I.3.v)

Ethel's words align with the grand themes of Kushner's play—immortality, historical fissures, impending cosmic shifts—but her affect remains decidedly out of step. It is declarative and punctured with "a little laugh," neither a guffaw of wisdom nor chortle of contempt. In this, Ethel is less prophet of the future than heckler of history. She and Roy are the Waldorf and Statler in Kushner's *Muppet Show*.

Ethel's final, astonishing line in Part One resonates with her actual last words in print. Over the course of her prison letters from Sing Sing, the actual Ethel Rosenberg began to think of herself as a figure in the history books. As her execution neared, Ethel developed a habit of signing letters to her lawyer, "Love, Ethel." She communicated her love to her sons, her wishes for their care, and the words and tokens by which she wished to be remembered. In her final letter she writes, "All my heart I send to all who held me dear—I am not alone—and I die 'with honor and dignity'—knowing my husband & I must be vindicated by history." She concludes by reprising one of her husband's refrains, "We are the first victims of American Fascism."[37] To this final prison house letter she appended a scrap of paper with a handwritten note to her psychiatrist. She writes, "I cry for my self as I lie dead—how shall they know all that burned my brain & breast." She imagines herself a corpse and laments the inability to speak. She ends with something of a premonition and terrifying curse: "the fat's in the fire to say nothing of the books." The phrase "fat is in the fire" is a Yiddishism meaning trouble is about to start. This makes the image of book burning all the more ominous.

The Rosenbergs saw their prison letters as one way to write their own script, which prompted Julius's near-obsessive attempts to correct and preserve the documentary record, certain of his rightfulness. The resulting archive presents two hauntingly complex people stiffened by political principles, but also buckled by fear, self-doubt, and weariness, especially in their role as anguished parents trying to balance their finite time pursuing appeals, securing arrangements for their children, and following the unfolding historical narrative in which they found themselves. A highly edited (or altered) selection of the letters was first published the month of their execution in *Death House Letters of Ethel and Julius Rosenberg*. In 1994, Michael Meeropol, one of the sons they left behind, published a complete edition. Regarding that collection, literary critic David Thorburn notes that Julius remains prolific in his vigorous blending of Marxist, religious, and patriotic arguments, but as the execution nears, "Ethel, in contrast, falls into near silence."[38] Some speculate about the psychological reasons for the silence—depression in particular[39]—yet it also creates a literary opening for Kushner: the silence carves out a space for posthumous voice.

In the published letters, the real Ethel never mentions Cohn by name, while Julius mentions him only twice, both times to their lawyer, Emanuel Bloch. In the first mention, dated February 1, 1953, Julius attempts to correct the trial record and therefore improve their chances at exoneration in the historical record, if not in court. "D. A. Cohn said the name of each scientist will be directly related to the two of us," he notes as he pores over the transcripts of their trial. "I don't believe he connected it up."[40] Even more so than Ethel, Julius exhibits a keen awareness of the contest to write their historical narrative. He recognizes how he has become an indeterminate symbol in various high-stakes stories playing out in the press, from imperialism to constitutional rights to anti-Semitism.[41] In this endeavor, Julius confronts the limits of time and the human body. In a letter dated December 3, 1952, Julius opens in part, "Dear friend I have permitted myself certain luxuries today for I must confess I am only mortal."[42] The "certain luxuries" include sleeping late, rather than tending to such matters as figuring out where the press stood on "key issues of the day" as their case wended its way through various appeals. Julius's concession of his own mortality stands in marked contrast to Ethel's declaration of immortality in Kushner's play.

Julius's second direct mention of Cohn is of an entirely different order, more in line with Ethel's prophetic bouts in the play. Julius first adopts a collective voice in a grand, ominous, almost oracular register designed for the history books:

> We do hereby indict for a conspiracy to commit murder all those who have had a hand in our case in violating the laws of Nature and the Constitution of the United States before God and Man; in that said individuals did conspire, combine, confederate and agree with intent and reason to believe, to bear false witness, directly or indirectly, to deprive of freedom, liberty and life, to innocent people, to incite the public mind, by chicanery and by fraud, to misinform, mis-lead and coerce people to conform to official policies, to create fear and hysteria that inevitably leads to war abroad and a police state at home.[43]

This letter is dated February 12, 1953, the day after President Eisenhower denied their first petition for executive clemency. Julius adopts the voice of a dead man cursing his enemies, in good company with the eviscerating imagination of Walker's curse-prayer. Julius is aware of his letter as not only a historical and political document but also a literary one in its consonance (e.g., "conspire, combine, confederate") and purposeful use of official forms such as the legal indictment and allusion to founding documents. He echoes with bitter irony the promises of life, liberty, and the pursuit of happiness in the Declaration of Independence. Like that and other political manifestos, the letter goes on to chronicle with righteous indignation the details of his charges, which includes the second mention of Cohn as but one detail among many. In adopting a grand voice of principled abstractions—"Man and God"—the letter also resonates uncannily with Kushner's own play four decades later, especially its conceit of the angels suing God for abandonment in something akin to a cosmic family court.

In the play, Kushner replaces Julius the confident politico with Ethel, the more conflicted maternal figure prone to bouts of silence. Kushner affords her the opportunity to write her own historical record and see if she can secure the justice that will stop Julius's curse. While Cohn is something on the order of a footnote in the prison letters, Kushner amplifies this sparring match. The ensuing encounter is ultimately more about Kushner's contemporary audience and their capacity to create a more just future. Prior ends the play, "This disease will be the end of many of us, but not nearly all, and the dead will be commemorated and will struggle on with the living, and we are not going away. We won't die secret deaths anymore. The world only spins forward. We will be citizens. The time has come" (Epilogue).

It is no surprise that Kushner ends on the note of citizenship. In his 1994 essay "American Things," Kushner explains the origins and tenets of his political lineage, which is diverse and radical but merits the shorthand "liberal." Kushner professes, "This liberalism at its best held that citizenship was bestowable on everyone, and sooner or later it would be bestowed."[44] The result is a multicultural humanism whose expansive vision is able to include posthumous citizenship. Later in the essay, Kushner avers, "The recovery of antecedents is immensely important work."[45] In *Angels,* Ethel can finally be a citizen among the living, even if she herself is dead. Roy? Not so much.

7

Dead Women Gossiping

Randall Kenan's *Let the Dead Bury Their Dead*

In *The Satanic Verses*, a masterpiece of magical realism, Salman Rushdie famously asks, how does newness enter the world? The tradition of dead women talking prompts a follow-up question: what if that which is new mingles with the dead, the half-buried, the forgotten, and the reviled? The fantastic standoff between Ethel and Roy in *Angels in America* is more than a proxy wrestling match with history; it also helps us reorder our present, and in turn our future. Harper asks, "Imagination can't create anything new, can it? It only recycles bits and pieces from the past."[1] It turns out that the imagination is the special province of humans, whose capacity for change may have spurred God to abandon them. While dead women who talk necessarily truck with the bits and pieces of the past, the convention also allows writers to narrate newness, and thereby make it imaginable.

We see this play out to different effect in gay black Southern writer Randall Kenan's story "Clarence and the Dead," in which a very young orphan can converse with a small Southern town's dead. Little Clarence's abilities capture the attention of a particularly persistent resident, an eccentric old farmer named Ellsworth who comes to believe that Clarence embodies his long-lost wife Mildred. The grief-wracked old man pursues a relationship with the young boy because he believes it to be a socially sanctioned coupling, even if the community doesn't see it that way. In other words, Ellsworth wants to be in a romance novel, but Kenan has other designs. The story opens *Let the Dead Bury Their Dead*, a 1992 short story collection that mixes sex, death, and religion in a stew of necromancy, miscegenation, incest, and all that is forbidden. Kenan is known for drawing masterfully on elements of traditions such as magical realism and the Southern gothic, even science fiction according to one literary critic.[2] He uses these traditions to reinvent key African American forms, such as the folk tale, the segregation narrative, and, most important in this book, the passing narrative. The result is a new kind of passing narrative, one that fully draws on passing's three main associations—race, sexuality, and death. Thus, Kenan makes possible new kinds of community without forfeiting the old.

In African American literature especially, the passing narrative has long been a go-to vehicle to explore who does and doesn't belong in a community when characters cross—or don't cross—heavily policed lines. The most crucial line Kenan crosses in "Clarence and the Dead" is not one of race or sexuality, but rather between the dead and the living. By breaching that ultimate uncrossable line, Kenan forges a place in the present for the past that has not passed. With Clarence's tale, Kenan reinvents the passing narrative for a post–civil rights, post-Stonewall project: to reach for what theorist José Esteban Muñoz calls the "then and there" of queer futurity,[3] or perhaps what Christopher Castiglia and Christopher Reed call "the promise of the queer past."[4] In this venture, he employs a dead woman and a living child. On the one hand, a dead woman literalizes what it means to pass (as in, to die), a conflation we also see in well-known racial passing narratives. As for the living child, queer theorist Lee Edelman identifies such a figure as a recurring trope in heteronormative discourse,[5] though Kathryn Bond Stockton has recently posed the "queer child" as a countertradition.[6] When a dead woman talks to and through a queer child such as Clarence, the community is asked to accept not just those who cross normative boundaries of identity, but also the departed, whether actively remembered or not, deceased or simply gone away. Thus, Kenan makes room in the present for the new as well as the buried, the unknown and seemingly alien, and the heretofore unthinkable. In short, his reinvented passing narrative makes social change possible.

Passing, Passed, Past

Passing's dual association with race and death is no mere linguistic coincidence. The twinned tropes of racial impersonation and death are prevalent in the African American passing narrative. In the most iconic example, Nella Larsen's 1929 novella *Passing*, Clare Kendry returns to the black community of Harlem after years spent living in bourgeois white society. Larsen presents Clare as if she is back from the dead. Upon finally recognizing her, Irene Redfield thinks, "It must be, she figured, all of twelve years since she, or anybody that she knew, had laid eyes on Clare Kendry."[7] The connection between racial passing and death is clear in the very next line: "After her father's death she'd gone to live with some relatives, aunts or cousins two or three times removed, over on the west side: relatives that nobody had known the Kendry's possessed until they had turned up at the funeral and taken Clare away with them."[8] The moment Clare first begins to pass into white society is also in a passage about her father's funeral. When she returns to Harlem years later, Clare is a woman resurrected. Clare's severed connection to the black community is made possible by, and understood through, death and ruptured racial kinship. Kenan's collection takes an inverse approach: to imagine new models of community made possible when the living commune with the returned dead.

Let the Dead Bury Their Dead is narrated from the collective point of view of Tims Creek, an imaginary town in rural North Carolina that seems simultaneously contemporary, timeless, and a throwback to Jim Crow–era race relations. Kenan opens with "Clarence and the Dead," whose parenthetical subtitle, "(*And* What Do They Tell You, Clarence? *And* The Dead Speak to Clarence)," underscores the central role of community lore and conversational modes of interaction—in a word, gossip. This leads Trudier Harris, an influential scholar of African American literature, to place Kenan in a tradition steeped in oral storytelling and folklore, which she signals as "the power of the porch." She argues, "The southern soil of *Let the Dead Bury Their Dead* is the soil of the past influencing the present, of realistic and extranatural characters, of morality and immorality, of striking restrictions and excessive liberties."[9] Yet Clarence's connection to the past is not always welcome, especially when it requires a recalibration—or even fundamental change—of his community. Further, newness resides in that same soil, a messy metonym for the stuff of death (graves), life (crops), and cross-generational inheritance (land).

Clarence is born from a very recently deceased mother. He emerges from the corpse's womb covered in a sticky caul everywhere but his face, a faithful inversion of the folk trope for a child who will have connections to the dead. The imagery also recalls W. E. B. Du Bois's famous description of the colorline as not only a veil but also a caul covering one's face at birth,[10] thereby aligning double consciousness with birth and death, funereal and bridal imagery. Despite his rather macabre entrance into the world, Clarence becomes yet another instance of mundane specialness in Kenan's matter-of-fact depiction of the fantastic yet routine world of Tims Creek. "Nothing much happened to point out that Clarence was different," Kenan writes, "not until the summer three years later when he began to talk, the day Ed Phelps found him out in his cow pasture surrounded by buzzards and talking in complete sentences."[11] Thus, Clarence enters the world of the gothic, the deathly, and the uncanny. That is the place where the known and the unknown meet, when the seemingly foreign becomes the familiar. Harris describes these moments as juxtapositions between the ordinary and the extraordinary. Likewise, Freud's concept of the uncanny would frame them as meeting the unhomely in the realm of the homely, or vice versa. At these moments, Clarence incites the nether regions of the passing narrative where racial or sexual passing mixes with passing's other pools of meaning, namely, connotations of death in the sense of *passing away* or *passing on*, as well as passing as a breach from one's community, to be in but not of, to pass by.

Kenan goes beyond metaphorical death in the racial passing narrative and makes it literal. His passing narrative forges the very connections to history and community that Clare Kendry must sever in Larsen's novella. Further, Clarence's necromantic connections contrast a backdrop of genealogical disruption as Kenan litters his landscape with Clarence's dead mother, his reluctant adoptive grandparents, Mr. George Edward and Miss Eunice, handwringing over retarded heirs, and a family hog with human eyes that allegedly talks. Like Clare Kendry, Clarence goes to live with relatives after a parent's death, but he remains within the community, a known quantity who nonetheless brings back knowledge of other worlds. Clarence knows about people and details from decades back and buried in private memories, out of view even from the leering, curious, gossiping porch community. Clarence speaks of "secrets no people had shared with no living person, much less a boy who could do well to stand and walk at the same time and who refused to give up his bottle" (8). Like Clare's tales of a life of white leisure in *Passing*, Clarence's knowledge of another world is alluring but not entirely welcome. Kenan writes, "Mr. George Edward gave Clarence a few extra licks for lying, all the while wondering how on earth the boy'd come to know about a woman long dead before Clarence was even thought about" (6). While Larsen's novel ends in Clare's physical death, the narrative had already posed her as a metaphorical dead woman returned from the other side. On the other hand, having never left his community, Clarence's possible connections to the other side are even more troubling.

In the passing narrative tradition, the protagonist is a liminal figure who can move back and forth across fiercely policed lines so that, as literary critic M. Giulia Fabi explains, the passer's body "turns what was once conceived of as natural opposition into a societal one."[12] Clarence limns the line between life and death, as much as race or sexuality. Thus, he refutes the injunction in the very title of the collection, *Let the Dead Bury Their Dead*, which recalls Jesus's fabled admonition to his disciples to dwell on more pressing issues than corpses.[13] Clarence's tale insists that the past is not passed, that the dead, along with the once known and the never known, occupy the realm of the living. With Clarence, Kenan explores what it would mean to truly form a community across long-cemented lines of social division, when the distance between a live boy and a dead woman isn't so great.

I must note that Clarence's story is not a racial passing narrative per se. In fact, the narrator conspicuously buries mention of race, only for it to erupt when the living interact with the dead. The first overt reference to race of any kind is well into the story, and therefore jarring. We learn Mr. George Edward's backstory, of which Clarence has uncanny knowledge: "Well, the long and short of it is that one payday while enjoying the end of the week them boys got themselves into a piece of trouble with a bunch of white sailors in Wilmington" (11). Under pressure, George Edward fingered the fellow black man who ended up killing a white sailor, an act of racial treason for which the now-dead acquaintance seeks revenge. Kenan thus establishes a pattern throughout the short story cycle of delaying mention of race and U.S. histories of segregation until an instance of high-stakes cross-racial contact. Furthermore, such events most often happen well after the story is into the thick of the plot and the dead and other fantastical figures have been long chattering away.

Kenan's story predates a contemporary resurgence in racial passing narratives. Michele Elam, a scholar of multiracial literature, considers the peculiar endurance of the racial passing narrative in a post–civil rights era, even though its concerns and its very existence may seem quaint, even obsolete, in an era that likes to think of itself as the "mulatto millennium." She notes that contemporary passing narratives by both black and nonblack authors "have risen seemingly from the dead not to bear witness to past issues but to testify in some of the fiercest debates about the viability of race in this 'beyond race' era."[14] Kenan's new kind of passing narrative offers neither a critique nor celebration of a particular identity. Nor is it interested in portraying identity as mere fiction, which Elaine Ginsberg argues is a dominant aim in the tradition.[15]

Kenan's reinvented passing narrative is more about the communities into which characters pass, or pass back. In fact, Kenan breaks altogether from the tradition of American individualism, which Kathleen Pfeiffer argues traditionally drives racial passing narratives. That is, passing narratives traditionally reject constricting ideas about racial identity and origins such as one-drop rules in order to advocate an individual's right to determine one's place in the world, or to expose the horrors of not being able to do so.[16] Much the same can be said of sexual passing narratives and their brash cousins, coming out narratives, which focus on the individual who passes or comes out. Kenan, on the other hand, maintains a focus squarely on the community of Tims Creek, even at the level of the narrative voice speaking collectively as "we," even if prone to internal dissent and bickering.

Clarence is the community's reluctant connection to its past, and to each other. He inhabits the terrain of the Southern gothic and its penchant for the odd, off-kilter, necromantic, and, most pertinently, the eerily anachronistic—that is, the lingering past amid the decaying present. Yet Clarence is no Addie Bundren. Addie's dying wish is to be buried away from the rural family home and in Jefferson so as to sever her ties with her non-blood family. The woman talking through Clarence, on the other hand, doesn't pass on or pass away so much as pass *back into* the community. In this, Clarence is closer kin to Beloved. Kenan's adult-talking, bottle-sucking young boy who communes with the dead evokes Morrison's strange-talking adult-baby of Sethe's murdered child returned. Still, Clare Kendry, Addie Bundren, Beloved, and Clarence all share a function: conduit between present and past, as well as between those who would otherwise not interact.

As any student of the uncanny knows, figures of the past are likely to pop up in unexpected places if repressed, be it a white-looking woman with a cat-like allure on the roof of the Drayton Hotel in the case of Clare Kendry, a talking corpse confessing her masochism toward children in the case of Addie Bundren, a girl-woman with a familiar scar on her neck in the case of Beloved, or a three-year-old boy at home with buzzards in the case of Clarence Pickett. Beloved and Clare Kendry, if not Addie Bundren, both return from the world of the half-forgotten, be it the Middle Passage or white society. The two women are cautiously half-welcomed back into their respective black communities, if only for a time. Clarence's engagements with the other side, however, lead to his expulsion from the community he never left. The reasons have to do primarily with passing's other vehicle: sexuality.

Kenan's Queer Child of Death

While Clarence is not passing in the racial sense, a decidedly queer passing narrative disrupts this tale of cross-generational connection and kinship. Ellsworth becomes infatuated with Clarence because the boy is speaking to and as his dead wife. Eventually, Mr. George Edward "come to feel a touch uneasy. . . . Tweren't the sort of look a grown man shows to a five-year-old boy" (18). With Ellsworth's persistence and increasing audacity, Clarence's grandparents begin to protect him from "what begun to look like courting and sparking" (19). At this point, we readers have a decision: is this a fantastic tale of a dead woman talking, or a story of pederasty passing clumsily as a heterosexual romance? The community chooses the latter. In doing so, it attempts to foreclose the possibilities Clarence opens. The community opts for a normative script to describe "Ellsworth Batts' 'unnatural affection' for Clarence Pickett" (19). When Ellsworth attempts to kidnap Clarence, the community deems the grieving widower "a true menace" (20). The most salient factor in the community's disapproval is Clarence's age: he is still only five years old, even though his knowledge from the dead makes him uncannily adult. The three components of passing coalesce into a pressing question of whether the community has room for any of these actors—the necromantic child, the lascivious would-be kidnapper, or the dead wife talking—all of whom are bound up in a romance the community thought long buried.

Narratives of racial and sexual passing have long converged, which we now recognize thanks in large part to pathbreaking queer readings of Larsen's *Passing*. In a seminal essay, Deborah McDowell argues, "Though, superficially, Irene's is an account of Clare's passing for white and related issues of racial identity and loyalty, underneath the safety of that surface is the more dangerous story—though not named explicitly—of Irene's awakening sexual desire for Clare."[17] In *Bodies That Matter*, Judith Butler further examined the inseparable, rather than layered, relationship between queer desire and racial passing in Larsen's novel.[18] Since then, scholars have reclaimed Larsen's queer contemporaries, such as Bruce Nugent, and fomented a wholesale "queering of the color line," to use Siobhan Somerville's formulation.[19] Still, McDowell famously noted the strange way many critics missed for so long the queer reading of *Passing*. She concludes that Larsen baits us to look for the familiar plot of race so that lesbian desire can be hidden in the open.[20] Such an open-secret model, however, is not possible in a gossipy town like Tims Creek where everyone has a loose tongue, including the dead.

As a child, Clarence adds a troubling element to even the queerest understanding of the passing narrative. By communing with the past, he becomes the antithesis of the omnipresent innocent child, a near-sacred figure in contemporary culture and the bugaboo in Lee Edelman's influential treatise *No Future: Queer Theory and the Death Drive*. Edelman positions "queer oppositionality" against "the Child as the emblem of futurity"[21] and advocates instead the death drive, which in queer theory becomes associated with non-procreative sex. Edelman rejects the "Ponzi scheme" of procreation because it bars the queer subject from participating in the community's perpetual regeneration. He advocates that rather than uttering lofty and endlessly deferred promises for future equality or arguing for rights not for current citizens but for that Child on the horizon, the national community must instead insist on the salience of the queer subject himself or herself. But Clarence is a different kind of child. He is not exactly a figure of innocence in need of community protection from the non-procreative, deathly queer subject. Yet the Tims Creek community ultimately deems him so.

Kenan creates a queer protagonist who is also a child, perhaps even *the Child*. Clarence is simultaneously a figure of futurity and death, of queerness and heterosexual desire. He serves the sort of redemptive, if dangerous, role against which Edelman tends to oppose the Child. Clarence is, instead, a queer child. I say this in the way Kathryn Bond Stockton imagines such figures: eerie, strange, disorienting. It is not clear that such children will "grow up" to become proper citizens and thus replicate civil society as we know it. Stockton encourages us to think instead of children who grow sideways. "Growing sideways," she explains, "suggests that the width of a person's experience or ideas, their motives or their motions, may pertain at any age, bringing 'adults' and 'children' into lateral contact of surprising sorts."[22] Such children don't self-perpetuate, but are instead ghostly figures haunting our normative, forward-moving history books. Queer studies has eschewed the procreative bias embedded in futurity. By tangling with the strange, decidedly uninnocent past, Clarence provides alternative possibilities for kinship and connection, ones that ignite the passing narrative's long-standing concerns with communal belonging, identity, and genealogy. Thus, he may foster the queer utopianism that José Muñoz argues is bound up in the past more so than the present.

Clarence is not only a queer child but also a child of death. In *Passed On*, black cultural critic Karla FC Holloway explores the black funeral business, cemeteries, memorials, and other ways of memorializing the prematurely departed, often victims of white violence or social neglect. The result is a celebrated and beguiling study in which she finds that "racial memory and racial realization is mediated through the veil of death."[23] Of course, African American literature has long engaged matters of the past and racial inheritance, as I explore in the chapter on Suzan-Lori Parks's *Getting Mother's Body*.[24] Scholars such as Sharon Holland position death as central to black subjectivity itself,[25] while Holloway helps us connect such concerns to the figure of the child. Mortality is such a pervasive cultural haunting, she argues, that African American children become "forlorn legatees of the cultural experience of black death."[26] Clarence, then, becomes the consummate child of not only Tims Creek but African American folk culture more generally.

By featuring a queer child of death, Kenan's passing narrative questions a community's normative lines. We learn that "at one point, forgetting himself, Ellsworth grasped the boy's hand. Mr. George Edward had to clear his throat to reacquaint Ellsworth with the impropriety of doing what he was doing" (19). This is a funny moment, to be sure, but it is also odd in the way it singles out for censure one breach among many in this myth-laden town. Stockton emphatically calls our attention to the tremendous amount of infrastructure, legal apparatus, and cultural training that goes into ensuring that children grow up properly in America: "*evidently, we are scared of the child we would protect*."[27] Ellsworth's advances lead to the townsfolk "keeping an extra eye on their womenfolk and children" (19), yet the talking pig, for instance, gives them little pause—at least, not until its owner brings it to church. It is also important to point out that nonconsensual heterosexual sex is not pathologized in Kenan's story. For instance, after a town member wakes from a dream about how her husband would have left her had she not followed Clarence's advice to bake him a pie, "she went back to sleep, to be waked up not by the rooster but by Joe Allen rocking on top of her, singing in her ear" (7).

Kenan's queer passing narrative does not advocate for the merits of sexual minority identity—it is not about LGBT empowerment, as we might expect in a sexual passing narrative or a coming out story. In fact, it is important to distinguish between queer and gay in this story because Ellsworth is not gay in any meaningful sense and because Clarence is a child. When critics see the relationship between Clarence and Ellsworth as homosexual, they are probably thinking more about Kenan's own identity or other stories in the collection. For instance, Harris explores how "a ghost story is overlaid with homosexuality"[28] and suggests that the Ellsworth episode is largely humorous in the way Tims Creek chooses to do battle with homosexuality rather than the talking dead. This reading captures the playful spirit of Kenan's storytelling, but it does not account for Clarence's status as a child. I suggest that the townsfolk's reaction is better understood by attending more to the relationship between the living and the dead, Clarence and Mildred, rather than Clarence and Ellsworth. Much more so than homosexuality or even pederasty, the taboo at stake is a necrophilic version of community. Other stories in the collection deal more directly with homophobia, especially "Run, Mourner, Run," but Clarence's story in particular insists on the uncanniness of such a young child with such adult knowledge and activities. After all, what is so curious about him is that he "would talk to Miss Eunice and Mr. George Edward *like an adult*" (5, emphasis mine).

In the end, Kenan's community banishes Clarence's story to mere myth, if remembered at all. The community deems the relationship with Ellsworth "crimes against nature" (19), and Kenan writes, "The likelihood of him conversing with his dead Mildred through the boy paled next to the idea of him fermenting depraved intentions for young and tender boys" (19). At this moment, the collective-speaking narrator begins to pull away from the community. Ellsworth may be wrongheaded in his attempt to normalize the relationship as a conventional heterosexual romance, if not a bit necrophilic, but Kenan suggests that the community is even more wrongheaded in its reluctance to acknowledge the fantastic in its midst. When Ellsworth jumps off a bridge to his death, Kenan writes, "We were all mostly relieved seeing what we considered a threat to our peace and loved ones done away with; a few of us—the ones who dared put one iota of stock in believing Clarence and his talking dead folk—figured it to be a kind of happy ending, seeing as Ellsworth would now be reunited with his beloved beyond the pale" (21). The description "beyond the pale" signals how the passing narrative breaches lines of color, community standards, and death. It is up to the community to decide what to do about the breach.

This community ultimately banishes Ellsworth and Clarence from its lore, which is the ultimate form of exclusion. Yet in recounting the banishment, the narrator evokes Morrison's concept of "disremembering" in *Beloved*. When the residents of Tims Creek—but not Kenan—banish Clarence from communal memory, the resulting blank spot demarcates a failure of imagination with consequences graver than Clare Kendry's death. The work of the ensuing collection of stories is to fill in that blank space of possibility.

Queer Children of the Future

Accounting for all its layers of passing, "Clarence and the Dead" is best described as an otherwise pedestrian heterosexual romance narrative passing as a ghost story tucked within a queer short story cycle. The past is dangerous and compelling territory in this multilayered passing narrative, not because it threatens an innocent child—Ellsworth's lovelorn kidnapping is, after all, supposed to be humorous—but because the realm of the dead harbors possibilities for other forms of kinship and community. As characters cross seemingly inviolable lines, citizens of Tims Creek encounter the heretofore alien, unknown, or buried. Where Freud locates a "peculiar feeling" of dread in such uncanny moments,[29] Kenan finds the tantalizing possibility of social change. Harris celebrates the assurance with which "citizens of Tims Creek see and have conversations with ghosts, interact with angels, and create mythical characters,"[30] and she, too, sees the collection as one that asks, "Can people change? If so, how do they change?"[31] Encounters between the real and the fantastic—the living and the dead, in this instance—do not just allow connections to and breaks from the past, but also the not yet known. The community then decides whether or not to make room for the new.

All this is to say, Clarence makes change possible. He becomes not only a queer child of death but also a queer child of the future. Death and dying become sources of social change . . . *if* the living community allows it. The community thinks, "We figured there was more to it than that, something our imaginations were too timid to draw up, something to do with living and dying that we, so wound up in harvesting corn, cleaning house . . . really didn't care about or have time or space to know. Why mess in such matters?" (22). Kenan pushes to break from the expected and the explicable so that we see Clarence through Ellsworth's eyes: as his dead wife returned. Matters of death and desire have defined a generation of queer studies, whether as cause to celebrate or resist, from Leo Bersani's foundational essay "Is the Rectum a Grave?" to Edelman's embrace of the death drive. Stockton goes so far as to link queer attraction and death, or more specifically living, decomposing corpses, a trope in such iconic black queer works as James Baldwin's *Giovanni's*

Room.[32] Clarence, on the other hand, emerges from a dead womb and may harbor the community's future.

How can a narrative that trucks in corpses and the realm of the dead bring life to a reimagined community? Holloway notes that "African Americans' particular vulnerability to an untimely death in the United States intimately affects how black culture both represents itself and is represented."[33] This heightens the observation by Sarah Goodwin and Elisabeth Bronfen in *Death and Representation* that death "grounds the many ways a culture stabilizes and represents itself, and yet it always does so as a signifier with an incessantly receding, ungraspable signified, always points to other signifiers, other means of representing what finally is just absent."[34] As Clarence's talking dead upset the finality of death, Kenan troubles the community's grounds for stability and ignites social crises. By engaging a simultaneous realist and mythic mode—assuming the folkloric mantle of Zora Neale Hurston more so than the earnest realism of Richard Wright—Kenan creates a community that lives with, but never fully acknowledges, the talking dead in their midst. The community must confront those they might wish to remain silent and removed from the community. In Clarence's story, for instance, the narrator reports, "We just shrugged and accepted [Ellsworth's] crazy behavior as one of those things that happen" (17). Thus, Kenan provides a strange model of acceptance of that which cannot be, not unlike the silence that tends to surround unacknowledged racial origins or sexual desires in more conventional passing narratives.

When a dead woman talks to a queer child, the challenge Kenan poses to readers is to listen. "Clarence and the Dead" ends with the banishment of the main character from community lore. Yet by the third story of the collection, "The Foundations of the Earth," Tims Creek has begun not only to tolerate the new, the forgotten, and the excommunicated, but also to invite them. In that story, Mrs. Maggie MacGowan Williams comes to terms with her gay grandson, Edward, who goes north and never returns. Upon Edward's death, Miss Maggie invites to her porch Gabriel, his white lover from the North. Her other guests remain silent, uninquisitive, and seemingly uninterested, save for some sidelong glances. Miss Maggie, however, attempts a feat of imagination. "How curious the world had become," she thinks, "that she would be asking a white man to exonerate her in the eyes of her own grandson; how strange that at seventy, when she had all the laws and rules down pat, she would have to begin again, to learn" (72). Miss Maggie tries to make room in her life for the new and the dead—without mistaking one for the other. Harris argues,

"Kenan shakes up the quiet land, as well as the quiet patterns of living."[35] I would add that it is too late for Miss Maggie to directly engage her gay grandson because he died in exile. But we have been primed to follow the lead of the necromantic queer child in the opening story. He shows us how to hear the voices of the dead through the living.

Kenan's project is more about the viability of community in Tims Creek than proffering a feel-good story of any particular identity. The rural South is often relegated to the past in a master national narrative of the Great Migration of black people to the urban North during the Jim Crow era.[36] This resonates with Leigh Anne Duck's observation that in U.S. modernist literature, the Jim Crow South served as a region imagined as temporally distinct from the modern nation, a relic of its past. Far from a relic, the porches of Tims Creek are rich, interesting, and perhaps even sophisticated perches from which to view the modern world. Kenan playfully blends history and mythology to create a community that feels simultaneously past and present, urgent and removed. In Tims Creek, post–civil rights concerns of multiculturalism, gender equality, and sexual inclusivity are not necessarily newer, more urban imports; they are central to the soap opera lives of the native porch communities. We see this with the elderly Miss Maggie, who "would sometimes sit by herself on the patio late of an evening, in the same chair she was sitting in now, sip from her Coca-Cola, and think about how big the earth must be to seem flat to the eye" (49–50). From this folksy perch, Miss Maggie is profoundly self-aware, a prime example of what Kwame Anthony Appiah might describe as rooted cosmopolitanism.[37]

The prospects for creating an inclusive community lie in our ability to hear the voices of the dead in the bodies of the living, even if such bodies are surprising or unexpected locations. Throughout *Let the Dead Bury Their Dead*, citizens commune with not only the dead but other seemingly alien bodies. For instance, in the collection's second story, "Things of This World (Or; Angels Unaware)," Mr. John Edgar, a longtime black resident of Tims Creek, forms an unexpected friendship with Chi, a man of ambiguous descent, perhaps Asian or Latino. Within a regime of compulsory race segregation, this might constitute what Marlon Ross frames as "aggressive mobility" in his influential study of gender, sexuality, and Jim Crow.[38] In fact, such a cross-identitarian friendship requires fantastical intervention. In a move reminiscent of *The Satanic Verses*, Kenan plunks Chi into Tims Creek by way of the sky, presumably an unaware fallen angel who disrupts an otherwise straightforward parable of Jim Crow justice. With such unexpected connections, Kenan charts new territory for the passing narrative's ability to transgress identitarian lines. Further, such uncanny bodies help us resist identitarian siren songs, or what Ross might call "racial claustrophilia,"[39] so that we do not endlessly replicate past social divisions into the future.

Kenan caps his story cycle with the titular "Let the Dead Bury Their Dead," a heavily footnoted pseudo-history of Tims Creek. Unlike Clarence's one-sided conversations with the dead, the concluding story is a conversational oral history teeming with digressive footnotes, faux historical references, and interruptive spats with the narrator's wife, who remembers it differently. The wry pseudo-history presciently troubles Kenan's own earnest ethnographic project seven years later in *Walking on Water: Black American Lives at the Turn of the Twenty-First Century*. In that nonfiction exploration, critic George Hovis argues, the collective autobiography is not told through the lens of black gay experience, thereby conceding an arms-length distance with which the black community holds its gay sons.[40] Seven years earlier, in *Let the Dead Bury Their Dead*, Kenan shows us how to embrace them, even if it requires a bit of necromancy. Kenan's technique of collective narration distinguishes between the speaking "we" and individual town members, including especially its queer subjects, from Clarence to Gabriel and others. Even if the community responds to Clarence's untimely death at age five with relief—"No one talks about Clarence, and God only knows what lies they'd tell if they did" (22)—Kenan uses Clarence to unearth the dead, buried, or repressed of Tims Creek to tell a new story of community, one that is also old.

Even when no one talks about the dead, banished, or reviled, they remain. They may be passed, but they are not in the past. This means that future citizens of the present may one day welcome them back onto their porches and into their homes. We experience a counter-text in the penultimate story, "Tell Me, Tell Me," which recounts a dead black boy creeping around and haunting a seemingly innocent elderly white woman, Mrs. Ida Perry. As the black boy encroaches on Ida's field of vision and domestic space, she considers calling the police to report an intruder. Eventually, Ida remembers the boy: he was murdered long ago by her now-deceased husband when the boy inadvertently stumbled upon the couple making love in the bushes early in their courtship. The story ends, "All are guilty, none is free" (269). Kenan indicts white culpability by puncturing its postures of innocence, a familiar theme in African American literature. However, this pastoral scene strikingly reverses famous scenes of black sexual innocence defiled by white interlopers, from Richard Wright's 1941 protest story "Big Boy Leaves Home" to Morrison's 1970 Black Arts novel *The Bluest Eye*. Kenan avoids polemicism by including the full range of community members in multiracial Tims Creek. When Ida's story joins the rest in the collection, Clarence's ability to commune with the dead offers a way to till the graveyard of the past, including its horrific injustices, in search of the seeds of the future.

With a cast of quirky characters who cross so many seemingly inviolable lines, Kenan imagines an inclusive community beyond niche identities. There is room for all manner of folk in Tims Creek, including philandering preachers and incestuous siblings, a talking pig and an ethnically ambiguous angel, a white woman haunted by a dead black boy, and a boy who communes with the dead. But Kenan cannot—or perhaps chooses not to—imagine a place in Tims Creek for someone most like himself: an out gay black man. The 1980s and 1990s saw the explosion of a niche market for LGBT narratives of empowerment and visibility, into which such writers as E. Lynn Harris tapped. Yet Kenan largely opts out of directly chronicling contemporary Southern black gay experience, leading to what Holland elsewhere identifies as the "absent gay black man." The closest Kenan comes is Gabriel. Miss Maggie observes, "Gabriel had come with the body, like an interpreter for the dead" (56). Gabriel serves a similar function as Clarence: to connect Tims Creek's living with its dead, especially the sort that Tims Creek has not yet figured out how to fully include.

Literary criticism has not yet fully caught up to Kenan's mythically inclusive community, though scholars are starting to follow Harris in this regard.[41] Throughout his fiction, Kenan mischievously creates characters whose identities cross, reject, or belie cemented identitarian lines. Literary critic Suzanne Jones considers Kenan's depiction of intolerance in multiracial Southern communities still haunted by Jim Crow, singling out the black community in particular as failing to include sexual minorities. She concludes, "Kenan demonstrates that identity politics, of any stripe, can function to create community but that communities so formed continue to function only by negating differences of the individuals within them."[42] Further, Éva Tettenborn traces how the gay protagonist of Kenan's 1989 novel *A Visitation of Spirits* returns south and "starts considering death as a liberating event," ultimately leading him to suicide.[43] Kenan himself articulated a paradoxical repulsion and connection to the Southern landscape by thinking about the case of his predecessor, William Faulkner. In a 1995 interview, Kenan observes, "Being in the South, writing about it through your self, through your own responses to it, and so often reflecting about wanting to get out of the South, but at the same time knowing—and it's a horrible paradox—that this is what sustains you, this is what makes you who you are; there's a very fine line there."[44] Out of this paradox arises Tims Creek, in part a mythical recreation of Kenan's own hometown of Chinquapin, North Carolina, and in part a fundamental reimagining of it.

Let the Dead Bury Their Dead stands as a new kind of passing narrative that allows the new to pass as the old, the old to pass as the new, and the dead to pass back into the world of the living. When a dead woman talks in the body of a queer child, Kenan wakes the passing narrative from its Jim Crow coffin, rescuing it from a box bound for the rummage sale. The denizens of Tims Creek fancy themselves *very* aware of racial cartographies and *very* able to talk matter-of-factly about who is and isn't black. But when Clarence speaks with and for the dead, and when Ellsworth takes him up on the offer, the community must reassess its standard of who belongs and who doesn't. At such moments, the fantastic seeps into the everyday and the expected. Clarence's tale sets in motion an ensuing short story cycle in which the community gets another chance to include the dead, the absent, and the departed. Americanist scholar James Nagel demonstrates that the short story cycle form is particularly suited to such a project because "there is the effort to create a community of tellers and listeners who share a nucleus of concerns and values inherent in the tales."[45]

In Kenan's world, stale identitarian lines fall away while newness enters the world through the womb of a corpse. Atrophied belief systems that value the familiar, the known, and the always-done-that-way become flexible. If the residents of Tims Creek can acknowledge the fantastic in their midst—if they can see Clarence as a dead woman talking—they need not define a community against its outcasts, but rather by its ability to welcome those with whom one may not share blood kinship or even direct interaction. Or in Kenan's terms, if pigs can talk, Clarence can commune with the dead, and an immigrant angel can fall from the sky, surely there is room in Tims Creek for a gay white stranger such as Gabriel and, if the community succeeds in reimagining itself, a gay native son like his dead lover Edward.

8

Dead Women Healing

Ana Castillo's *So Far from God*

We have seen that when dead women return home in American literature, they allow—or sometimes force—a community to confront the presence of past injustices. But how, Chicana writer Ana Castillo asks, might such women advance the presence of justice, rather than merely mark its absence? For Castillo, the route toward a more just world turns out to be grief. Her 1993 novel *So Far from God* tells the story of Sofia and her four daughters attempting to live meaningful lives in Tome, New Mexico, a place of material poverty and political powerlessness "so far from God, so near the United States."[1] All four daughters die over the course of the narrative: La Loca passes away as an infant only to be resurrected at her funeral, Caridad is raped and horribly mutilated after leaving a bar alone, Esperanza is kidnapped and murdered while a Gulf War correspondent, and Fe dies of radiation exposure from dutifully performing her low-wage factory job. In Castillo's world, however, death is rarely a finite event, but rather a new state of being. Three of the daughters remain active members of the community: La Loca resurrects to become a recluse who cannot stand the stench of the living, Caridad miraculously heals and trains to become an indigenous healer herself, and Esperanza returns as an ectoplasmic, transparent daughter. Fe, on the other hand, just dies.

Who becomes a dead woman talking and who simply dies marks their degree of allegiance to the improbable world that Castillo imagines, one that harbors the capacity to value a "woman who lived alone with her four little girls by the ditch at the end of the road" (20). Thus, Castillo recasts what counts as a life in the first place. Feminist and human rights theorist Judith Butler frames this as a question of when life is grievable. "Without grievability," she argues in *Frames of War*, "there is no life, or, rather, there is something living that is other than life."[2] This continues her argument in *Precarious Life* that "specific lives cannot be apprehended as injured or lost if they are not first apprehended as living."[3] Castillo counters such conditions by imagining a world that allows posthumous healing and radicalizes collective grief. Sofia goes so far as to create a counterpublic that can recognize dead women as active citizens, first in her capacity as the unofficial La Mayor of Tome, then as founding president of an international organization called M.O.M.A.S, Mothers of Martyrs and Saints. In this counterpublic, anthrophobic resurrected babies, de-mutilated lesbian healers, and transparent returned daughters are not only possible but central. In fact, they're written into the bylaws.

Castillo's Telenovela Realism

Like so many of the dead women talking in American literature, when each of Castillo's dead women rejoins her community, she creates new possibilities while also prompting crises of belief. The first death and resurrection occurs in the opening passage when three-year-old Loca pops out of her casket, "as if she had woken from a nap" (23), then flies to the top of the church. As the disbelieving congregation looks on, the priest wonders if this is an act of God or Satan while asking his fold to pray for the girl. "'No Padre,' she corrected him. 'Remember, it is *I* who am here to pray for *you*.' With that stated, she went into the church and those with faith followed" (24). Loca joins such uncanny figures as the adult-talking toddler in Randall Kenan's *Let the Dead Bury Their Dead* and the baby-talking adult in Morrison's *Beloved*. Loca shifts settled matters of faith and power in her community by upsetting not only who is supposed to say what but also the natural order of life preceding death—not the other way around. Loca herself acknowledges such matters of sequence: "Only in hell do we learn to forgive and you got to die first" (42). In Castillo's world, a dead woman speaking from experience is prerequisite in a novel of healing, restoration, and perhaps Kushnerian forgiveness.

Caridad's return is equally miraculous. "She came home one night as mangled as a stray cat," the narrator recounts, "having been left for dead by the side of the road" (32–33). After months of recovery at home in her destroyed body, which the narrative describes as a corpse, she inexplicably glides through the room. "It wasn't the Caridad that had been brought back from the hospital," the narrator reports, "but a whole and once again beautiful Caridad, in what furthermore appeared to be Fe's wedding gown" (37). The image of Madeline Usher is unmistakable, but Caridad won't meet her demise as a wailing corpse in a pile of rubble. This is a narrative of healing. Esperanza repeats,

"Caridad was whole. There was nothing, nothing that anyone could see wrong with her, except for the fact that she was feverish" (38). In turn, the third dead sister, Esperanza, experiences an equally incredible ectoplasmic return after having been kidnapped and murdered in the war-torn deserts of Saudi Arabia.

Castillo holds fast to the stuff of everyday Chicano life while also brashly flaunting departures from the real. When each dead woman returns, she pushes the bounds of credulity—less on the part of the reader (it is fiction, after all), and more on the part of her home community. Some deny that the deaths occur in the first place or relegate the talking dead to the outskirts of civil society as figures of myth or madness. The community's response to Loca's resurrection, for instance, is neither credulity nor denial. "She seemed serene, and though a little flushed, quite like she always did when she was alive," the narrator reports. "Well, the fact was that she *was* alive, but no one at the moment seemed quite sure" (24, emphasis in original). Note the slippery "was"—does it designate the moment before or after the resurrection? The grammar is as elusive as the congregation's faith. The narrator playfully offers explanations based in reason, science, and Western medicine, such as when the hospital "diagnosed that she was in all probability an epileptic" (25). Fe, for one, believes—insists upon—such explanations, but we readers are not so certain. The narrator continues, "Epilepsy notwithstanding, there was much left unexplained and for this reason Sofi's baby grew up at home, away from strangers who might be witnesses to her astonishing behavior, and she eventually earned the name around the Rio Abajo region and beyond, of La Loca Santa" (25). Reason, science, and Western medicine may explain away the improbable, but they are unconvincing—and uninteresting.

To create this world in which dead women return, talk, and heal, Castillo bastes her story in what I propose to call *telenovela realism*. The term is deliberately playful as it picks up on Sandra Cisneros's cheerful blurb for Castillo's "Chicana telenovela." It also follows feminist theologian Gail Pérez, who calls it a Mexican *cuenta* and quips, "Sometimes I think that people haven't any sense of humor."[4] Still, my term is a serious attempt to capture Castillo's simultaneously urgent and fun politics, as well as her place in the American literary tradition of dead women talking. In telenovela realism, the unfurling of long, complicated, and at times improbable story lines is delightful—in no small part *because* of brassy departures from the likely or expected. Its credibility, which is to say its realism, depends on Castillo's ability to invent new scenarios and even new natural rules. When the melodramatic and impossible become the pedestrian, Castillo shifts the grounds on which we come to value life, or particular lives, in an outpost of the former Spanish empire and current U.S. imperial map.

It is important to distinguish Castillo's telenovela realism from magical realism, a popular but fraught way to describe much Latino literature after the "boom" of the 1960s and 1970s, including by such wildly popular writers as Gabriel García Márquez. Critics have long questioned the political efficacy of magical realism.[5] Latino literature scholar Frederick Luis Aldama worries that it has come to be marked as both "exotic" and expected so that it is "an easily swallowed pill." He contends, however, that Castillo "de-form[s] such conventions" into what he calls *bent frames*.[6] Similarly, ecofeminist critic Kamala Platt discusses the novel in terms of *virtual realism*, "a realism that virtually encompasses lived experience and propels it into postmodern fiction, avoiding the depoliticization common in 'magical realism.'"[7] So too, critic Marta Carminero-Santangelo points out that the novel's most direct political engagement appears in scenes distinctly lacking in magical realism, such as the environmentally conscious cooperative and Fe's death by exposure to toxic waste. She argues, "The 'driving force behind collective activism' is distinctly different, in terms of the possibilities for agency and empowerment, from the driving force of miracles."[8]

Need realism and magical realism be so opposed? Castillo's telenovela realism plays with the natural order, but it never loses sight of very real conditions of material poverty, racism, working-class exploitation, and foreign wars. So too, throughout the tradition of dead women talking in American literature, the heretofore unreal both disrupts *and seeks a place in* the real. Castillo herself politicizes such an opposition in the title of her nonfiction work *Massacre of the Dreamers*, published around the same time as *So Far from God*. Her telenovela realism is able to speak of injustices—be they magical, mundane, or both—as well as fuel an alternative order. Castillo's best critics get at how she enlists any cultural tradition available—Catholicism, magical realism, Chicano nationalism, even telenovelas and mass-produced Goya foods—in service of a social justice vision. For instance, Pérez considers why working-class Chicanas in particular may be ripe for exploitation in nonunion factories, while their very same roles in the home also hold the promise of reinventing the world through cultural memory, indigenous values, and revisionist Catholicism. "With great respect," she argues, "[Castillo] will reject the Catholicism of the mothers for the curanderismo of the grandmothers."[9] Still, Castillo does not simply swap the home for the shop floor in an uncritical Chicano nationalist stance.

Perhaps the most salient distinction to be made between telenovela and magical realism is how it embeds the possibility of disbelief *within the story itself*, as we see in Fe's Western medical explanation for her sister's resurrection. The narrator's delivery may be matter-of-fact, as in magical realism, but in our midst are disbelieving community members. The eldest sister, too, harbors initial skepticism because "spontaneous recoveries were beyond all rhyme and reason for anyone, even for a reporter like Esperanza," Castillo writes. "It was time to get away, Esperanza decided, far away" (39). Skepticism is a potential political stance, one often paired ironically against faith. For instance, Doña Felicia, the curandera who has been practicing at least since the 1848 U.S.-Mexico War, has little patience for a faith accepting of miracles but blind to injustice. "Felicia was a non-believer of sorts," the narrator explains, "and remained that way, suspicious of the religion that did not help the destitute all around her despite their devotion" (60). Francisco el Penitente, a santero in his own right, is equally suspicious of traditional Catholicism and its unearned credulity. Nonetheless, he avers, "Despite what anyone wanted to say or not about the elusive younger daughter, she could not be of this world, having returned from the dead before a hundred witnesses" (192).

Castillo's ambivalent relationship to Catholicism is widely acknowledged. She herself reports, "I don't think like a Catholic at all. So even though it was part of my upbringing, I haven't practiced it as an adult."[10] Castillo's playful, revisionist Catholicism nevertheless runs throughout the novel as the glue holding together her world. For instance, when Caridad and Doña Felicia visit a church, "They lined up to go through small rooms adjacent to the chapel where there is a pozito opened to the holy earth with which, since the early part of the nineteenth century, Catholics (really, it wasn't their fault that they came so late to this knowledge, being such newcomers to these lands) have healed both their bodies and spirits" (75). Castillo's insouciance is contagious and, in its own way, reverent. After all, any alternate world order that expects the Tome community to participate can't discard Catholicism or Xicana indigena practices like some outmoded television.

In the end, it is the reader who adopts a posture of credulity. We don't have to believe that these dead women could inhabit our real world. But we want to. While Castillo may offer several platforms for rejections of telenovela realism—journalistic verity, Catholic piety, leftist politics, or allegiance to the dominant order under the banner of "common sense"—we as readers come to embrace the improbable as both better and possible. In this world, a place like "Santa Fe" can be made over into "Fanta Se" (114). The word play is as silly as it is serious. When given the choice, who wouldn't want to live in Fanta Se?

Fe wouldn't. Fe remains the willful, dutiful citizen of the dominant order almost until her end. She denies the Pueblo blood in her flat butt and harbors little patience for the ways of her home community. In order to secure "the long-dreamed-of automatic dishwasher, microwave, Cuisinart, and the VCR" (171), Fe leaves her dead-end job at the local bank in favor of Acme International. The factory pays well but requires secret, unregulated, and unprotected toxic waste disposal. When Fe meets her inevitable end from cancer, she simply dies. The narrator recounts, "The rest of the story is hard to relate. Because after Fe died she did not resurrect as La Loca did at age three. She also did not return ectoplasmically like her tenacious earth-bound sister Esperanza. Very shortly after that first prognosis, Fe just died. And when someone dies that plain dead, it is hard to talk about" (186). Neither faith, nor magic, nor a feat of literary imagination can bring her back. Having rejected telenovela realism, there is no place left in this story for Fe. She meets her end on the grounds of the dominant order: a nameless, unofficial victim of the privatized military industrial complex. Many critics would like to characterize Fe as yet another martyred sister in the name of global capitalism.[11] Yet Fe is no martyr. She is instead one of Russ Castronovo's *necro citizens*, the perfectly obeisant subject demanded by the state. By the time Fe understands her place in the dominant order and begins to speak to injustice, it is too late.

Unlike Fe, most characters eventually embrace the improbable and find a comfortable place in a world of resurrected babies, psychic surgeons, and winged devils, which is, after all, not a far leap from the more pedestrian world of curanderas and their remedies of salt, eggs, black hen meat, and massage for all manner of ailments. Esperanza is perhaps the most significant case given that she initially rejects telenovela realism as an aspiring journalist. She spends much of the novel as a prisoner of war as readers, like the family, await word. It is Loca, not the government, who eventually reports that Esperanza "is died," a curious phrase she twice repeats (158, 162) despite Fe's exasperated correction of her grammar. After that, there are Esperanza sightings around Tome and family members eventually incorporate her into their daily lives as a full participant. La Loca often meets her by the river, and Sofia is occasionally comforted by Esperanza in bed at night. Don Domingo sees her "from the front window, although he didn't dare go out and call to his transparent daughter" (163). Caridad is less reticent and begins "having long discussions, even if mostly one-sided, with Esperanza about war, about the president's misguided policies, about how the public was being fooled about a lot of the things that were going on behind that whole war business" (163). Doña Felicia is happy to welcome Esperanza, though she complains to Caridad, "What a know-it-all that sister of yours was . . . and still is" (164). Even Fe, with some reluctance, invites all of her sisters to her wedding, including the dead ones. There, some see Esperanza's ectoplasmic body, while some cannot.

In Castillo's telenovela realism, death becomes a metaphor of women's oppression, such as when the plucky narrator muses, "There were transitional years where [Esperanza] felt like a woman with brains was as good as dead for all the happiness it brought her in the love department" (26). So too, the response to Caridad's rape and mutilation speaks to the dominant order's disregard for vulnerable women as the media and police lose interest in pursuing her case. "She was left in the hands of her family," Castillo writes, "a nightmare incarnated" (33). For a time, Sofia's house is filled with fatal embodiments of injustice, "a permanently traumatized daughter, another who was more ghost than of this world, and a third who was the most beautiful child she had given birth to and who had been cruelly mutilated" (34). The distinction between death and trauma is unclear, if relevant at all. More important is the question of how to create a home, and eventually a community, that welcomes them, be they traumatized or whole, faithful or disbelieving, alive or "is died."

Grieving That Which "Is Died"

How might we welcome someone like Esperanza who "is died"? First, we must be able to grieve for them. Such a prospect gets at what it would mean to build a world that values any resident of Tome, living or dead. Within the dominant order of the United States, the lives of such women are simply not valuable. Butler contends, "We might think of war as dividing populations into those who are grievable and those who are not. An ungrievable life is one that cannot be mourned because it has never lived, that is, it has never counted as a life at all."[12] Castillo's novel is framed by war, both an official war in the Middle East and more domestic forms of war: colonial land grabs, cultures of sexual terrorism, economic systems that see workers as expendable, and the material poverty that renders them vulnerable in the first place. The death of someone like Fe is viewed more as collateral damage than a moment of human loss. In a way, according to Acme International and the U.S. government, Fe was never living. Political theorist Achille Mbembé also looks at national power and war in terms of its capacity to expose bodies to death. "War, after all," he explains," is as much a means of achieving sovereignty as a way of exercising the right to kill."[13] Fe is the logical embodiment of Mbembé's "necropolitics," in which the "ultimate expression of sovereignty resides, to a large degree, in the power and the capacity to dictate who may live and who must die." A political subject, then, must always imagine herself in relation to death and the state's power to confer it upon her.

Fe pledges allegiance to the dominant order in the way she adheres tenaciously, painstakingly, maddeningly to the tenets of mainstream U.S. culture and late capitalism. Her goal is to "have a life like people do on T.V." (189). Fe's television dream has no room for the home cultures of Tome. We see Fe's allegiance in her utter devotion to her boring bank teller job, and then her single-minded quest to become the model employee at Acme. "Fe was intent on moving up quick at Acme International," we learn, "therefore from the start she took on every gritty job available, just to prove to the company what a good worker she was" (178). As Fe moves up in pay, she moves downward through layers of secrecy until finally she is alone, unprotected, inside a bin deep underground "cleaning" glow-in-the-dark parts. Her symptoms increase in severity, from headaches and nausea to fatigue, miscarriage, a deadly permeating scent, and eventually incurable cancer. Similar ailments plague her coworkers, but the money is too good. So they listen credulously to the factory nurse who tells them about women's problems and postmenopausal changes, despite hysterectomies before thirty.

From the outset, Fe's allegiance to the dominant order is clear in her pathological adherence to the heterosexual marriage plot. When her fiancé pens a Dear Jane letter, Fe screams incessantly for months in a catatonic state. Her narrative ceases at the point it goes off the rails of a conventional romance novel; so too, her voice. "Fe had severely damaged her vocal cords during the days when she had so violently and ceaselessly screamed," the narrator reports; "as a result, when she spoke now her voice was scratchy-sounding, similar to a faulty World War II radio transmitter, over which half of what she was trying to say did not get through, something like talking to Amelia Earhart just before contact was broken off altogether and she went down" (85). Rather than finding a place for herself in telenovela realism, she recedes from the world altogether, as inaccessible as Amelia Earhart. Her broken voice renders her particularly exploitable. "What she was finally told," at the bank, "was that although the company did not want to discriminate against her new 'handicap,' her irregular speech, really did not lend itself to working with the public." She responds, "What do ____ mean, handi____?" (177). Fe does not understand herself as others see her; her story—not just her voice—is unintelligible in the dominant order. In the end, Fe is forbidden to use what is left of her voice when the federal government bars her from talking about her work at Acme. Her plight is, quite literally, not subject to grievance.

As Fe seeks recognition within a dominant order that cannot hear her, she is on the losing end of what Butler contends any political system does: "maximize precariousness for some and minimize precariousness for others."[14] Precariousness is a basic human condition, she explains, because bodies are inherently, intractably perishable despite money, wealth, or power. "Yet," Butler argues, "precisely because each body finds itself potentially threatened by others who are, by definition, precarious as well, forms of domination follow . . . the shared condition of precariousness leads not to reciprocal recognition, but to a specific exploitation of targeted populations."[15] The level of Fe's precariousness reflects the value accorded her body and her life. It also indexes the injustices afflicted upon Tome and the very earth around it. The narrator reports, "Most of the people that surrounded Fe didn't understand what was slowly killing them, too, or didn't want to think about it, or if they did, didn't know what to do about it anyway and went on like that, despite dead cows in the pasture, or sick sheep, and that one week late in winter when people woke up each morning to find it raining starlings" (172).

Without telenovela realism, such stories go unexplained, perhaps untold. Borderlands scholar Carmela Delia Lanza suggests that the daughters find voice in home spaces whereas the dominant culture cannot or will not listen.[16] Voice connotes not only what it means to have standing in the political realm, but also what is narratable in the literary realm. I would note that silence is not confined to the dominant culture. Caridad's violent rape, for example, also results in silence, which works hand in hand with the police department's decision not to pursue the assailants (they don't know it was actually a winged devil). "Caridad had never talked about that night to anyone," the narrator reports, "but there were two people besides herself who know what had happened because she had let them know through dreams and that was La Loca and doña Felicia" (77). Even within a home space, Caridad's voice fails, requiring the possibilities of telenovela realism to tell her story.

Not only do the voices of the sisters diminish and disappear from the dominant order over the course of the narrative, but so do their bodies, the sites of their precarity. Fe's body, like that of Addie Bundren, deteriorates before our eyes as she wastes away and undergoes painful procedures to remove cancerous lesions, a process she describes as torture. La Loca also slowly wastes from what we learn is AIDS, a curious outcome for someone who avoided nearly all human contact since the age of three. Eventually their bodies disappear altogether. For example, Fe's "cremation was approved of by the Church (and paid for by Acme International) because at the time of her death there was so little left of Fe to be buried anyway" (186). Fe's funeral is another form of waste disposal, leaving no evidence as Acme makes over its factory for a new set of nameless, ungrievable workers. So too, "Sofia buried La Loca, or what was left of the body (it would be no exaggeration to say in this case 'the remains')" (246). Esperanza's body also cannot be located because "without no one important enough on their side to help them do it, Esperanza's missing body remained a mystery" (160). Eventually, "the Army said that although they knew she was dead they never produced a body for [Sofia] to bury" (243).

Caridad joins these missing bodies in her fate as a mythical woman. When she jumps off a mesa with her paramour Esmerelda, the tourists "take a peek at the results down below just out of curiosity. But much to all their surprise, there were no morbid remains of splintered bodies tossed to the ground, down, down, like bad pottery or glass or old bread. There weren't even whole bodies lying peaceful. There was nothing" (211). They become pure myth "deep within the soft, moist dark earth where Esmerelda and Caridad would be safe and live forever" (211). Critics compare this scene to the controversial ending of *Thelma and Louise*, the 1991 Hollywood film in which the two heroines have no place in a male-dominated world and so elect to drive off a cliff. The film ends with the car in midair so that the audience is spared the gruesome outcome below. So too, we are left with the image of Caridad and Esmerelda in their free fall of freedom. Meanwhile, the "soft, moist dark earth" elicits grave imagery (sans corpses) as well as life-giving and female-centered womb imagery. As a woman of myth, Caridad will live on in Tome, if not the dominant cultural order.

Castillo's ultimate task is to create a world in which the humanity of these women is recognized before, during, and after they lived. Grieving is not a process of recognition, Butler clarifies, because recognition of life is a precondition. This requires the future anterior, she argues, the recognition at that outset of a life that it *will have been* lived. "But there can be no celebration," Butler explains, "without an implicit understanding that the life is grievable, that it would be grieved if it were lost, and that this future anterior is installed as the condition of its life." She continues, "Grievability precedes and makes possible the apprehension of the living being as living, exposed to non-life from the start" (15). Butler is primarily concerned with grievability at birth, or the moment we recognize the commencement of life, which we see contested in pro-life/pro-choice discourse. Castillo goes one step further by extending such recognition posthumously. This results in a new and corollary dimension of political recognition in the register of the present anterior: recognition that one *is died*. To recognize and welcome Esperanza as "is died" is to secure for her a place not just in the present political community but also in the ever-present political community, the one in which she will *always* be "is died." The grammar of justice ends up being the same as the grammar of history: the presence of the past.

Lest we lose ourselves in the fog of theory and high-minded verb conjugations, I should note that Castillo herself considers the grammar of healing along the same lines as Butler. In addition to Esperanza's perpetual "is died" status, for instance, La Loca reports meeting a nun at her "final death" in similar terms. "But she didn't smell like nothing," Castillo writes, "so Loca was not sure if she was a present nun or a past nun or maybe hasta una future subjunctive nun" (244). The linguistic play aside, this is quite serious: Castillo's telenovela world bears the responsibility of not losing these daughters to the silent ether of the dominant order, not unlike the disappeared bodies of Argentina's "Dirty War" or the young women who perennially go missing around the maquiladoras of Juarez, Mexico. If a woman like Esperanza can be welcomed in Tome as "is died," how, Castillo asks, does one harness this instance of life-giving grief into collective action?

La Mayor Sofia's Counterpublic

The first answer lies in Castillo's narratives of healing; the final answer lies in the institutionalization of radical collective grief. As the daughters wither and perish in the dominant order, they maintain a place in Tome via healing, including of the posthumous variety. In fact, both Caridad and La Loca themselves become healers after their initial deaths. The narrator informs us, "Caridad was incapable of hating anyone or anything, which is why doña Felicia had elected her heiress to her healing legacy" (77). In this legacy, healing and death are integral, not opposed. La Loca also comfortably mixes matters of life and death when, for instance, she occasionally "cures" her sisters via abortions. La Loca's role as a healer is curious given her repulsion to the stench of the living, which inverts the imagery of corpse and living bodies. "Only her mother and the animals were ever unconditionally allowed to touch her," we learn. "But without exception, healing her sisters from the traumas and injustices they were dealt by society—a society she herself never experiences firsthand—was never questioned" (27). Healing becomes not just a response to injustice; it fuels an alternative, more just world.

The opposite of healing becomes the novel's way of imagining injustice. Regarding Fe's cancer, the narrator reports, "Fe did not understand none of it. Especially what she did not understand was how the Attorney General's Office could be so concerned about who was to blame for the illegal use of a chemical but it was not the least bit concerned about her who was dying in front of their eyes because of having been in contact with it" (187). If Fe represents an ungrievable life as far as Acme is concerned, then there is nothing to heal. Castillo writes, "But Fe, who had stroked Caridad's brow so tenderly on that night of restoration when she had returned to the living after her encounter with the malogra, was really dead. And you couldn't bring back something that was so dead no matter how much you sat on your ankles before your candles and incense and prayed for a word, a sign, no matter what you did" (205). Having renounced telenovela realism, Fe is also beyond the limits of its possibilities of healing. La Loca's disease also resists the best efforts of psychic surgeons and curanderas, or "doctors invisibles" (235), suggesting that AIDS is a source of earth-bound injustice, akin more to Acme and its place in late capitalist economies than to an itinerant *malogra*.

The prospect of healing versus simply dying is perhaps Castillo's most sustained break from the dominant cultural order. Aldama argues, "The fact that Western medicine could not heal her allows Caridad the opportunity to self-heal and then re-create herself." Further, "Caridad's crossing over into a same-sex borderland space begins after her rape and disfigurement."[17] La Loca finds herself in a similar oppositional space. Castillo writes, "She had grown up in a world of women who went out into the bigger world and came back disappointed, disillusioned, devastated, and eventually not at all. She did not regret not being a part of that society, never having found any use for it. At home she had everything she needed" (152). This leads ethnic literatures scholar Theresa Delgadillo to argue that "a Chicana feminism fueled by a woman-centered spirituality emerges to challenge the subjugation of women within and without Chicana/o cultures, the marginalization of other sectors of U.S. society, and the destruction of the environment."[18] Men's stories play a role in this female-centered world, but they are ancillary—and often outright disruptive. For example, Francisco el Penitente's backstory is described as an "interlude" (94), whereas a chapter describing a road trip by two female lovers is playfully called "What Appears to Be a Deviation of Our Story, but Wherein, with Some Patience, the Reader Will Discover That There Is Always More Than the Eye Can See to Any Account" (120).

While Castillo may initially set Sofia's female-centered home in opposition to the dominant order, the two worlds necessarily commingle. The seemingly mundane or the purely spiritual becomes the stuff of potential radical politics. We see this in a final scene with La Loca, the ultimate recluse. Within a world of resurrected babies, flying lesbian healers, and psychic surgery, La Loca becomes politicized from a curiously mundane source: watching television. She learns of a factory's unfair working practices and heeds the call to rip off the tag of her jeans produced by the factory. "Sofia stared at her daughter in amazement," the narrator reports, "although that might sound hard to believe after everything Sofia had experienced with her youngest" (222). La Loca's sole interaction with the larger world is through television, filled with telenovelas, daytime talk shows featuring devil worship in Los Angeles, and corporate-sponsored cooking shows. Such television solidified Don Domingo's apathy and filled Fe with fatal dreams of middle-class assimilation. But for La Loca, it prompts a political conscious.

Telenovela realism and the future anterior by themselves are insufficient to sustain a viable community. Sofia resolves to institutionalize them. She becomes the first mayor of Tome, even if unofficially so. As La Mayor, Sofia initiates a utopian community of "economic self-sufficiency" via cooperatives, pesticide-free agriculture, and equally organic livestock, even including the Anglo neighbor who auspiciously raises peacocks—useless yet fascinating creatures. Castillo creates a new frame in which to recognize the humanity in lives heretofore deemed ungrievable. Butler avers that "a life has to be intelligible *as a life*, has to conform to certain conceptions of what life is, in order to become recognizable" (7). For Castillo, the dominant order simply lacks the capacity to deem Sofia and her family as anything but marginal and invisible at best, exploitable and expendable at worst. "I have a very conscious commitment to Latino people, here in this country," Castillo reflects in an interview with Hector Torres. "I feel very motivated by the fact that, as a Chicana, we are torn into a rather countryless state of existence—not to have a point of reference—which works on your head philosophically, spiritually" (182). In response to a "countryless state of existence," Castillo imagines a world of telenovela realism in which to recognize—celebrate!—such lives, both pre- and post-death. Otherwise, Caridad, Esperanza, and La Loca would simply be dead. As dead women talking, they are as active and interesting as their pre-death selves in the counterpublic of Tome. Perhaps more so.

I am being neither hasty nor glib when I say Sofia creates a counterpublic. First, we must address what it means to speak of a public. "Publics are queer creatures," social theorist Michael Warner explains; "You cannot point to them, count them, or look them in the eye. You also cannot easily avoid them. They have become an almost natural feature of the social landscape, like pavement." Yet despite their immaterial nature, "much of the texture of modern social life lies in the invisible presence of these publics that flit around us like large, corporate ghosts."[19] These phantom publics shape our relations to one another—kin, stranger, citizen—as well as how we interact. A counterpublic, in turn, consciously adopts *new* relations and *new* modes of interactions. To some extent, this is true of any public because, as Warner explains, "when people address publics, they engage in struggles—at varying levels of salience and consciousness, from calculated tactic to mute cognitive noise—over the conditions that bring them together as a public."[20] Therefore, any public, as opposed to *the* public, is an ad hoc creature, a contingent entity that crystallizes as it circulates and continually takes on new shapes. A counterpublic must do something more. "Their members," Warner explains, "are understood to be not merely a subset of the public but constituted through a conflictual relation to the dominant public. . . . A counterpublic maintains at some level, conscious or not, an awareness of its subordinate status."[21]

The distinction between public and counterpublic is important because we witness the transition of Tome from one public among many to a fully fledged counterpublic. Castillo's critics focus on the importance of valuing the Chicana ways of being that we find in Sofia's home from page one. However, the problem is that this home space exists more or less comfortably among all the other publics of the novel, including the late capitalist system in which Acme operates and in which Esperanza travels to Saudi Arabia to cover the latest American war. How to make a public into a functioning counterpublic? Butler's discussion of precariousness illuminates a way. When we recognize our shared precariousness, we are able to see humanity even within those frames that might deem certain bodies ungrievable. "The precarity of life," Butler explains, "imposes an obligation upon us. We have to ask about the conditions under which it becomes possible to apprehend a life or set of lives as precarious" (2). When Sofia runs for unofficial mayor of Tome, the residents begin to inquire into the conditions that render them vulnerable, exploitable, and ultimately ungrievable. "The truth was that most people had not been able to live off their land for the better part of the last fifty years," the narrator reports. "Outsiders in the past had overused the land so that in some cases it was no good for raising crops or grazing livestock no more" (159). As Tome comes to think of itself as a counterpublic and institutionalizes itself into a quasi-municipality, the systems of exploitation become visible, narratable.

Where the power of healing stops in this counterpublic, the importance of grieving begins. La Loca may end in a failed healing, but the novel does not end there. It ends instead in the institutionalization of radical grieving, which has the power to maintain the "is died" status of Sofia's daughters, as well as those daughters and sons of other mothers who disappeared without a second thought or glance from the dominant culture. First, there is a grassroots Holy Friday procession of direct political engagement. "No brother was elected to carry a life-size cross on his naked back," Castillo writes. "There was no 'Mary' to meet her son. Instead, some, like Sofi, who held a picture of la Fe as a bride, carried photographs of their loved ones who died due to toxic exposure hung around the necks like scapulars, and at each station along their route, the crowd stopped and prayed and people spoke on so many things that were killing their land and turning the people of those lands into an endangered species" (241–42). The procession engenders discussions of AIDS, pesticides, nuclear power, the Gulf War, and other world events, reminiscent of the private conversations between Caridad and her "is died" sister.

As an ad hoc demonstration, the march is ephemeral. Nevertheless, the procession sparks the birth of a sustainable counterpublic built around radical collective grief. "In the years to come," the narrator recounts, "la pobre Sofia—encouraged not only by vecinos and comadres, but by the hundreds of petitions she received in the mail every day, asking for prayers from the mother of the little crazy saint who died twice and her similarly ethereal sisters—became the founder and la first presidenta of what would later be known worldwide as the very prestigious (if not a little elitist) organization M.O.M.A.S., Mothers of Martyrs and Saints" (246–47). M.O.M.A.S. is explicitly woman-centered but eventually opens to mothers of male saints. It is presided over by female priests, even married ones. The organization allows for, even thrives on, the participation of the dead so that La Loca, for instance, "made very occasional ectoplasmic appearances at the national and international conventions" (249).

M.O.M.A.S. is a very different kind of public. It turns out to be a fantastic inverse of Mbembé's *death-worlds*, which are "new and unique forms of social existence in which vast populations are subjected to conditions of life conferring upon them the status of *living dead*."[22] In Castillo's counterpublic, dead women talking are not ghosts, but citizens. "Is died" daughters—and eventually sons—"came to converse with their moms, as well as with each other. They brought all kinds of news and advice that was, as part of the bylaws, generously passed on to relatives, friends, the petitioning faithful, and community agencies, as well as to relevant local or federal governments" (251). The "is died" citizens of M.O.M.A.S. are fundamentally different from the ghosts populating so much multiethnic literature. Literary critic Kathleen Brogan argues, "Possession in haunted American fiction marks a continuity with the past over which one has little control: history lodges within, swollen bodies (a recurring image in this literature) give birth not to the future but to a nightmarish repetition of the past."[23] The "is died" children of M.O.M.A.S., however, need not chain Sofia and her fellow grieving mothers to a past over which they have little control, nor to a dominant order that would seek to ignore, cremate, or disappear their children. Instead, Castillo's "is died" citizens facilitate very real political activity, such as drafting petitions and calling elected representatives. Such actions may be mundane, but they harbor the capacity to alter the course of the present, as well as the future.

All this leaves open the question of whether or not Castillo's counterpublic is real. In a way, the answer is yes. Castillo bases M.O.M.A.S. on very real—not to mention effective—organizations founded on grief. Critics note that M.O.M.A.S. invokes important groups such as the Mothers of the Plaza de Mayo, formed in response to the disappeared of Argentina's "Dirty War," as well as more local and contemporaneous groups, such as the Mothers of East L.A. and the Southwest Organizing Committee in Albuquerque.[24] The resonance with actual grassroots organizations allays, at least in part, those critics who worry about the viability of Castillo's fantastic sensibilities. Carminero-Santangelo, for instance, suggests that the Holy Friday scene remains primarily religious and not invested in direct action or "realist" politics.[25] Warner also cautions, "Analysis can never begin simply with the text as its object, as literary criticism is wont to do."[26] That said, my work is nonetheless primarily and unabashedly literary, as is, I think, Castillo's telenovela realism and the counterpublics it helps us imagine.

Castillo opts for the register of the improbable and present anterior over lamenting what was. In an interview, she reveals that the original ending of the novel portrayed Sofia in a posture of conventional grief. "At the very ending of that story," Castillo recounts, "Sofia is on the grave crying for her three martyred daughters. So that's how I originally ended my story. But my agent who was reading the manuscript commented that 'Well, this is very depressing. You know, you promised Norton a happy ending.' So I thought, 'what would [Sofia] do to change that, particularly as a religious figure. What would she do?' She takes over. She doesn't submit to that point in history when patriarchy took over her authority."[27] The M.O.M.A.S. ending transforms conventional grief into the radical collective grief necessary to change the conditions in which lives are deemed grievable in the first place. This counterpublic is organized around recognition of shared precarity, which Butler suggests offers a more viable model of human rights than multiculturalism or pluralism.[28] As La Mayor of Tome, then founding president of M.O.M.A.S., Sofia seeks to redistribute precariousness via cooperatives, organized protest, and enfranchising the unjustly dead.

Not that M.O.M.A.S. is perfect. The conventions become rife with charlatans, as well as vendors of T-shirts, pens, novelty tarot decks, and so on, similar "to what a tourist could find on a given day at Disney World" (249). But all this means that the conventions are incorporated into everyday life. M.O.M.A.S. becomes a rapidly expanding counterpublic in which dead daughters—and sons—not only talk but advise, protest, testify, and even gossip. In other words, they are typical citizens, as flawed and persnickety as the rest of us.

9

Dead Woman Coming of Age

Alice Sebold's *The Lovely Bones*

It is a dubious proposition to presume the wishes of the dead. When we take our cues from the dead themselves, their visions of justice may surprise us. For Addie Bundren, for instance, justice is being buried away from the husband and children that violated her aloneness. With Addie's lesson in mind, we can approach Alice Sebold's popular 2002 novel *The Lovely Bones*. The novel's distinguishing feature is that its narrator is dead. Susie Salmon is a suburban fourteen-year-old who was raped and brutally murdered while walking home from school before the story begins. Susie narrates from an "Inbetween" place, a weigh station for heaven from which she watches her living family, unable to directly help them identify her killer (the weird neighbor, Mr. Harvey), locate her remains, or salve their grief. The result is a reverse crime drama that transforms the hard-boiled whodunit formula into Susie's quest to point the living to the details of her opening-chapter murder. As such, we are primed to understand justice as the crime story would: nabbing, or perhaps killing, the bad guy.

But a funny thing happens on that route toward justice. In the climactic scene, Sebold jumps the rails of convention and leaves the tract-home setting, first to a crumbling gothic house, an anachronism amid late twentieth-century urban sprawl, then to a sinkhole at the edge of encroaching residential development where Mr. Harvey discarded the safe containing her bones. The sinkhole becomes not only the site of Susie's removal from the present, and therefore the future, but also an inaccessible pre-suburban past. At the edge of the sinkhole and late in the novel, Susie inhabits the body of Ruth, a willing former classmate obsessed with the world of the dead. Susie is no longer a mere posthumous narrator—by now something of a gimmick—but rather a fully fledged dead woman talking, one with a body and agency among the living. She does not search for the nearest phone, however, to culminate her quest for criminal justice; she reaches instead for the dreamboat nearby. And she has sex with him. Susie decides she is in neither a crime drama nor a protest novel, but rather a teenage coming-of-age novel. If the killer cut short her entrance into womanhood and her middle-school crush, Susie resolves to retake the reins of her narrative. This would be *Sweet Valley High* or some other saccharin teen drama if not for the inconvenient fact that she is dead. Though Susie never reveals the location of her body, the narrative achieves its sense of closure so that Susie is able to fully enter a heaven unhooked from worldly concerns.

The Lovely Bones has a genre problem: can a dead girl be the protagonist of a coming-of-age novel? If so, it is surprisingly typical in that it ends in consummated romance. (Dear reader, I slept with him.) Thus, Sebold reshuffles genres that have driven much feminist literary criticism: the bildungsroman and questions about its capacity to narrate women's lives, as well as the domestic novel whose sentimental leanings literary critic Leonard Cassuto suggests are deeply entwined with the American crime novel. The result is a suburban coming-of-age story that requires a ghost story to facilitate it within a murder plot. Within the tradition of dead women talking, Sebold may unwittingly pose one of the most difficult challenges, especially for skeptics of this wildly popular novel: to accept social justice on Susie's terms. Susie is not interested in justice within a legal framework, political calls for systemic change in response to cultures of sexual vulnerability and predation, or a critique of suburban fictions of safety and the economic inequality and razing of history that sustain them. Rather, in Susie's posthumous words, "I wanted to be allowed to grow up."[1]

The Problem of the Dead Narrator

Scholars tend to focus on the dead narrator conceit in *The Lovely Bones*, especially from a how-to angle of narrative technique, which one critic calls "unnatural" and impossible"[2] and another deems "non-natural" and "preposterous."[3] While the posthumous narrator may raise questions of credibility in a novel otherwise committed to a realist mode, it is not an unfamiliar entity. Susie is close in kind to the melodramatic narrator of *Desperate Housewives*, conventional ghosts, and the speaking cadavers in nineteenth-century lyric poetry. The technique is especially old hat in the ghost story tradition, which often features newly dead narrators speaking beyond or outside their recently deceased bodies. A good example is Elizabeth Stuart Phelps's 1873 local color tale "Since I Died," in which the ghost story structure allows a sort of posthumous culmination of a lesbian romance.[4] The result is more a narrative of mourning, conveniently sans body and therefore sex.

For the most part, Sebold's dead narrator updates the classic ghost story for a postmodern age of self-conscious narrators and ecumenical spiritualism. Susie exhibits traits common to occult fictions, such as indirectly affecting material objects in a familiar poltergeist motif. When her father destroys his collection of ships in a bottle in a fit of grief, Susie, "without knowing how, revealed herself" (46) in the glass shards, after which she is also able to perform such small tasks as blowing out a candle. This inevitably recalls Patrick Swayze's character in the 1990 blockbuster film *Ghost* when he learns to move small objects in an abandoned subway station. Susie's presence as a "watcher" also takes on classic tropes of haunting, though of a benevolent variety as her younger brother Buckley matter-of-factly reports seeing her. Her desire to be among the living also manifests in classic tropes of possession, even if unwitting and more sinister. When Lindsey, Susie's younger sister, breaks into Mr. Harvey's in search of evidence, Susie "was pushing so hard on the Inbetween to get to Lindsey that I suddenly felt I might hurt her when I meant to help. . . . She knew that our father had walked into the cornfield possessed by something that was creeping into her now" (180). This trope of a dangerously benevolent presence eventually results in Jack Salmon's heart attack, caused by Susie wanting her father for herself.

The ghost story serves as a vehicle of grief and mourning. In the hospital after his heart attack, Jack reports seeing Susie in his hospital room. "I see her everywhere," her mother Abigail also confides. "Even in California she was everywhere. Boarding buses or on the streets outside schools when I drove by. I'd see her hair but it didn't match the face or I'd see her body or the way she moved" (281). Here the stories of Susie's posthumous travels and those of parental grief mingle. The ghost story becomes first and foremost about the living, not the dead. This includes Susie. She may narrate from heaven, or at least the Inbetween, but her story remains fundamentally centered on Earth. In Sebold's pleasant cosmology for a seemingly post-theological age, heaven consists of overlapping personal visions created by the dead themselves out of their individual experiences and desires while living. For Susie, this looks initially like high school without classes, save for art or band. "Eventually I began to desire more," she reports. "What I found strange was how much I desired to know what I had not known on Earth" (19). Susie's ultimate wish is to come of age among the living, her premature death notwithstanding.

Susie wants to be in a coming-of-age story, preferring a bildungsroman to a serial killer novel. The bildungsroman and its cousins, the novel of development, formation, or apprenticeship, are quintessential Enlightenment genres chronicling a young subject's march toward a coherent self in the world. Feminist literary critics have long contended that that model does not hold for many female literary traditions. In fact, Elizabeth Abel, Marianne Hirsch, and Elizabeth Langland long ago found that female novels of development tend to portray the attainment of conventional womanhood—marriage, children, and so on—as an interruption of, even threat to, autonomous selfhood.[5] That is, the romance diverts or quashes the quest narrative. On the other hand, in *Unbecoming Women*, critic Susan Fraiman considers the use of the bildungsroman by such celebrated nineteenth-century women writers as Jane Austen, Charlotte Brontë, and George Eliot alongside conduct books. She finds that the female novel of development is less "a young lady's entrance into the world," as in the subtitle of a novel by Frances Burney, and "might be more accurately described as a young lady's floundering on the world's doorstep." As a result, she "imagine[s] the way to womanhood not as a single path to a clear destination but as the endless negotiation of crossroads" in a given culture.[6]

In contemporary America, stories about women coming of age are no longer devalued, dismissed, or relegated to the shadow of a male tradition. They are celebrated, even expected, in a post–women's movement era that has developed an appetite for first-person testimonial, from literary shelves to Oprah's couch. In this environment thrive stories of women who, in the words of feminist literary critic Christy Rishoi, "resist negative constructions of womanhood and actively create oppositional identity for themselves."[7] Such narratives, she explains, draw from not only the novel of development but also autobiography and the slave narrative. "The subjects of coming-of-age narratives, like those of the earlier genres, construct themselves as outsiders," Rishoi argues, "but unlike them, they choose to remain marginalized at the end of their texts."[8] Susie is an outlier here because she wants desperately to be at the center not only of her narrative but of social conventions.

The ghost story is able to deliver Susie's coming-of-age wish by proxy, if not through direct experience. Susie's younger sister provides a step-by-step vicarious emergence into womanhood through her evolving relationship with a first boyfriend. "She kissed him; it was glorious," Susie reports. "I was almost alive again" (71). Then, during Lindsey's first sexual encounter a couple years later, Susie opines, "At fourteen, my sister sailed away from me into a place I'd never been. In the walls of my sex there was horror and blood, in the walls of hers there were windows" (125). Susie's vicarious coming-of-age narrative culminates in a marriage proposal in core ghost story terrain: an abandoned Gothic Revival house during a crushing rain storm. Susie is elated and claims her sister's story as her own: "My sister! My Samuel! My dream!" (241). In this proprietary shout, the echo of Beloved's chilling refrain—"I am Beloved and she is mine"—is unmistakable, if not intended.

Susie's mother Abigail, on the other hand, underscores her dead daughter's inability to directly experience her own coming-of-age narrative. In describing a tryst with the detective in charge of the murder case, Susie realizes, "My mother had my body as it would never become" (197). Then, when Abigail returns to her husband's side after his heart attack, "I realized how much I wished I could be where my mother was. His love for my mother wasn't about looking back and loving something that would never change" (280). As Susie becomes aware of her never-aging status, her vicarious role as a mere watcher in a ghost story becomes increasingly insufficient. She reports in frustration, "All I could do was talk, but no one on Earth could hear me" (32). Later, Susie reveals that all denizens of the Inbetween carry on such one-sided conversations with the living. Eventually, Susie's quest is to come of age neither vicariously nor as an apparition.

The same problem drives the crime story. In the words of Jack, "But there is no body" (28). Instead, Susie's detached elbow stands as synecdoche for the whole body. Its symbolic value is more important than its contribution to the crime plot, especially since the very idea of a detached elbow jeopardizes the realism that is the crime story's main currency. Think about it: how (not to mention why) would Mr. Harvey use his knife to cut through Susie's ulna, radius, and humorous bones rather than severing the elbow joint itself, thereby rendering the two pieces no longer an elbow but parts of an arm? In any case, other objects also turn up to stand in for Susie's missing body, such as a school book and her homemade hat with jingly bells. Literary critic Ann Bliss argues that the school photograph also "functions as a metaphorical corpse in the absence of an actual corpse."[9] It stands in for the body at her public memorial, complete with extra ruddy cheeks that uncannily take on the exaggerated looks of preserved corpses at funerals. Furthermore, the novel's title itself refers to another proxy body: the family ties that knit around Susie's absence. Literary critic Laura E. Tanner suggests that this metaphor reflects a tendency in contemporary American literature and culture not only to blur the boundary between death and life but also to embody loss, to mark the presence of absence. The lovely bones of the title, she points out, form a metaphorical body of community only possible by Susie's death.[10]

Much of the plot of *The Lovely Bones* follows crime story conventions, including the slow accrual of evidence—severed elbow, knitted hat, handwritten journal, and eventually a telltale Pennsylvania keystone charm. Sebold goes so far as to signal the crime story genre in a self-aware ironic twist. Lindsey's honors camp special project is "CAN YOU GET AWAY WITH CRIME? HOW TO COMMIT THE PERFECT MURDER" (121). (Answer: stab your victim with an icicle, which will melt.) Sebold also trucks in the genre's cliché portraits of serial killers, complete with a long list of victims and a backstory of paternal abuse and maternal abandonment. Susie reports Mr. Harvey's childhood trauma of his mother barely escaping a rape attempt: "He had had a moment of clarity about how life should be lived: not as a child or as a woman. They were the two worst things to be" (190).

The dead narrator conceit works well within the crime story. As Cassuto argues in *Hard-Boiled Sentimentality*, Sebold "borrows the character of the serial killer from the crime genre and transplants him into a fantastic tale told from beyond the grave by his final victim."[11] Further, according to Cassuto, the American crime novel bears deep roots with the nineteenth-century sentimental novel and its fictions of domesticity. "The imaginary serial killer," he argues, "therefore stands for prominent and widely held fears of the disintegration of family ties in the United States after the fifties gave way to times of more open social conflict." Ultimately, American crime stories "are essentially family stories, but they are stories that communicate an extreme discomfort with an outdated family ideal in a postindustrial urban society."[12] Sebold goes one step further by setting her 2002 novel in 1973 so that that the nostalgic thrust is double-layered.

The absence of Susie's body becomes the crux of the ghost story, the coming-of-age narrative, and the crime novel. This poses a problem for the literary tradition of dead women talking because their bodies are often what distinguish them from such stock figures as ghosts. Moreover, their bodies form the basis of their bids for posthumous citizenship because, as I discuss in the cases of Beloved and Addie Bundren, Western legal understandings of personhood are inextricably linked with the body. To return to intellectual historian Ed Cohen's reminder, "It seems a simple enough formula: *to be* a person means *to have* a body."[13] He frames this in terms of "self-possession" or "self-ownership" by drawing on legal concepts of property and self-defense. From this angle, Sebold's dead narrator is the ultimate inadequate citizen: a person without body, having failed to protect it.

Borrowed Bodies and the Problem of Consent

The ghost story offers another kind of self-possession, one that can deliver on Susie's coming-of-age desires. She divulges, "I wanted so badly to kiss Ray Singh again" (286). For that, she needs a body. In the climactic penultimate chapter before a coda about heaven, Susie takes possession of Ruth's body. Susie feels a "pitiful desire. To be alive again on this Earth. Not to watch from above but to be—the sweetest thing—beside" (301). "I came to realize," Susie reports, "that the marvelous weight weighing me down was the weight of the human body" (301). Ray is in on the body swap. "You're not Ruth" (307), he says while in the shower with her body. Curiously, his first reaction is neither amazement nor fear. Rather, he is horny. To be fair, this is not a wholly alien concept for them. In adolescence, Ray and Ruth practiced kissing while each pretended she was Susie. Still, the sex scene is a disruption or even a departure from the three genres Sebold had set in motion. It is no surprise, then, that when critics explain the posthumous narration, they tend to describe Susie as narrating from the grave, beyond the grave, or as a corpse,[14] which accounts for all but the chapter in which Susie acquires a body not her own.

When she possesses Ruth, Susie fully enters the fold of dead women talking in American literature. She is no longer a mere ghost and closer in kind to a citizen of the present. From early in the novel, Sebold sets up the romance with Ray as unfinished and in need of closure. First, we learn that Ray "had written me a love note, which I never read" (25). We also learn that their first kiss was interrupted. "If I had known this was to be the sex scene of my life," Susie recounts, "I might have prepared a bit, reapplied my Strawberry-Banana Kissing Potion as I came in the door" (75). Then, the relationship develops posthumously as Susie gushes in full teenage-girl crush fashion. For instance, when Ray interacts with Ruth, Susie swoons, "It made Ray more attractive to me than he had ever been. His eyes were the darkest gray. When I watched him from heaven I did not hesitate to fall inside them" (81). The conventional end point of this teen romance—sex with the dreamboat—competes with that of the crime drama, bringing the killer to justice.

The possession scene poses a problem bigger than narrative credibility regarding bodily ownership: namely, the problem of consent. "Ruth pushed up against her skin, wanting out," Sebold writes. "She was fighting to leave and I was inside now, struggling with her. I willed her back, willed that divine impossible, but she wanted out. There was nothing and no one that could keep her down. Flying. I watched as I had so many times from heaven, but this time it was a blur beside me. It was lust and rage yearning upward" (301). The description becomes less a ghost story scene worthy of exorcism and more uncomfortably reminiscent of Susie's violent demise. The rape imagery is unmistakable, portraying Susie as the violent penetrator, a reversal of her own rape in the underground chamber in the cornfield.

This is an odd turn of events for the author of *Lucky*, Sebold's first book and bestselling memoir of surviving stranger rape while an undergraduate at Syracuse University. To cast the possession as consensual is dubious at best. First, Ruth's consent can only be inferred. Susie avers, "What [Ruth] had wished for her whole life happening, finally." Ruth asks, "Don't you want anything, Susie?" (295) after which Susie's apparition vanishes, never having spoken the terms of the contract Ruth is about to enter. Second, while the specific request is unspoken, the imagery of permanent trauma *is* clear. Susie describes, "Ruth had been a girl haunted and now she would be a woman haunted. First by accident and now by choice" (321). Finally, if we follow the central conceit of the book that Susie remains a girl of fourteen, this is statutory rape given that Ray is now in his early twenties. Despite these factors, some critics go out of their way to paint the scene as one of consent, perhaps to paper over the weird possibilities opened by the possession-as-rape imagery. For instance, Bliss describes the scene as "bizarre" but insists that "this possession happens with Ruth's consent and Ray's awareness that he is sexually intimate with Susie, not Ruth."[15]

How are we to think about social justice when the rape narrative and the coming-of-age narrative collide? The novel poses a predicament for a generation equally well versed in narratives of self-fulfillment such as *Eat, Pray, Love*, on the one hand, and also stories of women done wrong by men, from *Thelma and Louise* and *The Brave One* to *The Girl with the Dragon Tattoo*. We see this play out to odd effect in the film version of *The Lovely Bones* directed by Peter Jackson, known for such Hollywood epics as *The Lord of the Rings* and cult horror films such as *Dead Alive*. Jackson's film exacerbates the problems of the possession scene by filming it within the conventions of steamy romance. In reviewing the film for the progressive Christian publication *Commonweal*, Richard Alleva writes, "The scene was embarrassing enough in print but the movie verges on the obscene as the twenty-two-year-old Ruth morphs into the fourteen-year-old Susie with the adult Ray on top of her." He asks, "What was Peter Jackson thinking? When pedophiles die and go to perverts' heaven, will they watch this scene on their celestial DVD players?"[16] This is no mere sex-phobic rant. It gets at the backflips required to reconcile the competing modes of coming-of-age drama, horror film, and crime story. The scene prompts the same questions sparked by the collision of fantastical and realist modes in *Let the Dead Bury Their Dead* when grieved widower Ellsworth Batts courts five-year-old Clarence as a stand-in for his long-dead wife.

As a visual medium, film has an inherent problem with such bi-level scenes. Once again the best corollary is *Ghost*, in which Whoopi Goldberg acts the reluctant medium who reunites lovers played by Patrick Swayze and Demi Moore. In the film's famous climax, the medium allows the wife to kiss the murdered husband in a beautiful, cathartic confirmation of love. But who is Moore kissing—the actual body before her, which we all know to be that of Whoopi Goldberg, or the entity for which she stands, the husband? In a visual medium, one frame necessarily trumps the other—the actual body can be Swayze or Goldberg, but not both at that crucial moment. Lest too many queer (not to mention interracial) possibilities fracture the conventional romance, Swayze plays the body that kisses Moore. That iconic image ends up on the movie poster. The fantastical mode of the ghost story displaces the realist mode of the crime story, even if the viewer understands perfectly well that Goldberg is playing a heterosexual white man in that moment. In *The Lovely Bones*, Jackson makes this same choice. At the crucial moment, he replaces the actress whose body is in the realist plot (Ruth) with the one for whom it stands (Susie). Susie, however, is a fourteen-year-old, not unlike the actress playing her, Saoirse Ronan, who began filming at the age of thirteen. Fiction, by contrast, need not choose one over the other. That is why narrative theorist Jan Alber suggests that readers of such "physically impossible scenarios" are able to make sense of them by blending or combining multiple existing frames.

Nonetheless, the predicament of consent persists in the novel, too. To salve the dilemma, if not solve it, Sebold offers Ruth not just as a willing medium but as a cardboard cutout version of 1970s protofeminism. Ruth reads women's liberation texts on the sly, draws alluring sketches of nude women for art class, reads *The Bell Jar* and women's poetry, does not wear makeup, complains when something "demeans women," and declares herself a political vegetarian. In the world of the novel, she alone pines for the gothic terrain of the ghost story as she writes poetry about graves and journal entries about seeing the dead. After Susie brushes past Ruth in a posthumous flight from her fresh corpse, Ruth's life goal becomes connecting with the dead, especially female victims of violence. By the time she moves to New York City, "the world she saw of dead women and children had become as real to her as the world in which she lived" (227). As an aspiring feminist poet, Ruth decides "that her words had the power to resurrect" (117).

All that being said, Susie takes possession of Ruth's body not for communion with the necrophilic poet but for physical consummation with her now-grown middle-school crush. As such, Susie's possession of Ruth is inescapably troubling, no matter how many feminist signifiers Sebold attaches and no matter how many bouquets of flowers the other murdered girls shower on Ruth in heaven while Susie temporarily inhabits her body.

Live Woman Fleeing

The feminist varnish on Ruth is merely an accessory to Susie's coming-of-age narrative. The more compelling feminist story is that of Susie's mother. While Susie is a dead girl developing, Abigail is a live woman fleeing. Susie's death allows Abigail to reclaim an identity eclipsed by her roles as wife and mother. To escape her role as grieving mother, Abigail turns first to an affair with Len Feterman, the police detective assigned to the case, and then leaves town altogether to start a new life. "The time she'd had alone," Sebold writes, "had been gravitationally circumscribed by when her attachments would pull her back" (265). In fact, we learn that she despises the word *momma* and seeks moments of aloneness for "a brief vacation from her life as Mrs. Salmon" (196).

The connection to Addie Bundren is striking in the conflation of marriage and motherhood as violations of cherished aloneness. Like Addie, Abigail has an extramarital affair in an unsuccessful bid to reclaim her destroyed solitude. "When she realized she was pregnant the third time, she sealed the more mysterious mother off," Susie recounts. "Bottled up for years behind that wall, that needy part of her had grown, not shrunk, and in Len, the greed to get out, to smash, destroy, rescind, overtook her. Her body led and in its wake would be the pieces left to her" (152). Abigail's kinship to Addie is particularly apparent in a batch of photographs by Susie in which her mother is "*not there* somehow" (42). Susie describes one photograph in particular, "the one taken of her unawares, the one captured before the click startled her into the mother of the birthday girl, owner of the happy dog, wife to the loving man, and mother again to another girl and a cherished boy. Homemaker. Gardener. Sunny neighbor" (43). In this photograph, Sebold reprises Addie's math problem. "She had a stare that stretched to infinity," Susie recalls. "She was, in that moment, not my mother but something separate from me. . . . My mother's eyes are oceans, and inside them were loss" (43). In a feminist reading of the photographs, Ann Bliss rightly argues that Susie is "unnerved by the awareness that her mother has an independent identity."[17]

If Abigail is trapped in this suburban novel, prone like Addie to begrudge incursions on her infinite void, Jack Salmon is akin to Anse Bundren, greedy for the mathematics of fatherhood. When he sees his slain daughter's face multiplied in glass shards, he feels "the strange sad mortality of being a father. His life had given birth to three children, so the number calmed him. No matter what happened to Abigail or to him, the three would have one another. In that way the line he had begun seemed immortal to him, like a strong steel filament threading into the future, continuing past him no matter where he might fall off" (48). Against Abigail's vision of maternity as violation, Jack views paternity as solace. The numbers work in his favor. Len Feterman, on the other hand, is the anti-Anse. He is not "a worshiper of children. He watched her carry the two boys, but did not stand to help or comment on them the way the other policemen always did, defining her by her children, both living and dead" (89).

Sebold is not kind to a mother who abandons her children and resents the petty tyranny of conventional suburban life. First, she tames Abigail. Whereas Addie was a quietly masochistic teacher in her pre-Bundren life, in her pre-Salmon life Abigail worked at a bridal shop—named Wanamakers, no less. She liked it, continues to take solace in it, and dreams of returning to the bridal shop as the moment when she was all potential, a woman with no past (207). Whereas Addie regains her aloneness in her final burial away from the Bundrens in *As I Lay Dying*, in *The Lovely Bones* Abigail returns to her identity as Mrs. Salmon. Her decision is sparked by a charged symbol of motherhood:

a lovely pink baby crawling near the ocean in California. The image squashes Abigail's romantic dreams of suicide à la Virginia Woolf or Edna Pontellier, the heroine of Kate Chopin's *The Awakening*, both recalled from Abigail's college days. Faced with two stark choices—feminist suicide or maternal return—she opts for the latter, having no other options in her index of possibilities. Bliss contends, "Abigail is finally able to acknowledge that she never wanted to be a mother and implicitly rejects the maternal role: she returns for her husband, not for her children."[18]

Abigail becomes the reverse negative of Addie, closer in kind to the new Mrs. Bundren, the nameless town woman who inexplicably chooses Anse in the final chapter of *As I Lay Dying*. Even on the level of geography, Abigail echoes the new Mrs. Bundren. On a walk with a neighbor to the edge of their subdivision, "they stood on a high hill that had never been cleared for houses and on which a few old farmers dwelled" (169). From that perch Abigail can see the place from which Addie escaped in an earlier century. Moreover, while death allows Addie to regain her aloneness for eternity, Sebold's vision of heaven likely offers only more of the same for Abigail. The Inbetween is a universe of perpetual mothers and caretakers, from Franny the intake counselor to Mrs. Utemeyer the Alzheimer's victim ever in search of her daughter. Bliss notes, "Women cannot escape the role of nurturer, even after death."[19] Further, Susie's murder removes Abigail's one shot at freedom. Susie will never come of age and leave the house, trapping Abigail forever in the role of ever-grieving mother and caretaking wife.

Competing Visions of Justice in a Suburban Novel

Abigail's flight from conventional motherhood and dutiful marriage is first pathologized and then thwarted in Sebold's novel. Hers is the inverse of Susie's development from dead girl into woman. This signals a larger trend of competing visions of justice among each active genre in *The Lovely Bones*. The crime novel genre comes with a ready-made vision of justice: nab the bad guy, be it through good police work or vigilante revenge. Susie initially wishes for the latter, "swift vengeance" like in a Charles Bronson movie (58). Ruana Singh counsels the same to Jack Salmon. "'I would talk to everyone I needed to, I would not tell too many people his name. When I was sure,' she said, 'I would find a quiet way, and I would kill him'" (88). Susie, however, deliberately opts out of this vision of justice. When in Ruth's body, she reports, "I knew I did not want to chase after Mr. Harvey and knew why I was there. To take back a piece of heaven I had never known" (304). The coming-of-age narrative offers her preferred vision of justice. "But I knew I would not go out," she declares. "I had taken this time to fall in love instead—in love with the sort of helplessness I had not felt in death—the helplessness of being alive" (309). Sebold eventually satiates the crime novel's desire for vengeance in a quiet deus ex machina: a falling icicle kills Mr. Harvey as he chats with his next unsuspecting victim-to-be in the final chapter. This oh-so-clever twist is meant to be a comforting aside, something between an afterthought and a nightcap. Mr. Harvey's death creates a feeling of closure around a loose detail, one that is no longer central to the plot once the crime novel cedes fully to the coming-of-age narrative.

It is no surprise that Susie's vision of justice is drawn from conventional girlhood given when the murder arrests her development. In his study of the coming-of-age novel in contemporary American fiction, Kenneth Millard argues, "Adolescents are important because of the ways in which they are at the forefront of social change, even while they are simultaneously the products of an adult social culture that shapes their development. . . . They have the potential to reconfigure the existing social structures and institutions to which they find themselves heir, and thereby in some senses change society."[20] So too, Rishoi argues, "By focusing on adolescence, by definition a time of rebellion and resistance, and by foregrounding contradictory desires and discourses, the coming-of-age narrative provides a congenial form for women writers to successfully question the power of dominant ideologies to construct their lives."[21] Susie, however, does not belong in that tradition because she is not questioning dominant ideologies—in fact, she pines for them.

Sebold's novel may teem with political signifiers, but its vision of justice ultimately does not follow in the directions such signs point. We see this in the way Ruth, not Abigail, is festooned with women's liberation iconography untethered to a feminist vision. A similar dynamic informs Sebold's portrayal of racism unhooked to an antiracist vision. Susie is race conscious inasmuch as she is aware of her own whiteness. She recalls in the opening passage, "In newspaper photos of missing girls from the seventies, most looked like me: white girls with mousy brown hair. This was before kids of all races and genders started appearing on milk cartons or in the daily mail. It was still back when people believed things like that didn't happen" (5). Also, Susie reports that her father "had to describe the lightness of my skin" (20) to the police.

Rather than lead to an examination of the currency of whiteness in the suburban economy of the 1970s, however, Sebold paints a nostalgic patina on her suburbs of lost innocence and shattered illusions of safety, a fiction that ostensibly only recently lost its fact status. Whiteness may be visible, but in these suburbs it is still desirable. The same is true of race in the Inbetween. Susie's first friend is an Asian American girl whose version of heaven includes no accent and the whitest name she can imagine: Holly, taken from the protagonist of *Breakfast at Tiffany's*.

Sebold includes a few halfhearted gestures toward antiracist critique. First, Susie's missing schoolbook is the civil rights classic *To Kill a Mockingbird*, in which a black man is unjustly convicted of raping a white woman. This resonates with the early characterization of Ray, who is targeted as the first initial suspect not only because his love note is found among Susie's belongings but also because of his status as a second-generation Indian immigrant. "They were fueled by the guilt they read into Ray's dark skin," Susie reports, "by the rage they felt at his manner, and by his beautiful yet exotic and unavailable mother" (26). Still, Ray's is a story of assimilation, one culminated in the consummation scene. He, too, desires Susie, the perfect image of lost whiteness. Further, his alibi positions him as the consummate suburban citizen. "At first Ray's absence from school had been seen as evidence of his guilt," Susie recounts, "but once the police were presented with a list of forty-five attendees who had seen Ray speak at 'Suburbia: The American Experience,' they had to concede his innocence" (26). Ray *belongs* in this version of suburbia in which Susie's house "looked exactly like the ones on either side of it" (27). It turns out that Susie's lost innocence and desirable whiteness fall in the mainstream of American crime fiction. According to critic Maureen Reddy, "Whiteness—its boundaries, its value, its meanings and perceived threats to its dominance—has been a primary concern of crime fiction throughout its history in the US."[22]

Together, the ghost story and crime novel present another possible resolution: posthumous communion among the victims. While Lindsey is in Mr. Harvey's house, Susie meets his prior victims. They engage in a three-page talk therapy scene worthy of any self-help recovery narrative. Susie reports, "Each time I told my story, I lost a bit, the smallest drop of pain. It was that day that I knew I wanted to tell the story of my family. Because horror on Earth is real and it is every day" (186). Sebold portrays posthumous narration as in and of itself empowering. In turn, we participate in this support group by hearing her story, even if her family cannot. However, the novel does not end here—we are only midway through. The therapeutic scene cannot culminate Susie's coming-of-age quest.

Amid all these competing visions of justice—conviction, vengeance, posthumous empowerment group, feminist autonomy—Susie's vision wins out. Her adolescent coming-of-age narrative trumps the ghost story, the crime drama, and the one story most heir to those of earlier dead women talking, Abigail's dream of aloneness. Susie's heaven is as safe as Sebold's vision for suburbia. Susie tells Ray he can talk to the dead because they're all around. "It doesn't have to be sad or scary" (309), she reassures. Crime novels, too, fit well into domestic ideologies of safety and belonging. "Stereotypical liberal compassion provides a pathological, disease-oriented explanation for human cruelty," Cassuto explains, "but this explanation leads to the exile of the murderer from the human community on the grounds that he's not one of 'us.'"[23] Susie and her neighbors suspect that Mr. Harvey, the creepy bachelor, does not belong; her murder confirms this sense of us versus them. There is of course a long and profitable tradition of women detective novels, in which literary scholars Priscilla Walton and Manina Jones divine a feminist impulse.[24] But Sebold does not partake in that tradition as she delivers on her dead protagonist's adolescent desires.

As a suburban coming-of-age narrative, *The Lovely Bones* is a middling novel prone to bouts of beautiful prose and compelling premises. It is weighed down with melodrama, a comforting spiritual imagination easily swallowed by believers and nonbelievers alike, and a decidedly unsurprising antagonist: the weird guy who lives alone in this otherwise safe little subdivision. Susie's father tells the police "how weird the neighborhood thought Mr. Harvey was with no regular job and no kids" (61–62). The results of this fiction of suburban safety are clear: the novel has sold over ten million copies and counting. Sebold makes no apologies about writing a suburban novel. "Ultimately, the East Village had nothing on Nowhere U.S.A.," Sebold writes in the reader's guide, "and I returned, after several failed attempts at 'the urban novel,' to the material I knew best."[25] This suburban vision leads to the fathers' greatest fear: "How could they both work to support their families and watch their children to make sure they were safe? As a group they would learn it was impossible, no matter how many rules they laid down. What had happened to me could happen to anyone" (206). The gender politics are strikingly uncritical, and the bourgeois dream of safety needs the titillation, even the promise, of terror to sustain itself. Mr. Harvey confirms that their way of life is desired by others, worthy of either envy or enmity. That is why, when Mr. Harvey drives surreptitiously by his old house, Susie sees "a neighborhood of potential victims" (297).

Sebold earned measured praise from such literary kingmakers as the *New York Times*, in which critic Michiko Kakutani acknowledged that "at first it sounds like a high-concept movie, one of those supernatural heart-tuggers like 'Ghost' or 'The Sixth Sense.'" However, he concludes, *The Lovely Bones* "is anything but hokey, Ouija-board mystery" in the way it delivers keen observations about suburban life in an elegiac register.[26] Katherine Bouton similarly suggested that Sebold "shakes off the thriller trappings and turns . . . many clichés upside down."[27] Such popular venues as *People*, *Newsweek*, *Time*, and *USA Today* offered fawning reviews, often featuring follow-up puff pieces and adoring author profiles. *USA Today* declared, "Sebold is sizzling. Reader's can't get enough."[28] When *The Lovely Bones* was released in 2010 as a major Hollywood film, however, it was nearly universally panned, with the exception of Stanley Tucci's Oscar-nominated performance as a credible killer. Critics lamented how the film fell short of the novel, often singling out the dead narrator conceit. In *USA Today*, for instance, Claudia Puig wrote, "But a device that works on the page comes off artificial and emotionless on-screen."[29]

The Lovely Bones works by confirming preexisting ideas about good and evil. The novel was praised in particular for wresting beauty and comfort out of a horrific opening act. In *Time*, Lev Grossman wrote pertly, "What happens to little girls after they die? They go to heaven—and that's exactly what Susie does" (62).[30] So too, Bouton praised the message "of hope, set against a grim reality" when Sebold "takes the stuff of neighborhood tragedy—the unexplained disappearance of a child, the shattered family alone with its grief—and turns it into literature."[31] For many reviewers, Susie's was the voice of the six o'clock news—JonBenét Ramsey, Chandra Levy, Elizabeth Smart. Writing in *People*, Karen Brailsford suggested, "After this summer's highly publicized rash of abductions of young girls, Sebold hopes her book may help their families, as well as teach the rest of us how to understand and comfort them."[32] The evening news may excel in obsessive attention devoted to individual cases, at least for a news cycle, but it has little appetite or apparatus to investigate underlying structures of injustice that might lead to the next little dead girl, not to mention the non-suburban girls who may face horrible and more frequent deaths. All this may be why otherwise favorable reviewers were not always kind to those moments when the suburban novel veers into the American literary tradition of dead women talking and its social justice concern. In particular, critics disliked the scene in which the dead narrator inhabits a body and also those moments when Sebold attempts to connect Susie's murder to a larger history of violence against girls and women. Kakutani, for instance, deemed these elements "lapses" and "stumbles" in his otherwise glowing review.[33]

The Lovely Bones is ultimately a story of creeping suburbia. It chronicles the expansion of what literary critic Catherine Jurca calls the *white diaspora* in twentieth-century American fiction.[34] As Susie notices her memory fading from everyday lives, including her family's, she recalls, "We had lived in one of the first developments to be built on the converted farmland in the area—a development that became the model and inspiration for what now seemed a limitless number—but my imagination had always rested on the stretch of road that had not been filled in with the bright colors of shingles and drainpipes, paved driveways and super-size mailboxes" (235). Against this suburban backdrop of shiny amnesia arise the old gothic house and the sinkhole, which, like Mr. Harvey's dollhouses, signal the presence of a history before the 1970s. When Samuel and Lindsey first enter the house, Susie's unspoken presence is palpable, even though "it was no longer a Susie-fest on Earth" (236). Samuel exhibits historical memory, a rarity in this novel. "I noticed cross-bracing on the gable trim," he reports, "so that means it was after 1860" (236). The classic ghost story and gothic tropes emerge, such as Samuel's offhand comment that one could wall off a body in the plaster. The legacy of Edgar Allan Poe is patent, complete with his motif of corpses inside walls. In such places, Susie can remain in the present, a presence.

Sebold's suburban imaginary builds a castle of safety on the sands of ahistoricity. The posthumous sex scene, however, tears a small hole in the suburban fabric through which we can see the tradition of dead women talking. The sinkhole is the kind of uncanny, unsteady place where metal safes with sacks of bones can disappear, while old stoves can also reappear. The setting resonates with Alice Walker's search for Zora Neale Hurston in the sunken earth of an overgrown cemetery. At the edge of the sinkhole, Ruth first sees Susie: "As clear as day, she saw me standing there beside her, looking at the spot Mr. Harvey had dumped me" (295). It is no coincidence that the sinkhole is the locale of the ensuing possession, not just because of the proximity to her bones but also because the sinkhole is fertile terrain for the suburban gothic. As literary critic Kim Ian Michasiw argues, the suburban gothic contains an interesting twist on gothic anxieties: "not fearing that the undead walk but rather that they don't, that the energies of enlightenment . . . have fully disinfected the landscape."[35] While Mr. Harvey's fear is that Susie's bones will turn up, Susie's fear throughout most of the novel is that they will not. The sinkhole devours Susie's bones just as the creeping suburb will extinguish Susie's memory and all remnants of the past. "Our place is going to be swallowed up in subdivision land" (286), Ruth tells Ray. Still, the possession and the consummation scenes remain glaring aberrations. They are unswallowable by the sinkhole in this otherwise pedestrian suburban fiction.

10

Dead Woman Singing

Suzan-Lori Parks's *Getting Mother's Body*

As *The Lovely Bones* demonstrates, by the twenty-first century the tradition of dead women talking is a familiar device, occasionally bordering on a gimmick. This may signal a new era in which such women become less uncanny and therefore less able to disrupt a community's sense of itself or suture unclosed wounds of history. Instead, they may be becoming mere convention once again, melodramatic salves for grieving families or cheerful sidekicks to the living. They risk becoming the very stuff of convention from which writers from Poe to Morrison work to distinguish their walking, talking embodiments of historical injustice. Nowadays, we might even *expect* the dead to talk, even outside the conventions of ghost stories and fantasy. Animate corpses and talking dead festoon mainstream one-hour dramas ever since the HBO series *Six Feet Under* featured them in a fantasy sequence nearly every episode in a show otherwise largely committed to a realist mode. And their more conventional kin have entered the mainstream, as encapsulated in the figure of the tamed zombie in *Fido*, a 2006 mock-horror film in which the undead are the new servant class in 1950s suburbia thanks to technology akin to a bark collar. So too, unwitting and chatty ghosts now populate the multiplex, from the 1999 film à clef *The Sixth Sense* to the much-panned 2008 Ricky Gervais vehicle *Ghost Town*.

Nonetheless, the more literary tradition of dead women talking persists. Writers are still able to launch questions of what it means to recognize the dead as one of our own, and thereby how to encounter unjust pasts rather than lose them to the sinkhole of history. Perhaps the best example is *Getting Mother's Body*, the 2003 novel by award-winning playwright Suzan-Lori Parks in which a dead woman not only talks but also sings the blues. Parks consciously enters the literary tradition of dead women talking by reinventing Faulkner's *As I Lay Dying* for a post–civil rights audience. She swaps Faulkner's

Bundrens for the Beedes, a black family living in material poverty at the outer edges of the Jim Crow South on the eve of the famed 1963 March on Washington for Jobs and Freedom. Rather than a quest to bury their matriarch, the Beedes embark from the small town of Lincoln, Texas, to the even smaller town of LaJunta, Arizona, to *unbury* Willa Mae. She died years prior in a hotel bathroom from a self-administered coat-hanger abortion while her six-year-old daughter, Billy, waited outside. Willa Mae's exhumation is prompted by a supermarket's plans to plow up the field where her lesbian lover, Dill Smiles, buried her in a makeshift grave. The Beedes head west ostensibly to rescue the corpse, but each has secret designs on the pearls and ring with which Willa Mae is rumored to have been interred. The novel becomes an unconventional treasure hunt to finance each character's private dreams against the backdrop of a historical moment when the nation's eyes turned east toward Washington in search of a different treasure: full citizenship and dreams of American promises made real.

As a dead woman singing, Willa Mae's bid for posthumous citizenship is a performance; it enacts the communal engagement she seeks. But will the living welcome the act? This gets at Parks's most conspicuous break from Faulkner: the dead mother seeks not to rid herself of the company of her living family, but rather to reconcile. The question is whether the Beedes, especially Billy, will claim Willa Mae as one of their own. Likewise, given Parks's historical designs, the question is whether the nation will write someone like her into its history. Willa Mae speaks early and often in the novel, unlike Addie's lone chapter that compels a wholesale reconfiguration of Faulkner's composite picture. Willa Mae does not bring down an entire manor and family line, prompt sudden deaths, eat anyone out of house and home, or reveal anything terribly surprising. She sings playful songs, relays colorful anecdotes, and occasionally fills in details of her larger-than-life memory. In all, Willa Mae merely seeks an active role in the everyday lives of this soap opera–worthy cast.

More so than any other story of dead women talking in American literature, the exhumation plot enacts a very literal encounter with the exiled, discarded, mistreated, and misunderstood of a nation's history. I have twice written about Parks's novel in pieces that consider the uncanny effect of recreating historical segregation signs in fictional terrain[1] and also why Parks revises America's civil rights narratives by reinventing a modernist classic.[2] But I have yet to address Willa Mae directly. She joins America's long and curious history of actual exhumations and reburials, from Abraham Lincoln in 1901 to Emmett Till when his federal case was reopened in 2004. By considering what drives a nation to exhume bodies, along with the context of African American funeral practices, we can appreciate the importance of providing a proper burial, however delayed, for a fast-living fictional woman like Willa Mae and the outcast women for which she stands.

Not-Such-a-Lady Sings the Blues

Getting Mother's Body is an earnest, playful homage to Faulkner. Rather than merely translate his characters across the color line and into a new historical era, Parks scrambles and redistributes memorable components to create an entirely new yet uncannily recognizable story. Cash's broken leg in *As I Lay Dying*, for instance, becomes Aunt June's peg leg, while his penchant for precise carpentry morphs into Snipes's outlandish line of custom-made coffins, featuring anything from a Cadillac shape to a yellow banana to a giant medical bag. Billy Beede is closest in kind to Faulkner's Dewey Dell, but she is now the gravitational center of the plot, first in her all-consuming desire to marry Snipes when she finds she is five months pregnant ("bigged" in her vernacular), and then in her equally all-consuming quest for an abortion when she discovers that Snipes's "sister" is actually his wife. The character named Addie is now a gossipy sidekick in a beauty shop, while the Faulknerian mathematics of parenthood come from a meddling woman on a bus who senses that Billy is "in trouble." I have elsewhere described the novel as Parks reshuffling Faulkner's deck.[3] Parks adds a few wild cards of her own, especially in the character of Dill Smiles, a butch woman who passes as a man even though the whole town is in on the secret. Dill is nonetheless at home in this Faulknerian universe. Her vulture posture and missing teeth directly evoke Anse Bundren, while her gender transgressions set up the punch line for Parks's own one-line chapter: "She pees standing up."[4]

Willa Mae's earnest and playful monologues, however, point to a project different from Faulkner's, one that reaches for justice rather than modernist irresolution. The posthumous monologue structure remains largely the same throughout: homespun philosophy accompanied by bouts of blues singing. Willa Mae's first turn as narrator is the seventh chapter, after Billy has twice taken the helm. She delivers her first words as if performing on stage: "This next song I'ma sing is a song I wrote about a man I used to know. It's called 'Big

Hole Blues'" (30). The time frame, like all of her monologues, is unclear. Is it a flashback, a posthumous appearance on that great blues stage in the sky, or an atemporal interlude from the goings-on in Lincoln, Texas? The last seems most likely, so that Willa Mae's chapters operate as a lyrical chorus in a picaresque prose novel. A chorus, be it in a blues song, a modern guitar lick, or an ancient Greek play, is stranded with but distinct from the rising action. It signals the work's overarching mood and themes. Such a structure holds Willa Mae apart from her community, a minor-key voice set off by time, mode, and everyday concerns.

Posthumous blues singer is a new role for Willa Mae given that in life she was a loose woman and a huckster, but not a stage performer. Still, the speaker in the ensuing number is pure Willa Mae, an unruly woman we can't help but love. She sings,

> My man is digging in my dirt
> Digging a big hole just for me.
> He's digging in my dirt
> Digging a big hole just for me.
> It's as long as I am tall, goes down as deep as the deep blue sea. (30)

The lyrics are classic blues: domestic tensions, even violence, in amorous affairs, often told through everyday conceits and sexual imagery. The ensuing stanzas speak of betrayal and wryly report "my man's" threat to dig a hole big enough for the singer and her boyfriend. The lyrics, tone, and delivery directly channel the rebellious and revered legacies of Ma Rainey and Bessie Smith, as well as the more polished stylings of Billie Holiday. Moreover, while promoting the book and on the audio version, Parks herself belts out the lyrics and accompanies herself on guitar, adding another layer of seriously playful performance.

The opening song also evokes the charm of midcentury popular jazz singers such as Dinah Washington. In 1953, Washington recorded the song "My Man's an Undertaker," whose speaker cheerfully threatens her pesky ex-lover with the refrain, "My man's an undertaker and he's got a coffin just your size." Historian Suzanne E. Smith suggests that "the song's humor offers one glimpse of the role funeral directors played in the cultural imagination of the black community,"[5] a group about which I shall say more in the next section. The humor of the number also suits Willa Mae's brand of spitfire pluck. Yet *her* man is not an undertaker—nor a man, depending on how strict the definition—and she doesn't need the protection, thank you very much. With her own opening number, Willa Mae retains the brazen independence of Bessie Smith, while able to slip on Washington's flirtatious air as easy as a silk dress.

The influential role of blues women and their descendants is now recognized and celebrated thanks in part to the work of black feminist scholars. In her groundbreaking work, Hazel Carby argues that "organic intellectuals" such as Ma Rainey, Bessie Smith, and Ethel Waters offered an empowering presence. Coming out of the experience of the new urban black proletariat, the blues depicted women as sensuous, sexual, autonomous subjects in contradistinction both to the respectable bourgeois women of Harlem Renaissance fiction and to the pervasive patriarchal images of black women as sexual exotics. The tradition arose out of the Great Migration when masses of African Americans moved from the rural South to the urban North, which challenged the ability of the talented tenth to represent the race from their enclaves in Boston, Harlem, and Chicago. "Being able to move both North and South," Carby argues, "the women blues singer occupied a privileged space: she could speak the desires of rural women to migrate and voice the nostalgic desires of urban women for home, which was both a recognition and a warning that the city was not, in fact, the 'promised land.' "[6] So too, noted black feminist theorist Patricia Hill Collins argues, "The growth of Black women's blues paralleled another dimension of the greatly expanded discourse on sexuality in the 1920s that also rejected 'bourgeois notions of sexual purity.' " While Jim Crow culture and black church teachings alike painted sexuality as dangerous and prone to deviance, blues culture made sexuality public and possibly fun. Collins continues, "The blues took on themes that were banished from popular music—extramarital affairs, domestic violence, and the short-lived nature of love relationships all appeared in Black women's blues. The theme of women loving women also appeared in Black women's blues, giving voice to Black lesbianism and bisexuality."[7]

Parks takes up this last point in earnest through the curious pairing of Willa Mae, notorious for her sexual exploits with many a man, and Dill, the butch woman everyone treats as a man. (The barber's highest compliment is to offer her a shave.) Dill's open secret points to another key divergence from Faulkner: there are fewer discrepancies between internal and external monologues, between public faces and private realities—though everyone acts like they are not in on a communal secret, such as Dill's true sex. As a father figure for Billy Beede, Dill is as unconventional as Willa Mae in her maternal role.

While the town members never quite understand their relationship, Willa Mae provides the explanatory backstory in her own moment of posthumous revelation that comes closest to Addie's confessional mode. Willa Mae, we learn, first mistook Dill for a man. "One night we was going at it and I got bold," she recounts. "I felt around down there and then I knew and Dill knew that I knew but we didn't mention it" (225). Their silence neither masks a hypocrisy, as with Faulkner's adulterous preacher, nor indicates a non-lingual sibling bond, as with Darl and Dewey Dell. In Parks's novel, mutually agreed silence is a gift to a fellow citizen. Eventually, Willa Mae goes so far as to flatter Dill that she could be Billy's father. What is more, this lovingly comic scenario directly evokes the real-life story of Billy Tipton, the successful jazz musician who, upon his death in 1989, was discovered to have been born female.

Dill turns out to be the woman-done-wrong in this story. Willa Mae continues to sleep with another man, pushing Dill to go so far as to lie in bed with them during the act—to keep an eye on her woman. While unconventional to say the least, the arrangement could work, except that Willa Mae reveals Dill's secret to the whole town. "I found out but I didn't tell nobody for a long time and when I did," she admits, "I felt bad but once words leave your mouth you can't get them back in" (225). Willa Mae has a different kind of word problem than Addie Bundren: words mean exactly what she says they mean. Once the words are spoken, Dill no longer has the right to author her own standing in the community. And so we appreciate anew how the town participates in Dill's charade, never daring to call her out and rescind her preferred status. As for the usually unabashed Willa Mae, the surprisingly contrite dead woman is a direct contrast to the surprisingly defiant one in Faulkner's novel. To reconcile with Dill requires not the airing of truths long buried, but rather the restoration of a benevolent fiction that endows someone like Dill with the male civic status she desires.

Like Dill and the blues women of history, Willa Mae is not a conventional lady. Yet her quest is to be claimed as a mother. Billy, in turn, frequently and vociferously denies her this status by calling Willa Mae by anything but her first name—at least, out loud. Radical scholar Angela Davis addresses such seeming inconsistencies in her work to position black feminism within a blues legacy. "What gives the blues such fascinating possibilities of sustaining emergent feminist consciousness," she argues, "is the way they often construct seemingly antagonistic relationships as noncontradictory oppositions." The social consciousness that arises from the blues turns out to be as slippery and improvisational as the performances themselves. Davis explains, "A female narrator in a women's blues song who represents herself as entirely subservient to male desire might simultaneously express autonomous desire and a refusal to allow her mistreating lover to drive her to psychic despair."[8] This is a perfect description of Willa Mae as lover, con artist, and mother. To recognize Willa Mae as a mother, not to mention Dill as a father figure, is a quiet political act, even if it requires that we merely expand conventional categories, rather than jettison them—a queer coupling in heterosexual clothing.

While her singing places Willa Mae in a long and celebrated blues legacy, her chapters are also deeply entwined with the novel's core burial motifs, not to mention plot. Willa Mae shares her philosophy of the Hole. "Everybody's got a Hole," she explains. "Ain't nobody ever lived who don't got a Hole in them somewhere. When I say Hole you know what I'm talking about, dontcha? Soft spot, sweet spot, opening, blind spot, Itch, Gap, call it what you want but I call it a Hole" (30–31). This monologue evokes Addie's philosophy of aloneness and her violated void, but in colloquial language and a direct address to the reader. Willa Mae's opening chapter, like all of them scattered throughout the narrative, allows her entrance into the community and its (un)burial concerns, versus Addie's posthumous confession that she would like nothing more than to rid herself of the Bundrens. In fact, while Willa Mae's down-home advice may interrupt the real-time plot, her monologues often prove quite useful for the living, sometimes consciously and sometimes less so.

Willa Mae's opening chapter does not force us to realign pieces of a composite picture Parks has assembled thus far. Instead, she lends depth and charm to the rather coherent portrait. When Willa Mae first sings the posthumous blues, we are already keenly aware of the depth of Billy's dilemma and the devil-may-care posture she uses to cover her desperation. We are privy to other key deceptions, such as the financial troubles of Mrs. Faith Jackson and her husband's funeral home. We also appreciate how the Jim Crow landscape of bald racism and material poverty affects the daily lives of the Beede clan, such as Aunt June's desire to replace the leg she lost at sixteen. "I'd like a new leg," she confides, "but even if we could get the money together for it, I ain't yet seen one in my color" (19). Faulkner's morbid humor becomes a wistful pathos in Parks's world, one conscious of color and politics. It retains a hint of Faulkner's trademark humor, even if it is gentler and never distances us from the Beedes. Aunt June's monologue, for instance, happens while she "crutches around" with her hair only half pressed, the other half "still wild" because Billy had to get to the bridal shop. Unlike in *As I Lay Dying*, there is no detached onlooker to underscore the pitiable wretchedness of the image. After all, the townsfolk know that the rest of the world would see them as no different from the Beedes. This is a novel of community formation, not a wry take on the residues of the Old South lingering amid the new.

Parks's aim, then, is one of recovery: to accept as one of our own the outcasts, misfits, and forgotten who did not make it to Washington in 1963, or into the glossy history books illustrating a grand narrative of racial progress. Davis notes that the blues culture of the 1920s and its "race records" market did not survive the Depression, yet "these women nonetheless managed to produce a vast body of musical texts and a rich cultural legacy."[9] Carby also notes the short life span of the era, while cueing us to how the black woman blues singer has thrived in post–civil rights literary culture as a soulful, empowered icon, from Gayl Jones's 1975 novel *Corregidora* to Alice Walker's blockbuster *The Color Purple*.[10] Willa Mae belongs in this line. And Parks aims to put her there—even if it requires a shovel and a full tank of gas.

Americorpse

When we dig up the dead in the most literal sense, what kind of engagement with the past does that allow? What does it mean to bring Willa Mae's corpse into the terrain of the living? First, the fact that Willa Mae is a lively presence in the novel is not a terribly surprising conceit given that death and the presence of ancestors are central tropes in African American literature and culture. "Historically," historian Suzanne Smith explains, "death in the African American cultural imagination was not feared but rather embraced as the ultimate 'homegoing,' a welcome journey to a spiritual existence that would transcend the suffering and injustices of the mortal world."[11] She clarifies, "The dead are not 'alive' in the most literal sense; rather, they exist as powerful spiritual beings who continue to influence the living world through the actions of their descendants."[12] While that may be so, a reverential approach to death and ancestors is a far cry from Parks's novel. Billy's insouciance, for instance, reflects the tendency noted by other scholars, such as John L. Jackson Jr., to actively keep our past at arm's length, lest we be shackled by it. We see this tendency most overtly in announcements of a *post-racial era*, which paints anyone committed to confronting our racial past as "the walking dead," citizens of a bygone era who belong on a shelf next to the mammies, Uncle Toms, and other denizens of Jim Crow America. "These dead walk, talk, struggle, and strain," Jackson argues in *Racial Americana*. "In so doing, they also chain us to the scene of our past crimes."[13] So too, when Aunt June gently suggests kinship by reciting the adage about the apple not falling far from the tree, Billy responds curtly, "I ain't no goddamned apple" (19).

While the trope of dead women talking provides literal encounters with the dead, critical race scholars tend to think of death on a more metaphorical level. They cast African Americans as socially dead,[14] which in turn positions struggles for full citizenship as a struggle to bring the dead back to life. Furthermore, the world of the living is often seen as the world of injustice, a logical conclusion in an era of slavery, then compulsory race segregation, then de facto segregation and structural racism after the civil rights movement. That is why, for instance, Richard Wright's rich literary record of documenting racial injustice positions violence and death at the center of African American existence. Critic Abdul R. JanMohamed suggests that black people in Wright's United States are swaddled from infancy with the threat of death, so that they become "death-bound subjects."[15] If death is at the center of black and other minority subjectivity, black queer theorist Sharon Patricia Holland argues, the role of African American literature is to "raise the dead" so that we may hear and even seek out marginalized voices, rather than be haunted by them.[16]

To exhume a body is a different matter than communing with one's ancestors in a prayerful moment, visiting a monument on the national stage, or scouring junk stores for detritus of the Jim Crow era. In *Digging Up the Dead: A History of Notable American Reburials*, historian Michael Kammen tracks skirmishes over the corpses of such figures as Jefferson Davis, F. Scott Fitzgerald, Abraham Lincoln, James Monroe, Thomas Paine, Edgar Allan Poe, and Chief Sitting Bull. Kammen wonders what purpose is served when families, municipalities, private cemeteries, churches, and states vie over the final resting place. He asks, "Were they always and unambiguously seeking to do justice to the dearly departed?" Or, from a more postmodern angle, "Are reburials quite literally about the physical *re*constructedness of the past—a form of historical revisionism, setting the record straight in some sense"?[17] Across his examples, Kammen finds that, "historically considered, reburial has come to mean a figurative form of resurrection—primarily the resurrection of reputation, at least for a while." He continues, "It has also meant, with the passage of time, renewed honor and frequently some form of reconciliation, or at least movement in the direction of reconciliation—familial, sectional, and above all national."[18]

It is important to place the fictional Willa Mae alongside the very real tendency to rewrite national history through exhumation and reburial of citizens from past eras. While Kammen is primarily interested in notable personages, Willa Mae decidedly does not foot that bill. That is partly the point when Parks turns away from Washington to tell a story of a family squabble whose stakes are as low on the historical register as the drama is intricate and entertaining. To dig up someone like Willa Mae is not to restore her national reputation, but to bestow posthumous honor never available during her life. In this respect, Willa Mae is like Matthew Alexander Henson, the African American who accompanied Robert E. Peary to the North Pole in 1909. Peary was interred at Arlington National Cemetery with much fanfare in 1920. On the other hand, when Henson died in 1955, Kammen reports, "he was buried in a simple grave at Woodlawn Cemetery in the Bronx, having spent most of his post-Arctic years in obscurity as a clerk in the Customs House of New York City."[19] Henson was exhumed and reburied in Arlington in 1988, thanks to a long campaign to recognize this African American pioneer. It also required special dispensation from President Ronald Reagan because Henson was never enlisted in the military. Or, given the supermarket plot, perhaps Willa Mae is closer in kind to the Africans buried in a field in lower Manhattan in the eighteenth century, only to be discovered in 1991 when development for a new building turned up the remains, leading to a protracted effort to properly study and reinter them.[20]

Just as important as exhumation is the prospect of reburial. To accomplish this task, Parks adds the funeral director to her Faulknerian cast: Mr. Jackson and his none-too-smart son Laz. On the first matter, exhumation is rare enough that Laz, who is love-struck for Billy Beede, remarks, "I don't get much call to dig peoples up, but when you gotta do it, you dig them up the same way you would dig them down" (250). The charmingly matter-of-fact approach is noteworthy for a number of reasons. First, the exhumation is narrated, unlike Addie's burial in *As I Lay Dying*. Second, it requires the same care and precision as burying a body in the first place. Laz goes at the task of digging up a corpse as if it is another one of life's duties, a professional obligation and perhaps even a civic one. To get mother's body, as announced in the novel's title, is a preliminary step to bringing Willa Mae back into the community.

Laz says to Billy, "I'm gonna take your mother back to Lincoln. . . . I'm gonna get her a new coffin, a nice one, and a nice angel headstone. I'll put her in the ground real good and all at my expense" (253). Willa Mae will finally have a proper burial in the African American community of the novel, as well as the national imagination of the contemporary readership.

All this gets at the crucial role of the funeral director in black culture. Smith argues, "As individuals charged with orchestrating the African American funeral—often described as a 'homecoming celebration,' funeral directors have always been culturally valued for their ability to help their communities honor their dead with dignity and the requisite pageantry."[21] Mr. Jackson is aware of his station as Smith describes it and boasts, "Jackson's Funeral Home aint the most respected in Butler County for nothing. White or black, we the most respected. You seen the sign out front. 'Established in 1926.' We'll be fifty come 'Seventy-six" (16). Mr. Jackson's claim to cross-racial respect fits uneasily within the actual history of black funeral directors, who were icons of economic self-sufficiency in a Jim Crow economy. "As entrepreneurs in a largely segregated trade," Smith explains, "funeral directors were usually among the few black individuals in any town or city who were economically independent and not beholden to the local white power structure."[22] The politics of respectability and middle-class uplift cast "the funeral director as a symbol of the promise of black entrepreneurship as well as the custodian of the most revered African American homegoing traditions."[23]

The funeral director came to rival the black preacher as community leader. "Sometimes, he was the only one, other than the preacher, who wore a suit during the week," cultural theorist Karla FC Holloway adds, "and the fact that it may have been his only suit mattered less than the fact that his business gave him license to wear it on some day other than Sunday."[24] The black funeral director's spot at the head of the African American community was not inevitable, without strife, or enduring. "As the twentieth century began," Holloway explains, "the black undertaker emerged as a businessman in a community of few independent black-owned businesses."[25] Then, in a post–civil rights era, African Americans increasingly discarded racial loyalty and solicited white-owned funeral homes, often as a mark of social advancement. As a result, Holloway notes, "there was passionate resentment among many African American professionals about how white businesses were successful in ways that they themselves were not, especially with crossover clientele."[26] Further, bodies themselves can carry traits and obligations not always well understood across the color line. Holloway recounts a beleaguered white mortician's desperate attempts to restore one corpse's chemically curly hair, until finally a black journalist suggests hair spray. "A dead Jheri-Kurl is about as culturally specific as one can get," Holloway quips.[27] All of this colors Parks's portrait of burial and reburial so that as a black funeral director, Mr. Jackson stands as the embodiment of Jim Crow–era self-determination as well as civil rights–era commitments to integration, two enduringly warring ideals in American history.

It is fitting that a black funeral also serves as the stage for Parks's retrospective meditation on civil rights legacies. Willa Mae's initial burial was an ad hoc affair in the back of a small roadside motel. Yet it was done with some degree of reverence, such as Dill's gesture to wrap the body in a family quilt, a powerful family symbol in black culture. Likewise, Willa Mae's reburial is also a family affair, this time done right with a black funeral home and community sanction. Her modest reburial contrasts markedly from the important role of the civil rights funeral. "By the mid-1960s," Smith explains, "the civil rights funeral, a tradition that had begun with Emmett Till's ceremony in 1955, became a central stage on which the dramas and internal tensions of the movement play themselves out. . . . They revealed not only the obvious tension between blacks and whites but also the internal divisions among black activists who were increasingly in conflict about the future direction of the struggle."[28] Smith considers the eulogy for slain Mississippi freedom rider James Chaney to mark the moment when "it was no longer sufficient simply to bear witness to the loss of the movement's martyrs. The point of the civil rights funeral was not to wallow in grief but to take decisive action to continue the fight of those who had died for the cause."[29] On the other hand, grief in itself can be a political tool. Dora Apel, for instance, argues that Mamie Till staged a "spectacle funeral" for her murdered and mutilated teenage son Emmett Till in order to elicit public shame and counter the terror of spectacle lynching.[30]

In her study of reburials in post-Soviet Eastern Europe, Katherine Verdery considers efforts to properly bury and mark victims of mass injustice. "And so reburials revise the past," she explains, "by returning names to the nameless and perhaps endowing these revisions with feeling."[31] The result is not only historical revisionism, but also a new take on how we think time works, often by joining two disparate periods and excising the intervening era of injustice. Parks stages her own temporal feat with a 2003 novel about a civil rights–era quest to rebury someone who died six years prior, when the idea of a grand march on Washington may have been unthinkable. Parks not only restores the reputation of an unknown, fictional blues woman like Willa Mae but also returns to the black community a butch lesbian like Dill, who Aunt June had taken to calling "Miss He-She-It"; a slow but earnest son of a funeral director; a preacher with no church; and his wife, who long ago was cast off from her California family as a burden. Parks manages on a domestic scale to achieve the national reconciliation that Kammen and others suggest drive reburials of notable figures.

The reconciliation returns the Beedes to their hometown, rather than lighting out even farther west to start anew. This contrasts a repatriation scheme that Kammen finds Zora Neale Hurston proposed in a letter to W. E. B. Du Bois. "Why," Hurston asked, "do you not propose a cemetery for the illustrious Negro Dead?" She suggested Florida as the rightful location for such figures as Nat Turner and Frederick Douglass and any other African American of note.[32] Hurston's scheme resonates with the name where Willa Mae is initially buried: LaJunta, which means government by military coup. By bringing Willa Mae's body back to Lincoln, namesake of a founding father, Parks restores her station in the family, as well as the rest of the Beedes to their place in the national community.

My Mother, the Corpse

While Smith frames African American deathways through the colloquialism *homegoing*, Willa Mae's exhumation and reburial are explicitly a *homecoming*. In the novel, religious practices, not to mention theological beliefs about a non-worldly afterlife, are strikingly absent. Instead, this is a quirky story of domestic reconciliation with grand national repercussions. Literary critic Lisa Perdigao identifies exhumation as a postmodern trope following modernism's prevailing themes of burial and entombment.[33] Though she does not attend to Parks's novel in particular, the contrast holds. When Willa Mae finally gets a proper burial, Faulkner's modernist lack of resolution and embrace of fragmentation become Parks's postmodernist desire for justice, however manufactured and fictional.

Willa Mae's corpse is an active participant in this process. The reconciliation is neither metaphorical, nor merely ceremonial, nor symbolic, such as Walker's quest to mark Hurston's grave with a headstone and a beautiful essay. Initially, Dill is dead set against the exhumation, ostensibly to enforce Willa

Mae's wishes. Willa Mae's brother, Uncle Teddy Roosevelt, reports the family squabble:

> "Willa Mae wanted to be buried with her jewels and that's what she *still* wants," Dill says.
>
> "How you know what Willa wants *still*?" June says.
>
> "She ain't changing her mind once she's dead," Dill says.
>
> "She might," June says. June reads and knows things. (25)

The skirmish is humorous in its folksy exchange, but it also cues larger questions about life, death, and the prospect of posthumous agency. Of course, we know that Willa Mae's wishes are not necessarily enforceable, as I explored in my discussion of *As I Lay Dying*. How we treat bodies has more to do with the rights and needs of the living, not the dead who no longer have legal standing. In any case, the real reason Dill opposes the exhumation is to keep secret that she stole Willa Mae's jewels during the original burial and then sold off the pearls one by one to keep her pig business afloat.

The exhumation prompts a posthumous reconciliation between the two lovers. "I lay stomach-down in the dirt, my feet resting on the white-chalk grave-marking stones," Dill reports. "I know what Ma is thinking. She's thinking there's my daughter topping her woman one last time" (244). Parks then delivers one of the most beautiful and earnest images of intimacy and reconciliation: "Ma's teeth have disappeared and her skin has grown smooth. She looks young, like a child. I am a man, but an old old man, and Willa Mae, six feet underneath the top of the ground, unfolds her hands from where I laid them crosst her chest and, with a smile, takes me in her arms" (244). The necro-embrace is a beautiful image of reconciliation across time, one that fulfills Dill's cross-gender dreams. It also precedes the reshrouding of Willa Mae's body in preparation for her proper burial. Parks offers a model for how the African American community, as well as the whole nation, can reclaim the bodies of its own cast-off sons and daughters, be they dead or alive. In this, Dill may evoke such historical figures as Bayard Rustin, the architect of the March on Washington who did not ascend the podium that day to take his rightful role as race leader in part because he was gay.[34]

One reconciliation remains: Billy Beede and her dead mother. The reconciliation comes from not only her contact with the corpse but also interaction with Willa Mae's voice. As I mentioned, for the most part Willa Mae's monologues are occasional musical breaks to the linear plot. Yet one particularly colorful anecdote about the "ring trick" ends up helping Billy get out of a pickle in the real-time action. The ring trick is a con by which an unsuspecting mark, in this case a white filling station owner who is a racist and a rube, is tricked into paying big bucks for a ring he believes to be the jewel of the rich lady who just left his station. The ring, of course, is a fake and the young kid who hands it over for a fee is in on the con. The chapter conferring this motherly advice is the sole one in pure narrative sans blues lyrics. When Billy enlists her family members to pull off their own ring trick to finance their way to LaJunta, we are already privy to the mechanics of the ruse. Willa Mae lets us in on the joke so that we feel superior in our knowledge and vindicated in our sense of racial justice by way of con artist–driven reparations.

As readers, we see a direct connection between Willa Mae's monologue and Billy Beede's adjacent account of her own ring trick, even if Billy does not mention it. In fact, all of Billy's most intimate interactions with her mother go unspoken. For instance, Aunt June reports, "'I callt her "Mother" in my head, but not out loud,' Billy says. 'That was the way she wanted it'" (174). Amid all the novel's chatter—external and internal, living and posthumous—Billy's silence becomes a mode of familial connection. At the end she thinks, "If Dill stole things I don't got a need to talk about it. The truth, whatever it is, is gonna stay a secret" (256–57). Like Addie, Parks ends up embracing silence, but of a different kind. Everyone is in on the secret yet chooses not to say so. The result is curiously in alignment with Addie's vision: justice becomes when a dead woman need not talk, nor even the living.

11

When Dead Women Don't Talk

Maxine Hong Kingston's "No Name Woman"

Once we begin to account for all the dead women talking in American literature, we also notice when dead women don't talk—even when we might wish them to. After all, anything is possible in the realm of literature, so it should be conspicuous when corpses simply remain silent. When dead women don't, won't, or can't talk, this may crimp or even foreclose literature's ability to confront the past. On the other hand, as I suggest in this brief concluding chapter, we might find unexpected value in such impediments.

A telling example is Maxine Hong Kingston's 1975 feminist blockbuster *The Woman Warrior: Memoirs of a Girlhood among Ghosts*. "No Name Woman," the inaugural chapter, famously begins with a command for silence and willful forgetting: "'You must not tell anyone,' my mother said, 'what I am about to tell you.'"[1] Many have noted the core irony in this printed utterance of a spoken injunction against speech. The narrator first relays the bare facts of a fabled aunt who drowned herself in the family well after having been marauded, then banished, for becoming pregnant years after her husband left rural China for America. In its brevity, focus on secrets, and inability to piece together incongruent details, the ensuing narrative instills an urgent desire to recover this dead woman's story. We struggle to make it comprehensible, or in Kingston's phrasing, "to name the unspeakable" (5). As we see in any number of stories about women who die unjust deaths, language and voice arise as antidotes to the silence and shame that so often surround those who defy community conventions, be it having a child outside of marriage or not showing adequate penitence for social transgressions of any sort. This has led countless readers and critics, including Kingston herself, to celebrate *The Woman Warrior* under the long-standing feminist banner of "breaking the silence."[2]

The trouble is that the aunt is not there to tell her story. She is a silent, hungry ghost forever banished from the family table. The problem becomes one of both social justice and the genre of memoir. In terms of social justice, the aunt's death is a direct result of patriarchal structures and the community's intolerance for women who defy convention, which leads to silence and banishment from sanctioned family lore. In terms of genre, on the other hand, the narrator must speak from experience and that which she can infer from secondhand stories. In this, the narrator is deliberate about the importance of confronting her familial past to make sense of her present. "Unless I see her life branching into mine," the narrator notably asserts, "she gives me no ancestral help" (8). Despite the narrator's best efforts to recreate her aunt's story and to connect it to her own, this dead woman does not, cannot, and will never talk.

In the end, Kingston's narrator can only ventriloquize her dead, inert, absent aunt. She must sift through possible versions of the story to seek not the truth, but the version that is most satisfying. Is the no-name aunt violated, defiant, compliant, romantic, savvy, or responsible? She becomes not a dead woman talking but a dead woman talked about. This leads to the most striking, even terrifying, moment in the story. The narrator belatedly considers, "I do not think she always means me well" (16). Up to this point, the narrative compellingly portrayed the collective punishment of silence as a conspiracy of the highest order against women who flout patriarchal expectations. Now the narrator realizes that turning silence into voice is not necessarily a feminist empowerment narrative. If she ventriloquizes her aunt in an attempt to make the dead speak, that may be a further betrayal and another form of punishment.

As a whole, *The Woman Warrior* is immersed in matters of death, haunting, memory, and how characters interact with figures and relics of the past. The dead aunt who may not wish to talk sets in motion a series of ghost stories, a genre also signaled in the subtitle, *Memoirs of a Girlhood among Ghosts*. Some sections hew closely to conventional ghost stories, such as the stories Brave Orchid, the narrator's mother, tells of fending off ghosts in a deserted section of her dormitory while a medical student in China. For most of the narrative, however, *ghost* is more metaphor than category. It permeates the text, standing in for the uncanny, the excessive, the unknown, and generally as a figure of the outsider, a relative position in whichever dominant culture Kingston's characters find themselves. In this way, the trope helps us understand ethnic identity in multiethnic spaces. It also provides a source of possible ethnic empowerment. For instance, in a comical episode in which Brave Orchid encounters a racist laundry patron who mocks her, she deftly uses the skill she cultivated in China to name ghosts and thereby subdue them. "Noisy Red-Mouth Ghost she'd write on its package," the narrator reports, "naming it, marking its clothes with its name" (105).

The narrator of *The Woman Warrior* is haunted by figures from her mother's homeland in China, a land she herself has never visited and knows almost exclusively through "talk-story." For example, she cannot live up to the older sister and brother who perished before her mother emigrated, if they existed at all. She is also haunted by the mythic figures of female warriors and slaves in Chinese oral culture, and of course by her aunt with no name. Members of both generations also experience living family members as ghosts, especially across generational and immigrant lines. Brave Orchid surrounds herself with family portraits and craves her daughter's physical presence, "not wandering like a ghost from Romany" (107). Moon Orchid, Brave Orchid's sister, emigrates to Gold Mountain late in life and recoils from the "barbarian" children who don't speak human language (that is, her Chinese dialect). And when the two women confront Moon Orchid's long-emigrated husband, they realize that "she must look like a ghost from China" (153). In that encounter, the husband explains, "You became people in a book I had read a long time ago" (154).

Some critics accept Kingston's invitation to read *The Woman Warrior* not so much as memoirs but as ghost stories. Ken-Fang Lee suggests that ghosts are not just the "in-between" space of the immigrant, but also the difference between source and target inherent in translation, especially given Kingston's penchant to describe Chinese ideograms that never themselves appear in the text. For Lee, such acts of translation allow the narrator direct transactions with the silent dead woman because "she transforms pieces of writing into spirit money to appease her aunt."[3] Critic Gayle Fujita Sato also traces the "bewilderingly diverse" ghost theme by which "the narrator comes to identify with her nameless, outcast kinswoman." For Sato, the dead aunt is a ghost writer and the narrator's ventriloquist act is one of feminist "filiality" that allows her "to claim Chinese American identity while repudiating antifemale teachings and practices rooted in Chinese Confucian tradition and rehearsed in her own house."[4]

What say does the aunt have in this filial act? The "No Name Woman" section comes closest to a ghost story per se, complete with a corpse and spirit that haunts the present-day narrator. Given that story and voice are such overriding themes, it is odd that the dead aunt doesn't speak. In fact, the aunt's silence becomes a defining characteristic in one of the possible versions of her story. The narrator suggests, "She kept the man's name to herself throughout her labor and dying; she did not accuse him that he be punished with her. To save her inseminator's name she gave silent birth" (11). In this moment, the narrator considers the possibility that silence can be a conscious act, perhaps one of defiance as worthy as any other method of protest.

While the aunt's direct words remain inaccessible, Kingston focuses our attention on her body across multiple versions of her story: a mole ordaining unhappiness that the aunt digs out with a needle; a tendril of hair she lets fall from her bun in an act of individuality; and, of course, when Brave Orchid "found her and her baby plugging up the family well" (5). While the narrator emphasizes recovering the aunt's story to overcome the problem of her silence, Kingston quietly chronicles her body. Critic Jennifer Griffith positions the "no name aunt" as one of many uncanny bodies falsely inscribed by patriarchal codes. Recovering these traumatized bodies, she observes, instigates a "renewed connection between body and voice."[5] Even if this dead woman does not speak, her traumatized body may be her voice in another guise, a metonymic stand-in.

Throughout this book I have focused on the corporeality of dead women talking. Their bodies are often uncanny and unpleasant, as opposed to the disembodied voices and ethereal spirits of many ghost stories. Kingston's memoirs are filled with foul, rank, and defiled bodies, from the bloated body plugging up the family well to the maddeningly frail Moon Orchid whose body cannot withstand the heat and physical demands of the family laundry. At the heart of the memoirs is a damaged body. In a defining moment, Brave Orchid cuts the narrator's tongue, an act initially perceived as a violation. But Brave Orchid explains, "I cut it so that you would not be tongue-tied. Your tongue would be able to move in any language. You'll be able to speak languages that are completely different from one another" (164). With a cut tongue and ugly voice that "quacks like a pressed duck" (192), the narrator's body is as jarring and uncanny as many of the dead women talking in American literature. Critic Jeehyun Lim argues that the book "grapples with the question of what it means for a racialized body to acquire a language."[6] She contends, "Mutedness has served as a protective shield, but it turns into a stress factor the moment the narrator realizes that muteness is frowned upon by her teachers."[7]

By the end of *The Woman Warrior*, violated bodies and silent figures are unexpected sites of empowerment. The narrator learns that the demand for others to speak may be an imposition, perhaps even a violent one, such as when she tortures a silent classmate over the course of ten excruciating pages. "I hated the fragility" (176), the narrator reports, but no matter how much pain or shame she inflicts on her classmate, she will not speak. "Quarts of tears but no words" (179), she reports. In these spaces of silence, Kingston's work with voice happens somewhat out of sight, a magician's sleight of hand. The audience tends more to the spectacular and obvious on display—ghosts, crazy women, cut tongues, and communist revolutions. Meanwhile, voice may not be the best go-to solution, contrary to decades of feminist and minority thought linking it to agency, visibility, and empowerment. For the no-name aunt and the silent classmate, muteness may be a conscious refusal to do the work of bringing justice to the community that rendered them pariahs. If they speak, the community is off the hook. It need not diagnose and change systems that render these women speechless in the first place.

Stiff Corpses and Silent Women; or, My Mother Is Not a Cadaver

If the dead remain silent, what are descendants to do with the corpses in our midst? We need guidance in encounters with the dead where they should not be—floating in the family well, gossiping on the front porch, demanding sweets in the kitchen, riding on a wagon in the middle of July, standing on a church roof, hanging out by a hospital bed. What are we to do if they won't explain how they came to be there?

In her plucky bestselling book *Stiff*, Mary Roach traces "the curious lives of human cadavers." She explores willed body programs, anatomy labs, human crash test dummies, medicinal cannibalism, outdoor decomposition laboratories, and other ways dead bodies find a vocation. The line between person and cadaver is necessarily bright, she discovers. She opines, "You are a person and then you cease to be a person, and a cadaver takes your place." That is why Roach reflects on seeing her own mother's dead body and concludes, "My mother was never a cadaver; no person ever is."[8] The moments that are most creepy, and therefore most prone to Roach's gruesome humor, are when a dead body breaches that line between person and cadaver, such as when plastic surgeons attend seminars to practice their craft on well-preserved human heads severed just below chin level, assembled on folding tables buffet-style, and draped with lavender cloths—because that color is, apparently, soothing.[9]

Roach's subject may seem morbidly whimsical, perhaps closer kin to Ripley's *Believe It or Not!* than the literary or social justice endeavors examined throughout this book. Nonetheless, the same anxiety rears its head, so to speak: whether to recognize the dead as one of our own. "The problem with cadavers," Roach reasons with deadpan clarity, "is that they look so much like people." Roach finds that, to cope, those who work with cadavers—medical students, researchers, morticians—develop a variety of strategies either to objectify the dead body, such as seeing it as wax (the preferred method of one woman who severs the heads for cosmetic surgery seminars), or to honor the dead, such as giving them real names or holding a funeral service (a voluntary tradition of human anatomy students at the University of California, San Francisco, Medical School).[10] Such strategies would be less successful for a speaking cadaver. No matter how much Sethe's community ignores Beloved, the dead woman still wants. No matter how much Roy Cohn wishes Ethel Rosenberg would stay mum, she heckles. To quiet these dead women talking, the community cannot simply objectify or honor the individual dead body. Instead, the community must seek justice.

In *The Political Lives of Dead Bodies*, anthropologist Katherine Verdery asks, "What is it about a corpse that seems to invite its use in politics, especially moments of major transformation?" One reason, she explains, is the corporeality of the corpse, the fact that it is "indisputably there" as opposed to, say, intangible legal claims to property. It is not only corpses' mere materiality but also their role as repositories of symbolic capital as we endow them with grand associations, what she terms "cosmic" concerns.[11] Verdery turns to the bodies of key political leaders, such as Lenin on display in Red Square in Moscow, the ouster of Stalin's body from that mausoleum in 1961, and the debates about the fate of Lenin's corpse in a postsocialist world after 1989. Cadavers can help a society navigate times of great transition; Verdery explains, "By repositioning them, restoring them to honor, expelling them, or simply drawing attention to them, their exit from one grave and descent into another mark a change in social visibilities and values, part of the larger process of postsocialist transformation."[12]

Scholars Sarah Webster Goodwin and Elisabeth Bronfen suggest that the authority of a corpse comes from its intractable silence, the finality and therefore "the sense of nothing more to say."[13] As a prime example, they cite images of the Holocaust's infamous body count. In its silence, the mute corpse can also serve as a projection screen or ventriloquist dummy for the living. But when the dead speak for themselves—when dead women talk—this is neither reverence nor ventriloquism. It is a moment when the community must confront those they might rather remain silent. Instead of a prop to help a community navigate times of great change, as Verdery would have it, speaking cadavers bring social change to a community, whether they welcome it or not.

Cadavers are at the center of how we make meaning out of death, especially via highly orchestrated funeral and burial practices. Sociologist Clive Seale suggests that problems of death are particularly modern because explanations move from the religious to the medical sphere, which locates death not in theological narratives but rather in the body itself. He writes, "Social and cultural life involves turning away from the inevitability of death, which is contained in the fact of our embodiment, and toward life."[14] Mourning practices, he concludes, are attempts at resurrection because they locate a piece of the lost body within the griever's living self.[15] For such practices to work, the body must be put away, interred, removed from the living community. When a dead woman talks—or drowns herself in the family well—she demands a space of her own in the living community and its unjust world. Such cadavers demand a different kind of mourning or burial practice, one that will result in an alignment of justice and silence.

Toward a Just Silence

Kingston helps us ask why a dead woman might not talk, even if hers is a story of urgent injustice. At the end of "No Name Woman," the narrator avers, "There is more to this silence: they want me to participate in her punishment. And I have" (16). Worried primarily about her own complicity, the narrator does not pause to consider the wishes of the dead aunt. She celebrates voice for the sake of voice in order to counteract "the family's deliberately forgetting her" (16). But voice and collective memory are no panacea. Like Addie Bundren's cultivated aloneness, the aunt leaves behind no sign that she seeks or would even welcome public voice. Just as Addie felt profoundly violated when motherhood robs her of her void, the aunt has no recourse to privacy and aloneness. Marriage and motherhood breach Addie's void so that only death offers her a respite and a path toward her own story. So too, death offers resolution for the aunt, even if, or perhaps because, her "spite suicide" (16) poisons the community left behind.

Kingston tells a story about what it means to be a second-generation immigrant in a nation with profound ambivalence about assimilation, while making room for ambivalence about ethnic heritage, too. But in this task, the narrator violates her aunt anew if she ventriloquizes her posthumously. While the narrator imagines the no-name aunt as a hungry ghost, the aunt escapes the task of enforcing or breaking cultural traditions passed down through talk-story. That responsibility is up to descendants.

The answer is not necessarily to exorcise ghosts. "I have learned that writing does not make ghosts go away," Kingston explains in an interview about women and memory. "[T]he reader might be walking along very well in the present, but the past breaks through and changes and enlightens the present, and vice versa. The reason that we remember a past moment at all is that our present-day life is still a working-out of a similar situation."[16] It bears mentioning that the burden of remembering belongs to the living, not the dead. For the most part, Kingston wants us to value the concept of voice as a central conceit that can counteract unjust taboos and tell stories a community would rather not hear. But silence has a role to play in restoring dignity and autonomy to violated women. Perhaps the unnarrated story is the most fitting response to the decision by No Name Woman's community to turn her into a living ghost, a cast-out woman living among them. In other words, perhaps it is an injustice to ask this dead woman to talk.

Can silence, the bugaboo of so much feminist and minority politics, be allied with social justice? In the words of the slogan made popular by the AIDS Coalition to Unleash Power (ACT UP), SILENCE = DEATH. In fact, since the 1970s, the discourse of silence and voice has permeated feminist and minority recovery projects, which fueled the rallying cry to "break the silence." The logical answer, in the words of iconic black feminist poet-critic Audre Lorde, is to transform silence into language and action.[17] For critic King-Kok Cheung, silence in "No Name Woman" is a problem because it is imposed as a direct result of an oppressive social order that punishes subjects who defy social conventions.[18] Though the discourse of silence no longer holds the critical cachet it once did, the project of uncovering buried voices and listening to previously unheard groups remains a priority. In *Raising the Dead*, for example, Sharon Patricia Holland attempts to "harass the border between the living and the dead,"[19] especially because that porous boundary is often commensurate with the lines of power. For Holland, marginalized figures occupy a queer, black space equivalent to the cacophonous universe of the dead. In that vein, if we learn to raise the dead in literature, perhaps we can do the same for the socially dead who walk among us, what Russ Castronovo calls our necro citizens.

All this is to say, we have come to value voice and demonize silence. But this may be hasty. There may be something valuable to learn from mute corpses. We should ask what undue burdens we place on the dead if we ask them to speak. Perhaps Addie Bundren has it right in her distrust of words and desire for aloneness in death. To do her honor is to let her leave the perpetual present so that she can finally be laid to rest. While Faulkner conspicuously leaves the moment of her burial unnarrated, our role is to use our own voices to fill the silence, to eulogize the dead in a way that seeks just resolutions to the circumstances that lead to their unjust deaths. Our goal may be to recalibrate the equation so that SILENCE = JUSTICE. If we learn to recognize silence as a right of the dead, we restore to the realm of the living the obligation to seek justice. We learn not to punt such questions for the dead to field. In seeking justice, we must honor the right of the dead to remain silent.

NOTES

INTRODUCTION: Recognizing the Dead

1. C. Davis, "Can the Dead Speak to Us?," esp. 88–89.
2. Morrison, *Beloved*, 247. Further references are given parenthetically in text.
3. Castronovo, *Necro Citizenship*, 4.
4. Ibid., xii.
5. Patterson, *Slavery and Social Death*. Cf. V. Brown's use of Patterson in *The Reaper's Garden*.
6. Scholarship on citizenship and the body is large and diverse. See, for example, Berlant, *Queen of America*; Bosniak, *Citizen and the Alien*; M. Ngai, *Impossible Subjects*.
7. J. Roach, *Cities of the Dead*, xi.
8. Cubilié, *Women Witnessing Terror*, xii.
9. See Fuss, "Corpse Poem"; Hotz, *Literary Remains*; Jermyn, "You Can't Keep"; Kibbie, "The Estate, The Corpse"; Kristeva, *Powers of Horror*; Pile, "Revenge of the Exquisite Corpse"; Piper, "Signifying Corpse"; Presner, "'Fabrication of Corpses'"; Schwab, "Multiple Lives"; Schwenger, "Corpsing the Image"; Stockton, "Erotic Corpse"; Tambling, *Becoming Posthumous*; Zimmerman, "Psychoanalysis and the Corpse."
10. Holloway, *Passed On*.
11. Kammen, *Digging Up the Dead*.
12. See Brown and Burdett, *Victorian Supernatural*; Carpenter and Kolmar, *Haunting the House of Fiction*.
13. Gentile, "Supernatural Transmissions," 208. See also Carpenter and Kolmar, *Haunting the House of Fiction*.
14. Brogan, *Cultural Haunting*, 11.
15. Gordon, *Ghostly Matters*.
16. Holland, *Raising the Dead*. See also JanMohamed, *Death-Bound Subject*; Su, "Ghosts of Essentialism"; Wardi, *Arc of Mourning*.
17. V. Brown, *Reaper's Garden*.
18. Mbembé, "Necropolitics."
19. Adorno and Horkheimer, "On the Theory of Ghosts," 215.
20. See Fuss, "Corpse Poem"; Raymond, *Posthumous Voice*; Worthington, "Posthumous Posturing"; Caldwell, "Strange Death"; Perdigao and Pizzato, *Death in the American Texts*.

21. See Selley, “Satisfied Shivering”; Worthington, “Posthumous Posturing”; Zeitlin, *Phantom Heroine*.

22. Fuss, “Corpse Poem,” 2–3.

23. See C. Davis, “Can the Dead Speak to Us?”; Dufallo, *Ghosts of the Past*; Fuss, “Corpse Poem”; Johnson, “Apostrophe, Animation”; Kneale, “Romantic Aversions”; Loeffelholz, “Poetry, Slavery, and Personification.”

24. Raymond, *Posthumous Voice*, 13.

25. See Lacan, “L’Éclat d’Antigone,” 305–9.

26. Young, *Black Frankenstein*.

27. Blaine, *Death in the Novel*, 107.

28. Dever, *Death and the Mother*.

29. Bronfen, *Over Her Dead Body*. See also Klaver, *Images of the Corpse*.

30. See Broydo, “Attack of the Celebrity.” Cf. Caruth, “Claims of the Dead” for a more literary meditation.

31. I follow the numbering system in *The Poems of Emily Dickinson*, edited by R. W. Franklin.

32. Socarides, “Poetics of Interruption.”

33. Goodwin and Bronfen, *Death and Representation*, 20.

34. Raymond, *Posthumous Voice*, 22, 24.

35. Vendler, *Dickinson*, 268.

36. Raymond, *Posthumous Voice*, esp. 12.

37. Goodwin and Bronfen, *Death and Representation*, 6.

38. Freud writes, “It often happens that neurotic men state that to them there is something uncanny about the female genitals. But what they find uncanny [‘unhomely’] is actually the entrance to man’s old ‘home,’ the place where everyone once lived.” Freud, *The Uncanny*, 151.

39. Raymond also suggests that Plath is rewriting William Butler Yeats’s “Lapis Lazuli.” Raymond, *Posthumous Voice*, 10.

40. Goodwin and Bronfen, *Death and Representation*, 7.

41. Ibid., 14.

42. Fuss, “Corpse Poem,” 2, 6.

43. Ibid., 13.

44. Tanner, *Lost Bodies*, esp. 211–12.

45. A. Friedman, *Fictional Death*, 148.

46. Perdigao, *Modernist Entombment*.

CHAPTER ONE: Dead Woman Wailing

1. Lubiano, *House That Race Built*.

2. Rosenheim and Rachman, *American Face*, xii, xx.

3. See, for example, Kennedy and Weissberg, *Romancing the Shadow*.

4. Whalen, *Poe and the Masses*, esp. 76–108. See also McGill, *Culture of Reprinting*, esp. 187–217.

5. Poe, "Fall of the House of Usher," 322. Further references are given parenthetically in text.

6. For more on Poe and publishing, see McGill, *Culture of Reprinting*, esp. 141–86.

7. Savoye argues for Scotland. See his "Sinking under Iniquity."

8. Bergland, *National Uncanny*.

9. L. Jackson, " 'Behold Our Literary Mohawk, Poe,' " esp. 97–99.

10. Ibid., 113. For more on Poe's depictions of American Indians, see Etter, " 'Tawdry Physical Affrightments.' "

11. Faherty, " 'Legitimate Sources,' " 42.

12. Poe, *Collected Works*, 3:55.

13. Ibid., 56.

14. Weekes, "Poe's Feminine Ideal," esp. 149.

15. Royle, *Uncanny*, 1.

16. Freud, *Uncanny*, 124.

17. Ibid., 148.

18. Jentsch, "Psychology of the Uncanny."

19. D. Henderson, "Love and Fear of Death," 69. On this gothic trope in African American fiction, see Shockley, "Buried Alive."

20. Dayan, "Amorous Bondage," 202.

21. Weekes, "Poe's Feminine Ideal," 148, 150.

22. Ibid., 151.

23. Dayan, "Amorous Bondage," 183, 180.

24. Norman, "Historical Uncanny." The ensuing discussion of the uncanny draws from this piece.

25. Freud, *Uncanny*, esp. 152–54.

26. For a classic reading along these lines, see Robinson, "Order and Sentience." See also Coss, "Art of Sentience."

27. Dayan, "Poe, Persons, and Property," 107, 114–18.

28. Ibid., 119.

29. Ibid., 150–51.

30. Freud, *Uncanny*, 156–57, 158.

31. Goddu, *Gothic America*, esp. 88–93.

32. Cassuto, *Inhuman Race*, xv.

33. Ibid., 161.

34. See also Morrison, *Playing in the Dark*, esp. 57–58.

35. See Kaplan, *Anarchy of Empire*, esp. her discussion of Puerto Rico as officially "foreign to the United States in a domestic sense" (3).

36. Kaplan, " 'Left Alone in America,' " 17.

37. Levine, *Dislocating Race and Nation*, esp. 6–7.

38. Brooks and Warren, *Understanding Fiction*, 202.

39. Martin, "Imagination," 194.

40. Bieganowski, "Self-Consuming Narrator," esp. 182–85.

41. Peeples, "Poe's 'Constructiveness,' " 180.

42. Castronovo, *Necro Citizenship*, 148–49.

43. G. Brown, "Poetics of Extinction," 331.

44. See, for example, Greven, *Men beyond Desire*, esp. 152.

CHAPTER TWO: Dead Woman Dictating

1. James, *Turn of the Screw* (1908 New York edition), 174. Further references are given parenthetically in text.

2. See Smajic, "Trouble with Ghost-Seeing."

3. Robbins, "'They Don't Much Count,'" 378.

4. Ibid., 379, 381.

5. Caruth, "Claims of the Dead," 420. Caruth considers both actual and legal death, as in the doctrine of *civil death*. In either case, to restore property rights is equivalent to revivifying a subject in the eyes of the law.

6. Air Transportation Safety and System Stabilization Act (49 USC 40101).

7. Ripstein, "Philosophy of Tort Law," 658.

8. Coleman, "Practice of Corrective Justice," 72.

9. Over 98% of those eligible elected to participate. U.S. Justice Department, "September 11th."

10. Coleman, "Practice of Corrective Justice," 66–67.

11. Sperling, *Posthumous Interests*, 4–5.

12. "These rights may exist for at least as long as the deceased is still 'present' (symbolically existent) among the living," he argues, "but they may also exist for longer or shorter periods of time depending on the content of the interests whose protection and promotion is sought." Ibid., 236–37.

13. L. Friedman, *Dead Hands*, 181. See also Madoff, *Immortality and the Law*.

14. It is the parents who die in India in the 1898 version serialized in *Collier's*.

15. L. Friedman, *Dead Hands*, 180.

16. Robbins, *Servant's Hand*, 202.

17. Rowe, *Other Henry James*, 25.

18. Lynch, "Spectral Politics," 67–68.

19. Cole, "Hideous Obscure."

20. Other examples are on pages 171, 186, 223, 239, and 247.

21. On the circumstances of writing the manuscript, see Esch and Warren, *Turn of the Screw*, 87–89.

22. Julie Rivkin fashions a portrait of James "of displaced agency and intermediaries, of deputies, delegates, and substitutes." See her *False Positions*, 2. Psychoanalytic critic Shoshana Felman famously lights in particular on the letters (both epistolary and alphabetic) as James's mode of doubling, projection, and deferral. See her "Turning the Screw of Interpretation," 94–207.

23. Beidler, *Case Studies*, viii.

24. Banta, *Henry James and the Occult*, 114.

25. Ibid., 117.

26. See, for example, Beidler, *Ghosts, Demons*.

27. See, for example, Lustig, *James and the Ghostly*, 106–89.
28. Bann, "Ghostly Hands," 664.
29. Beidler, *Case Studies*, 152.

CHAPTER THREE: Dead Woman Rotting

1. Kincaid, "As Me and Addie," 586.
2. Ibid., 592.
3. Faulkner, *As I Lay Dying*, 172. Further references are given parenthetically in text.
4. See, for example, Bergman, "'this was the answer'"; Fowler, "Matricide."
5. For example, see Sheri Benstock's forum response and Stephen Ross's reply in *PMLA* for a skirmish over structuralist accounts of Faulkner's use of voice and language.
6. Blaine, "Abjection of Addie."
7. Gwin, *Feminine and Faulkner*, 153–54.
8. Liman, "Addie in No-Man's Land," 41.
9. Edwards, "Extremities of the Body," 745.
10. Schwab, "Multiple Lives," 212.
11. Perdigao, *Modernist Entombment*, 43–51. For a similar earlier project, see A. Friedman, *Fictional Death*, including his reading of Addie Bundren, 81, 266.
12. Baldanzi and Schlabach, "What Remains?," 38, 40.
13. Madoff, *Immortality and the Law*, 2.
14. Ibid., 6.
15. Ibid., 16–17.
16. Ibid., 2.
17. Holloway, *Private Bodies*, 139.
18. Ibid., 148.
19. Ibid., 137.
20. Madoff, *Immortality and the Law*, 13.
21. Hewson, "'My Children,'" 551.
22. Cohen, *Body Worth Defending*, 149, trans. Cohen.
23. Ibid., 149.
24. Holloway, *Private Bodies*, 9.
25. Ibid., 2–5.
26. See my "Historical Uncanny," 445.
27. Matthews, "Preface," 4.
28. Slankard, "'No Such Thing,'" 11.
29. Duck, *Nation's Region*.

CHAPTER FOUR: Dead Woman Cursing

1. A. Walker, *Mothers' Gardens*, 93–116. Further references are given parenthetically in text.
2. Ibid., 338–42. Further references are given parenthetically in text.

3. Washington, *Our Mothers, Our Powers*, 105.

4. Wall, *Worrying the Line*, 227–28.

5. Like Hurston biographer Robert Hemenway and other scholars, I borrow this phrase from Hurston in *Their Eyes Were Watching God*, 48.

6. On the trope of the South as a region outside national time, see Duck, *Nation's Region*.

7. On this last point, see Holloway, *Passed On*, esp. 15–20.

8. Ibid., 123.

9. *Mother Jones*, September/October 1982, 20–21.

10. Wall, "On Freedom," esp. 284–85.

11. Hurston, *Mules and Men*, 197–98. A. Walker also embeds the curse within her story "The Revenge of Hannah Kemhuff," collected in *In Love and Trouble*, 60–80.

12. See Washington, *Our Mothers, Our Powers*, 91.

13. Hurston, *Mules and Men*, esp. 191–205. On the difficulty of constructing Leveau's biography, see Allured, "Evaluating a New Orleans Icon."

14. See Lutz, "Save Me from the Fall."

15. Danet and Bococh, "Whoever Alters This."

16. See Cryer, "Magic in Ancient Syria," 118–19.

17. See Brichto, *Problem of the Curse*; Linafelt, "Undecidability of Barak"; Urbrock, "Blessing and Curse."

18. On the classical origins of the curse, see Gager, *Curse Tablets*.

19. Ogden, "Binding Spells," 10. See also Luck, *Arcana Mundi*, 48–49.

20. Thiselton, "Supposed Power of Words." I thank Tod Linafelt for this reference.

21. On how to read such texts, see Foley, *How to Read an Oral Poem*; Ong, *Orality and Literacy*.

22. Danet and Bogoch, "Whoever Alters This," 132.

23. Ogden, "Binding Spells," 18. See also Ogden, *Magic, Witchcraft, and Ghosts*, 210.

24. Danet and Bogoch, "Whoever Alters This."

25. Greenblatt, *Learning to Curse*, 25.

26. See, for example, Nair, *Caliban's Curse*; Coutinho, "Learning How to Curse."

27. Díaz, *Oscar Wao*, 1–2.

28. Newton and Stacey, "Learning Not to Curse," 66. They similarly praise the work of James Clifford.

29. Lioi, "End to Cosmic Loneliness."

30. On the essay as open-ended, see Adorno, "Essay as Form"; Kauffman, "Skewed Path"; Lopate, *Art of the Personal Essay*, esp. xxxvii–xxxviii; Norman, *American Protest Essay*, esp. 37–39, 124–27; Wall, *Worrying the Line*, 211.

31. Laurie McMillan points to *In Search of Our Mothers' Gardens* as an example of the social justice uses of autobiographical criticism. McMillan, "Telling a Critical Story." Cf. Allan, "Voice of One's Own."

32. Wall, *Worrying the Line*, 211. See also Mittlefehldt, "'Weaponry of Choice.'"

CHAPTER FIVE: Dead Woman Wanting

1. Morrison, *Beloved*, 149. Further references are given parenthetically in text.

2. Christian, McDowell, and McKay, "Conversation." On Beloved as the return of the collective repressed, see also M. Henderson, "Re-Membering the Body."

3. Schweik, *Ugly Laws*, 142.

4. Qtd. in ibid., 1–2.

5. Scarry, *On Beauty*, esp. 96–97.

6. Holland, *Raising the Dead*, 3–4.

7. See for representative examples Gordon, *Ghostly Matters*; Handley, "House a Ghost Built"; Holland, *Raising the Dead*; Krumholz, "Ghosts of Slavery"; Raynaud, "Shifting Shapes of Memory." For a full discussion of how critics categorize the Beloved character, see Plasa, *Columbia Critical Guides*, 57–85.

8. Holland, *Raising the Dead*, 4.

9. Harris, "Escaping Slavery."

10. See, for example, Brogan, *Cultural Haunting*, esp. 64–92; Gordon, *Ghostly Matters*, 181–83; M. Henderson, "Re-Membering the Body."

11. Harris, "Woman, Thy Name Is Demon."

12. Caruth, "Claims of the Dead."

13. For more on citizenship as a contested category with overlapping definitions, see Bosniak, "Citizenship."

14. Krumholz, "Ghosts of Slavery," 116.

15. E. Cohen, *Body Worth Defending*, 70.

16. C. Henderson, *Scarring the Black Body*, 92.

17. Darling, "In the Realm of Responsibility," 5.

18. Scarry, *On Beauty*, 57.

19. See Pocock, "Ideal of Citizenship," esp. 33.

20. Scarry, *On Beauty*, 100.

21. On *Beloved* as a healing narrative, see, for example, Krumholz, "Ghosts of Slavery," esp. 110–14, 117–19.

22. Scarry, *On Beauty*, 69.

23. Ibid., 112.

24. Nussbaum, *From Disgust to Humanity*, xvii.

25. Ibid., xvii.

26. Rushdy, "Daughters Signifyin(g) History," esp. 37–38. See also Byerman, *Remembering the Past*, 28–37.

27. Reinhardt, *Who Speaks*, 42.

28. A. Friedman, *Fictional Death*, 277. Friedman transcribes this as a quote, but it is his paraphrase of the final passage.

29. Reinhardt, *Who Speaks*, 117.

30. Ibid., 43.

31. Rich, *Poems*, 148–51.

32. I thank Rose Miola for this insight.

33. See, for example, Spillers, "'All the Things'"; Tate, *Psychoanalysis and Black Novels*, esp. 119.

CHAPTER SIX: Dead Woman Heckling

1. Kushner, *Angels in America*, I.3.v. Further references are given parenthetically in text.
2. S. Ngai, *Ugly Feelings*, 9.
3. Ibid., 10.
4. Cadden, "Strange Angel," 100.
5. Freedman, "Angels, Monsters, and Jews," 93.
6. Posnock, "Roy Cohn in America," 64.
7. Ibid., 66.
8. W. Schneir and M. Schneir, *Invitation*.
9. See Green, "Suffering Body."
10. Solomon, "Wrestling with *Angels*," 129–30.
11. Murphy, "Vows, Boast, and Taunts," 105.
12. Brinkman and Kirschner, *Dealing with People*, viii, 47.
13. Phillips and Alyn, *How to Deal*, 17–18.
14. Kowalski, *Complaining*, 164.
15. Ibid., 179.
16. Palca and Lichtman, *Annoying*, 9.
17. "Are You Annoying?," www.npr.org.
18. Palca and Lichtman, *Annoying*, 17.
19. See his "Some Questions about Tolerance," *Thinking*, 41–54.
20. Cadden, "Strange Angel," 102.
21. Solomon, "Wrestling with *Angels*," 128.
22. Neville, *Press*, 133.
23. Shewey, "Kushner's Sexy Ethics," 30.
24. Griswold, *Forgiveness*, 39.
25. N. Cohen, "Wrestling with Angels," 228.
26. Cadden, "Strange Angel," 102.
27. Lazare, *On Apology*, 168.
28. Posnock, "Roy Cohn in America," 72.
29. Konstan, *Before Forgiveness*, 11.
30. Ibid., 41.
31. Ibid., 73–77.
32. Cunningham, "Thinking about Fabulousness," 63.
33. See Pollack and Metress, *Emmett Till*.
34. See Metress, "'No Justice,'" 102.
35. Griswold, *Forgiveness*, 116.
36. Ibid., 209.

37. Meeropol, *Rosenberg Letters*, 704; presumably a note to Saul D. Miller, Ethel's psychiatrist.

38. Thorburn, "Rosenberg Letters," 180.

39. Thorburn cites Ilene Philipson, *Ethel Rosenberg: Beyond the Myth* (New York: Franklin Watts, 1988), 324–25, 337–38.

40. Meeropol, *Rosenberg Letters*, 585. For clarity, all quotations include Meeropol's notes as silent edits.

41. For an account of press coverage, see Neville, *Press*.

42. Meeropol, *Rosenberg Letters*, 488.

43. Ibid., 597.

44. Kushner, *Thinking*, 5.

45. Ibid., 9.

CHAPTER SEVEN: Dead Women Gossiping

1. Kushner, *Angles in America*, I.1.vii.

2. Costello, "Kenan beyond the Final Frontier."

3. Muñoz, *Cruising Utopia*. For more on queer futurity, see also Freeman, *Queer Temporalities*.

4. Castiglia and Reed, *If Memory Serves*, esp. 14–31.

5. Edelman, *No Future*.

6. Stockton, *Queer Child*.

7. Larsen, *Passing*, 152.

8. Ibid., 152.

9. Harris, *Power of the Porch*, 107.

10. Du Bois, *Souls of Black Folk*, 8.

11. Kenan, *Let the Dead*, 3. Further references are given parenthetically in text.

12. Fabi, *Passing and the Rise*, 5.

13. Matt. 8:21–22; Luke 9:59–60.

14. Elam, *Souls of Mixed Folk*, 98. Elam discusses Danzy Senna's *Caucasia* (1998), Colson Whitehead's *The Intuitionist* (1999), and Philip Roth's *The Human Stain* (2001).

15. Ginsberg, *Passing*.

16. Pfeiffer, *Racepassing*.

17. McDowell, Introduction, xxvi.

18. Butler, "Passing, Queering." See also Barbara Johnson, "Quicksands of the Self," for a psychoanalytic reading of Larsen's work.

19. Somerville, *Queering the Color Line*.

20. McDowell, Introduction, esp. xxx.

21. Edelman, *No Future*, 4.

22. Stockton, *Queer Child*, 11.

23. Holloway, *Passed On*, 7.

24. On the past in contemporary African American fiction, see Byerman, *Remem-*

bering the Past; Rushdy, *Remembering Generations*. On death in African American literature, see Castronovo, *Necro Citizenship*; Wardi, *Arc of Mourning*.

25. Holland, *Raising the Dead*. See also JanMohamed, *Death-Bound Subject*.

26. Holloway, *Passed On*, 3.

27. Stockton, *Queer Child*, 37, emphasis in original.

28. Harris, *Power of the Porch*, 126.

29. Freud, *Uncanny*, 124.

30. Harris, *Power of the Porch*, xii.

31. Ibid., 109.

32. Stockton, *Beautiful Bottom*, esp. 149–76.

33. Holloway, *Passed On*, 2.

34. Goodwin and Bronfen, *Death and Representation*, 4.

35. Harris, "Transformations," 161.

36. A good example is Patricia Hill Collins's sweeping narrative of gender and segregation from the Jim Crow to post–civil rights era (*Black Sexual Politics*, 61–85).

37. Appiah, "Rooted Cosmopolitanism."

38. M. Ross, *Manning the Race*.

39. M. Ross, "Beyond the Closet."

40. Hovis, "'I Contain Multitudes,'"103. Alternatively, Hunt thinks of *Walking on Water* as a travelogue that updates Du Bois's *The Souls of Black Folk*. See Hunt, "Conversation," 420.

41. See Holland, "(Pro)Creating Imaginative Spaces"; McCoy; "Rescuing the Black Homosexual"; McRuer, "Queer Locations" and "Visitation of Difference"; Tucker, "Gay Identity"; Wester, "Haunting and Haunted Queerness." Most focus primarily on Kenan's novel *A Visitation of Spirits*, though Tucker also attends to Kenan's short fiction.

42. Jones, *Race Mixing*, 291.

43. Tettenborn, "'But What If,'" 261.

44. Hunt, "Conversation," 414. On a similar theme, see Baker, *I Don't Hate the South*, among many others.

45. Nagel, *Contemporary American Short Story Cycle*, 255. Nagel discusses Louise Erdrich's *Love Medicine* (1984) in particular.

CHAPTER EIGHT: Dead Women Healing

1. Castillo, *So Far from God*, epigraph. Further references are given parenthetically in text.

2. Butler, *Frames of War*, 2.

3. Ibid., 1.

4. Pérez, "Castillo as Santera," 62.

5. For more on magical realism, including its definition, its political capacity, and the problems of pairing it against Western ontologies, see Christian, *Show and Tell*; Zamora and Faris, *Magical Realism*.

6. Aldama, *Brown on Brown*, 94.

7. Platt, "Ecocritical Chicana Literature," 79.
8. Carminero-Santangelo, "'Pleas of the Desperate,'" 84.
9. Pérez, "Castillo as Santera," 59.
10. Torres, *Conversations*, 154.
11. See, for example, Pérez, "Castillo as Santera," 66–68.
12. Butler, *Frames of War*, 38.
13. Mbembé, "Necropolitics," 1.
14. Butler, *Frames of War*, 2–3.
15. Ibid., 31.
16. Lanza, "Hearing Voices."
17. Aldama, *Brown on Brown*, 97. For more on healing in the novel, see Stanford, *Bodies in a Broken World*, 137–44, 158–70. On the lesbian as healer and saint, see Morrow, "Queering Chicano/a Narratives."
18. Delgadillo, "Chicana Feminist Resistance," 888.
19. Warner, *Publics and Counterpublics*, 7.
20. Ibid., 12.
21. Ibid., 118–19.
22. Mbembé, "Necropolitics," 40, emphasis in original.
23. Brogan, *Cultural Haunting*, 9.
24. See, for example, Pérez, "Castillo as Santera," 55.
25. For more on Castillo's vision of an alternative community space, see Michael, *New Visions of Community*; Rodriguez, "Chicana/o Fiction."
26. Warner, *Publics and Counterpublics*, 16.
27. Saeta, "*MELUS* Interview," 147.
28. Butler, *Frames of War*, 31.

CHAPTER NINE: Dead Woman Coming of Age

1. Sebold, *Lovely Bones*, 19. Further references are given parenthetically in text.
2. Alber, "Impossible Storyworlds," 79, 89.
3. Heinze, "Violations of Mimetic Epistemology," 287, 289.
4. See Poole, "Body/Rituals," esp. 246.
5. Abel, Hirsch, and Langland, *Voyage In*.
6. Fraiman, *Unbecoming Women*, x.
7. Rishoi, *From Girl to Woman*, 8.
8. Ibid., 63.
9. Bliss, "'Share Moments,'" 877.
10. Tanner, *Lost Bodies*, esp. 219.
11. Cassuto, *Hard-Boiled Sentimentality*, 269.
12. Ibid., 270.
13. E. Cohen, *Body Worth Defending*, 70.
14. See, for example, Alber, "Impossible Storyworlds," 90; Heinze, "Violations of Mimetic Epistemology," 289.

15. Bliss, "'Share Moments,'" 878.
16. Alleva, "Restless Spirits," 18.
17. Bliss, "'Share Moments,'" 866.
18. Ibid., 879.
19. Ibid., 863.
20. Millard, *Coming of Age*, 1–2.
21. Rishoi, *From Girl to Woman*, 9.
22. Reddy, "Race and American Crime Fiction," 135.
23. Cassuto, *Hard-Boiled Sentimentality*, 266.
24. Walton and Jones, *Detective Agency*, 4.
25. Sebold, "Oddity of Suburbia," 2.
26. Kakutani, "Power of Love," E1.
27. Bouton, "What Remains," 14.
28. Blais, "For Sebold," 4D.
29. Puig, "Between Book and Film," 2d.
30. Grossman, "Murdered, She Wrote," 62.
31. Bouton, "What Remains," 14.
32. Brailsford, "Shock Waves," 98.
33. Kakutani, "Power of Love," E1.
34. Jurca, *White Diaspora*.
35. Michasiw, "Suburban Gothic," 251.

CHAPTER TEN: Dead Woman Singing

1. Norman, "Historical Uncanny." See also B. Brown, "Reification, Reanimation."
2. Norman, "Jim Crow Faulkner," in *Neo-Segregation Narratives*, 133–54.
3. Ibid., 142.
4. Parks, *Getting Mother's Body*, 192. Further references are given parenthetically in text.
5. Smith, *To Serve the Living*, 79.
6. Carby, "It Jus Be's Dat Way," 476.
7. Collins, *Black Sexual Politics*, 110.
8. Davis, *Blues Legacies*, xv.
9. Ibid., xiii.
10. Carby, "It Jus Be's Dat Way," esp. 479. See also Wall, *Worrying the Line*, for a similar book-length argument, as well as M. Walker, *Down from the Mountaintop*.
11. Smith, *To Serve the Living*, 17–18.
12. Ibid., 19–20.
13. J. Jackson, "Little Black Magic," 400–401.
14. For the seminal work, see Patterson, *Slavery and Social Death*.
15. JanMohamed, *Death-Bound Subject*.
16. Holland, *Raising the Dead*.

17. Kammen, *Digging Up the Dead*, ix, x. See also Hausladen, *Places for Dead Bodies*.
18. Ibid., 7.
19. Ibid., 187.
20. See ibid., 189.
21. Smith, *To Serve the Living*, 8.
22. Ibid., 8.
23. Ibid., 103.
24. Holloway, *Passed On*, 23.
25. Ibid., 23.
26. Ibid., 42.
27. Ibid., 31.
28. Smith, *To Serve the Living*, 166–67.
29. Ibid., 169.
30. Apel, "Lynching Photographs," esp. 64.
31. Verdery, *Political Lives*, 115. For more on Verdery's work, see the concluding chapter.
32. Qtd. in Kammen, *Digging Up the Dead*, 26. The letter is dated June 11, 1945, and reprinted in *The Correspondence of W. E. B. Du Bois*, ed. Herbert Aptheker (Amherst: University of Massachusetts Press, 1978), 3:41–42.
33. Perdigao, *From Modernist Entombment*.
34. See D'Emilio, *Lost Prophet*.

CHAPTER ELEVEN: When Dead Women Don't Talk

1. Kingston, *Woman Warrior*, 3. Further references are given parenthetically in text.
2. See, for example, Boardman, "Voice and Vision"; Cheung, " 'Don't Tell' "; Danahay, "Breaking the Silence"; Garner, "Breaking Silence"; Morante, "From Silence to Song." Kingston adopts the phrase in Hoy, "To Be Able," 50. For a related discussion of secrecy and silence in literature, see Lewis, *Telling Narratives*.
3. Lee, "Cultural Translation," 114.
4. Sato, "Search for Ghosts," 140–41.
5. Griffith, "Uncanny Spaces," 354.
6. J. Lim, "Cutting the Tongue," 50.
7. Ibid., 52.
8. M. Roach, *Stiff*, 12.
9. Ibid., 19–20.
10. Ibid., 21, 37.
11. Verdery, *Political Lives of Dead Bodies*, 27.
12. Ibid., 19.
13. Goodwin and Bronfen, *Death and Representation*, 9.
14. Seale, *Constructing Death*, 1.

15. Ibid., 193.
16. Rabinowitz, "Eccentric Memories," 67, 68.
17. Lorde, "Transformation of Silence."
18. Cheung, "'Don't Tell.'"
19. Holland, *Raising the Dead*, 9.

BIBLIOGRAPHY

Abel, Elizabeth, Marianne Hirsch, and Elizabeth Langland, eds. *The Voyage In: Fiction of Female Development*. Hanover, NH: University Press of New England, 1983.

Adorno, Theodor W. "The Essay as Form." Translated by Bob Hullot-Kentor and Frederic Will. 1958. Reprinted in *New German Critique* 32 (1984): 151–71.

Adorno, Theodor W., and Max Horkheimer. "On the Theory of Ghosts." Reprinted in *Dialectic of Enlightenment*, 215–17. London: Verso, 1997.

Alber, Jan. "Impossible Storyworlds—and What to Do with Them." *Storyworlds* 1, no. 1 (2009): 79–96.

Aldama, Frederick Luis. *Brown on Brown: Chicano/a Representations of Gender, Sexuality, and Ethnicity*. Austin: University of Texas Press, 2005.

Allan, Tuzyline Jita. "A Voice of One's Own: Implications of Impersonality in the Essays of Virginia Woolf and Alice Walker." In *The Politics of the Essay: Feminist Perspectives*, edited by Ruth-Ellen Boetcher Joeres and Elizabeth Mittman, 131–47. Bloomington: Indiana University Press, 1993.

Alleva, Richard. "Restless Spirits." *Commonweal*, February 12, 2010, 18–19.

Allured, Janet L. "Evaluating a New Orleans Icon: Evidence and Reinterpretation." H-SAWH, March 2006, www.h-net.org.

Amenábar, Alejandro, dir. *The Others*. Dimension Films, 2001.

Andrews, William, and Nellie McKay, eds. *Toni Morrison's "Beloved": A Casebook*. New York: Oxford University Press, 2007.

Apel, Dora. "Lynching Photographs and the Politics of Public Shaming." In *Lynching Photographs*, by Dora Apel and Shawn Michelle Smith, 42–78. Berkeley: University of California Press, 2007.

Appiah, Kwame Anthony. "Rooted Cosmopolitanism." Chap. 6 in *The Ethics of Identity*. Princeton, NJ: Princeton University Press, 2004.

"Are You Annoying? Take the Quiz." www.npr.org/2011/05/17/135703137/you-bug-me-now-science-explains-why. Accessed May 18, 2011.

Baker, Houston. *I Don't Hate the South: Reflections on Faulkner, the Family, and the South*. New York: Oxford University Press, 2007.

Baldanzi, Jessica, and Kyle Schlabach. "What Remains? (De)Composing and (Re) Covering American Identity in *As I Lay Dying* and the Georgia Crematory Scandal." *Journal of the Midwest Modern Language Association* 36, no. 1 (2003): 38–55.

Bann, Jennifer. "Ghostly Hands and Ghostly Agency: The Changing Figure of the Nineteenth-Century Specter." *Victorian Studies* 51, no. 4 (2009): 663–85.

Banta, Martha. *Henry James and the Occult*. Indianapolis: Indiana University Press, 1972.

Beidler, Peter G., ed. *Case Studies in Contemporary Criticism: The Turn of the Screw*. 3rd ed. Boston: Bedford / St. Martin's, 2010.

———. *Ghosts, Demons, and Henry James:* The Turn of the Screw *at the Turn of the Century*. Columbia: University of Missouri Press, 1989.

Benstock, Shari. "'Voice' in *As I Lay Dying*." *PMLA* 94, no. 5 (1979): 957–58.

Bergland, Renée. *The National Uncanny: Indian Ghosts and American Subjects*. Hanover, NH: University Press of New England, 2000.

Bergman, Jill. "'this was the answer to it': Sexuality and Maternity in *As I Lay Dying*." *Mississippi Quarterly* 49, no. 3 (1996): 393–407.

Berlant, Lauren. *The Queen of America Goes to Washington: Essays on Sex and Citizenship*. Durham, NC: Duke University Press, 1997.

Bersani, Leo. "Is the Rectum a Grave?" *October* 43 (1987): 197–222.

Bieganowski, Ronald. "The Self-Consuming Narrator in Poe's 'Ligea' and 'Usher.'" *American Literature* 60, no. 2 (1988): 175–87.

Blaine, Diana York. "The Abjection of Addie and Other Myths of the Maternal in *As I Lay Dying*." *Mississippi Quarterly* 47, no. 3 (1994): 419–39.

———. Introduction to *Death in the Novel*. Special issue, *Studies in the Novel* 32, no. 2 (2000): 107–11.

Blais, Jacqueline. "For Sebold, Life is 'Lucky' and 'Lovely.'" *USA Today*, October 24, 2002, 4D.

Boardman, Kathleen. "Voice and Vision: *The Woman Warrior* in the Writing Class." In S. Lim, *Approaches to Teaching*, 87–92.

Bosniak, Linda. *The Citizen and the Alien: Dilemmas of Contemporary Membership*. Princeton, NJ: Princeton University Press, 2006.

———. "Citizenship." In *The Oxford Handbook of Legal Studies*, edited by Peter Can and Mark Tushnet, 183–201. New York: Oxford University Press, 2003.

Bouton, Katherine. "What Remains." *New York Times Book Review*, July 14, 2002, 14.

Brailsford, Katherine. "Shock Waves." *People*, August 12, 2002, 97–98.

Brichto, H. C. *The Problem of Curse in the Hebrew Bible*. Philadelphia: Scholars Press, 1963.

Brinkman, Rick, and Rick Kirschner. *Dealing with People You Can't Stand: How to Bring Out the Best in People at Their Worst*. Rev. ed. New York: McGraw-Hill, 2002.

Brogan, Kathleen. *Cultural Haunting: Ghosts and Ethnicity in Recent American Literature*. Charlottesville: University of Virginia Press, 1998.

Bronfen, Elisabeth. *Over Her Dead Body: Death, Femininity and the Aesthetic*. New York: Routledge, 1992.

Brooks, Cleanth, and Robert Penn Warren. *Understanding Fiction*. New York: Crofts, 1943.

Brown, Bill. "Reification, Reanimation, and the American Uncanny." *Critical Inquiry* 32, no. 2 (2006): 175–207.

Brown, Gillian. "The Poetics of Extinction." In Rosenheim and Rachman, *American Face*, 330–44.

Brown, Nicola, and Carolyn Burdett, eds. *The Victorian Supernatural*. Cambridge: Cambridge University Press, 2004.

Brown, Vincent. *The Reaper's Garden: Death and Power in the World of Atlantic Slavery*. Cambridge, MA: Harvard University Press, 2008.

Broydo, Leora. "Attack of the Celebrity Vacuum-Cleaner-Salesman Ghouls." *Salon.com*, July, 8, 1997, www.salon.com.

Butler, Judith. *Frames of War: When Is Life Grievable?* London: Verso, 2010.

———. "Passing, Queering: Nella Larsen's Psychoanalytic Challenge." Chap. 6 in *Bodies That Matter: On the Discursive Limits of "Sex."* New York: Routledge, 1993.

Byerman, Keith. *Remembering the Past in Contemporary African American Fiction*. Chapel Hill: University of North Carolina Press, 2005.

Cadden, Michael. "Strange Angel: The Pinklisting of Roy Cohn." In Garber and Walkowitz, *Secret Agents*, 93–105.

Caldwell, Janice McLarren. "The Strange Death of the Animated Cadaver: Changing Conventions in Nineteenth-Century British Anatomical Illustration." *Literature and Medicine* 25, no. 2 (2006): 325–57.

Carby, Hazel. "It Jus Be's Dat Way Sometime: The Sexual Politics of Women's Blues." In *The Jazz Cadence of American Culture*, edited by Robert G. O'Meally, 469–82. New York: Columbia University Press, 1998.

Carminero-Santangelo, Marta. " 'The Pleas of the Desperate': Collective Agency vs. Magical Realism in Ana Castillo's *So Far from God*." *Tulsa Studies in Women's Literature* 24, no. 1 (2005): 81–103.

Carpenter, Lynette, and Wendy K. Kolmar, eds. *Haunting the House of Fiction: Feminist Perspectives on Ghost Stories by American Women*. Knoxville: University of Tennessee Press, 1991.

Caruth, Cathy. "The Claims of the Dead: History, Haunted Property, and the Law." *Critical Inquiry* 28, no. 2 (2002): 419–41.

Cassuto, Leonard. *Hard-Boiled Sentimentality: The Secret History of American Crime Stories*. New York: Columbia University Press, 2009.

———. *The Inhuman Race: The Racial Grotesque in American Literature and Culture*. New York: Columbia University Press, 1996.

Castiglia, Christopher, and Christopher Reed. *If Memory Serves: Gay Men, AIDS, and the Promise of the Queer Past*. Minneapolis: University of Minnesota Press, 2012.

Castillo, Ana. *Massacre of the Dreamers: Essays on Xicanisma*. Albuquerque: University of New Mexico Press, 1994.

———. *So Far from God*. New York: Penguin, 1994.

Castronovo, Russ. *Necro Citizenship: Death, Eroticism, and the Public Sphere in the Nineteenth-Century United States*. Durham, NC: Duke University Press, 2001.

Cheung, King-Kok. " 'Don't Tell': Imposed Silences in *The Color Purple* and *The Woman Warrior*." *PMLA* 103, no. 2 (1988): 162–74.

Christian, Barbara, Deborah McDowell, and Nellie McKay. "A Conversation on Toni Morrison's *Beloved*." In Andrews and McKay, *Toni Morrison's "Beloved,"* 203–20.

Christian, Karen. *Show and Tell: Identity and/as Performance in U.S. Latina/o Fiction*. Albuquerque: University of New Mexico Press, 1997.

Cohen, Ed. *A Body Worth Defending: Immunity, Biopolitics, and the Apotheosis of the Modern Body*. Durham, NC: Duke University Press, 2009.

Cohen, Norman J. "Wrestling with Angels." In Vorlicky, *Tony Kushner*, 217–30.

Cole, Jean Lee. "The Hideous Obscure of Henry James." *American Periodicals* 20, no. 2 (2010): 190–215.

Coleman, Jules L. "The Practice of Corrective Justice." In *Philosophical Foundations of Tort Law*, edited by David G. Owen, 53–72. Oxford: Oxford University Press, 1995.

Collins, Patricia Hill. *Black Sexual Politics: African Americans, Gender, and the New Racism*. New York: Routledge, 2005.

Coss, David L. "Art and Sentience in 'The Fall of the House of Usher.'" *Pleaides* 14, no. 1 (1993): 93–106.

Costello, Brannon. "Randall Kenan beyond the Final Frontier: Science Fiction, Superheroes, and the South in *A Visitation of Spirits*." *Southern Literary Journal* 43, no. 1 (2010): 125–50.

Coutinho, Eduardo de Faria. "'Learning How to Curse in the Master's Tongue': Stratégies du postcolonialisme Amérique latine." *Revue de Littérature Comparée* 4, no. 316 (2005): 467–76.

Cryer, Frederick. "Magic in Ancient Syria, Palestine, and in the Old Testament." In *Witchcraft and Magic in Europe: Biblical and Pagan Societies*, edited by Bengt Ankarloo and Stuart Clark, 97–146. Philadelphia: University of Pennsylvania Press, 2001.

Cubilié, Anne. *Women Witnessing Terror: Testimony and the Cultural Politics of Human Rights*. New York: Fordham University Press, 2005.

Cunningham, Michael. "Thinking about Fabulousness." In Vorlicky, *Tony Kushner*, 62–76.

Danahay, Martin A. "Breaking the Silence: Symbolic Violence and the Teaching of Contemporary 'Ethnic' Autobiography." *College Literature* 18, no. 3 (1991): 64–79.

Danet, Brenda, and Bryna Bogoch. "'Whoever Alters This, May God Turn His Face from Him on the Day of Judgment': Curses in Anglo-Saxon Legal Documents." *Journal of American Folklore* 105, no. 416 (1992): 132–65.

Darling, Marsha. "In the Realm of Responsibility: A Conversation with Toni Morrison." *Women's Review of Books* 5 (1988): 5–6.

Davis, Angela. *Blues Legacies and Black Feminism: Gertrude "Ma" Rainey, Bessie Smith, and Billy Holiday*. New York: Pantheon, 1998.

Davis, Colin. "Can the Dead Speak to Us? De Man, Levinas, Agamben." *Culture, Theory, and Critique* 45, no. 1 (2004): 77–89.

Dayan, Joan. "Amorous Bondage: Poe, Ladies, and Slaves." In Rosenheim and Rachman, *American Face*, 179–209.

———. "Poe, Persons, and Property." In Kennedy and Weissberg, *Romancing the Shadow*, 106–26.

Delgadillo, Theresa. "Forms of Chicana Feminist Resistance: Hybrid Spirituality in Ana Castillo's *So Far from God*." *Modern Fiction Studies* 44, no. 4 (1998): 888–916.

D'Emilio, John. *Lost Prophet: The Life and Times of Bayard Rustin*. New York: Free Press, 2003.

Dever, Carolyn. *Death and the Mother from Dickens to Freud: Victorian Fiction and the Anxiety of Origins*. Cambridge: Cambridge University Press, 1998.

Díaz, Junot. *The Brief and Wondrous Life of Oscar Wao*. New York: Riverhead, 2007.

Du Bois, W. E. B. *The Souls of Black Folk*. 1903. Reprint, New York: Oxford University Press, 2007.

Duck, Leigh Anne. *The Nation's Region: Southern Modernism, Segregation, and U.S. Nationalism*. Athens: University of Georgia Press, 2006.

Dufallo, Basil. *The Ghosts of the Past: Latin Literature, the Dead, and Rome's Transition to Principate*. Columbus: Ohio State University Press, 2007.

Edelman, Lee. *No Future: Queer Theory and the Death Drive*. Durham, NC: Duke University Press, 2004.

Edwards, Erin. "Extremities of the Body: The Anoptic Corporeality of *As I Lay Dying*." *Modern Fiction Studies* 55, no. 4 (2009): 739–64.

Elam, Michele. *The Souls of Mixed Folk: Race, Politics, and Aesthetics in the New Millennium*. Stanford, CA: Stanford University Press, 2011.

Esch, Deborah, and Jonathan Warren, eds. *The Turn of the Screw*, by Henry James. A Norton Critical Edition, 2nd ed. New York: W. W. Norton, 1999.

Etter, William. "'Tawdry Physical Affrightments': The Performance of Normalizing Visions of the Body in Edgar Allan Poe's 'Loss of Breath.'" *American Transcendental Quarterly* 17, no. 1 (2003): 5–22.

Fabi, Giulia. *Passing and the Rise of the African American Novel*. Urbana: University of Illinois Press, 2001.

Faherty, Duncan. "'Legitimate Sources' and 'Legitimate Results': Surveying the Social Terror of 'Usher' and 'Ligeia.'" In *Approaches to Teaching Poe's Prose and Poetry*, edited by Jeffrey Andrew Weinstock and Tony Magistrale, 39–47. New York: MLA, 2008.

Faulkner, William. *As I Lay Dying*. 1930. New York: Vintage, 1990.

Felman, Shoshana. "Turning the Screw of Interpretation." In *Literature and Psychoanalysis: The Question of Reading: Otherwise*, edited by Shoshana Felman, 94–207. Baltimore: Johns Hopkins University Press, 1982.

Foley, John M. *How to Read an Oral Poem*. Urbana: University of Illinois Press, 2002.

Fowler, Doreen. "Matricide and the Mother's Revenge: *As I Lay Dying*." *Faulkner Journal* 4 (1988/1989): 113–25.

Fraiman, Susan. *Unbecoming Women: British Women Writers and the Novel of Development*. New York: Columbia University Press, 1993.

Franklin, R. W., ed. *The Poems of Emily Dickson*. 3 vols. Cambridge, MA: Harvard University Press, 1998.

Freedman, Jonathan. "Angels, Monsters, and Jews: Intersections of Queer and Jewish Identity in Kushner's *Angels in America*." *PMLA* 113, no. 1 (1998): 90–102.

Freeman, Elizabeth, ed. *Queer Temporalities*. Special issue, *GLQ* 13.2/3 (2007).

Freud, Sigmund. *The Uncanny*. Translated by David McLintock. New York: Penguin, 2003.

Friedman, Alan Warren. *Fictional Death and the Modernist Enterprise*. Cambridge: Cambridge University Press, 1995.

Friedman, Lawrence M. *Dead Hands: A Social History of Wills, Trusts, and Inheritance Law*. Stanford, CA: Stanford University Press, 2009.

Fuss, Diana. "Corpse Poem." *Critical Inquiry* 30, no. 1 (2003): 1–30.

Gager, John G. *Curse Tablets and Binding Spells from the Ancient World*. New York: Oxford University Press, 1992.

Garber, Marjorie, and Rebecca L. Walkowitz, eds. *Secret Agents: The Rosenberg Case, McCarthyism, and Fifties America*. New York: Routledge, 1995.

Garner, Shirley Nelson. "Breaking Silence: The Woman Warrior." In *The Intimate Critique: Autobiographical Literary Criticism*, edited by Diane P. Freedman and Olivia Frey, 117–25. Durham, NC: Duke University Press, 1993.

Gentile, Kathy Justice. "Supernatural Transmissions: Turn-of-the-Century Ghosts in American Women's Fiction: Jewett, Freeman, Wharton, and Gilman." In *Approaches to Teaching Gothic Fiction: The British and American Traditions*, edited by Diane Long Hoeveler, 208–14. New York: Modern Language Association, 2003.

Ginsberg, Elaine, ed. *Passing and the Fictions of Identity*. Durham, NC: Duke University Press, 2003.

Goddu, Theresa. *Gothic America: Narrative, History, and Nation*. New York: Columbia University Press, 1997.

Goodwin, Sarah Webster, and Elisabeth Bronfen, eds. *Death and Representation*. Baltimore: Johns Hopkins University Press, 1993.

Gordon, Avery. *Ghostly Matters: Haunting and the Sociological Imagination*. Minneapolis: University of Minnesota Press, 1997.

Green, Carol Hurd. "The Suffering Body: Ethel Rosenberg in the Hands of the Writers." In Garber and Walkowitz, *Secret Agents*, 183–96.

Greenblatt, Stephen. *Learning to Curse: Essays in Early Modern Culture*. New York: Routledge, 1992.

Greven, David. *Men beyond Desire: Manhood, Sex, and Violation in American Literature*. New York: Palgrave McMillan, 2005.

Griffith, Jennifer. "Uncanny Spaces: Trauma, Cultural Memory, and the Female Body in Gayl Jones's *Corregidora* and Maxine Hong Kingston's *The Woman Warrior*." *Studies in the Novel* 38, no. 3 (2006): 353–70.

Griswold, Charles L. *Forgiveness: A Philosophical Exploration*. New York: Cambridge University Press, 2007.

Grossman, Lev. "Murdered, She Wrote." *Time*, July 1, 2002, 62.

Gwin, Minrose. *The Feminine and Faulkner: Reading (beyond) Sexual Difference*. Knoxville: University of Tennessee Press, 1990.

Handley, William. "The House a Ghost Built: Nommo, Allegory, and the Ethics of

Reading in Toni Morrison's *Beloved*." *Contemporary Literature* 36, no. 4 (1995): 676–701.

Harris, Trudier. "*Beloved*: Woman, Thy Name Is Demon." In Andrews and McKay, *Toni Morrison's "Beloved,"* 127–58.

———. "Escaping Slavery but Not Its Images." In *Toni Morrison: Critical Perspectives Past and Present*, edited by Henry Louis Gates Jr. and Anthony Appiah, 330–41. New York: Amistad, 1993.

———. *The Power of the Porch: The Storyteller's Craft in Zora Neale Hurston, Gloria Naylor, and Randall Kenan*. Athens: University of Georgia Press, 1996.

———. "Transformations of the Land in Randall Kenan's 'Foundations of the Earth.'" In *South of Tradition: Essays on African American Literature*, 160–74. Athens: University of Georgia Press, 2002.

Hausladen, Gary. *Places for Dead Bodies*. Austin: University of Texas Press, 2000.

Hayes, Kevin J. *The Cambridge Companion to Edgar Allan Poe*. Cambridge: Cambridge University Press, 2002.

H.D. "Eurydice." In *Collected Poems, 1912–1944*, edited by Louis Martz, 51–52. New York: New Directions, 1986.

Heinze, Ruediger. "Violations of Mimetic Epistemology in First-Person Narrative Fiction." *Narrative* 16, no. 3 (2008): 279–97.

Henderson, Carol E. *Scarring the Black Body: Race and Representation in African American Literature*. Columbia: University of Missouri Press, 2002.

Henderson, Desirée. "Understanding the Love and Fear of Death in Three Premature Burial Stories." In *Approaches to Teaching Poe's Prose and Poetry*, edited by Jeffrey Andrew Weinstock and Tony Magistrale, 69–75. New York: MLA, 2008.

Henderson, Mae G. "Toni Morrison's *Beloved*: Re-Membering the Body as Historical Text." In Andrews and McKay, *Toni Morrison's "Beloved,"* 79–106.

Hewson, Marc. "'My Children Were of Me Alone': Maternal Influence in Faulkner's *As I Lay Dying*." *Mississippi Quarterly* 53, no. 4 (2000): 551–67.

Holland, Sharon Patricia. "(Pro)Creating Imaginative Spaces and Other Queer Acts: Randall Kenan's *A Visitation of Spirits* and Its Revival of James Baldwin's Absent Black Gay Man in *Giovanni's Room*." In *James Baldwin Now*, edited by Dwight A. McBride, 265–88. New York: New York University Press, 1999.

———. *Raising the Dead: Readings of Death and (Black) Subjectivity*. Durham, NC: Duke University Press, 2000.

Holloway, Karla FC. *Passed On: African American Mourning Stories*. Durham, NC: Duke University Press, 2003.

———. *Private Bodies, Public Texts: Race, Gender, and a Cultural Bioethics*. Durham, NC: Duke University Press, 2011.

Hotz, Mary Elizabeth. *Literary Remains: Representations of Death and Burial in Victorian England*. Albany: SUNY Press, 2009.

Hovis, George. "'I Contain Multitudes': Randall Kenan's *Walking on Water* as Collective Autobiography." *Southern Literary Journal* 36, no. 2 (2004): 100–125.

Hoy, Jody. "To Be Able to See the Tao." 1986. Reprinted in Skenazy and Martin, *Conversations with Maxine Hong Kingston*, 47–66.

Hunt, V. "A Conversation with Randall Kenan." *African American Review* 29, no. 3 (1995): 411–20.

Hurston, Zora Neale. *Dust Tracks on the Road*. 1942. Reprint, New York: Harper Perennial, 2006.

———. *Mules and Men*. 1935. Reprint, New York: Harper Perennial, 1990.

———. *Their Eyes Were Watching God*. 1937. Reprint, New York: Harper Perennial, 2006.

Jackson, John L., Jr. "Little Black Magic." *Racial Americana*. Special issue, *South Atlantic Quarterly* 104, no. 3 (2005): 393–402.

Jackson, Leon. "'Behold Our Literary Mohawk, Poe': Literary Nationalism and the 'Indianation' of Antebellum American Culture." *ESQ* 48, nos. 1–2 (2002): 97–133.

Jacobs, Harriet. *Incidents in the Life of a Slave Girl*. 1861. Reprint, New York: Oxford University Press, 1998.

James, Henry. *The Turn of the Screw*. 1908 New York edition. Reprinted in *The Turn of the Screw and The Aspern Papers*, 143–262. New York: Penguin, 1986.

JanMohamed, Abdul R. *The Death-Bound Subject: Richard Wright's Archaeologies of Death*. Durham, NC: Duke University Press, 2005.

Jentsch, Ernst. "On the Psychology of the Uncanny." Translated by Roy Sellars. *Angelaki* 2, no. 1 (1995): 7–16.

Jermyn, Deborah. "You Can't Keep a Dead Woman Down: The Female Corpse and Textual Disruption in Contemporary Hollywood." In *Images of the Corpse: From the Renaissance to Cyberspace*, edited by Elizabeth Klaver, 153–68. Madison, WI: Popular, 2004.

Johnson, Barbara. "Apostrophe, Animation, and Abortion." *Diacritics* 16, no. 1 (1986): 29–47.

———. "The Quicksands of the Self: Nella Larsen and Heinz Kohut." Chap. 2 in *The Feminist Difference: Literature, Psychoanalysis, Race, and Gender*. Cambridge, MA: Harvard University Press, 1998.

Jones, Suzanne. *Race Mixing: Southern Fiction since the Sixties*. Baltimore: Johns Hopkins University Press, 2004.

Jurca, Catherine. *White Diaspora: The Suburb and the Twentieth-Century Novel*. Princeton, NJ: Princeton University Press, 2001.

Kakutani, Michiko. "The Power of Love Leaps the Great Divide of Death." *New York Times*, June 18, 2002, E1.

Kammen, Michael. *Digging Up the Dead: A History of Notable American Reburials*. Chicago: University of Chicago Press, 2010.

Kaplan, Amy. *The Anarchy of Empire in the Making of U. S. Culture*. Cambridge, MA: Harvard University Press, 2003.

———. "'Left Alone with America': The Absence of Empire in the Study of American Culture." In *Cultures of United States Imperialism*, edited by Amy Kaplan and Donald Pease, 3–21. Durham, NC: Duke University Press, 1993.

Kauffman, Lane. "The Skewed Path: Essaying as Unmethodical Method." In *Essays on the Essay: Redefining a Genre*, edited by Alexander Butrym, 221–40. Athens: University of Georgia Press, 1989.

Kenan, Randall. *Let the Dead Bury Their Dead*. San Diego: Harcourt, Brace, 1992.

———. *A Visitation of Spirits*. New York: Grove Press, 1989.

———. *Walking on Water: Black American Lives at the Turn of the Twenty-First Century*. New York: Knopf, 1999.

Kennedy, J. Gerald, and Lilianne Weissberg, eds. *Romancing the Shadow: Poe and Race*. New York: Oxford University Press, 2001.

Kibbie, Anna Louise. "The Estate, the Corpse, and the Letter: Possession in *Clarissa*." *ELH* 74, no. 1 (2007): 117–43.

Kincaid, Nanci. "As Me and Addie Lay Dying." *Southern Review* 30, no. 3 (1994): 582–95.

Kingston, Maxine Hong. *The Woman Warrior: Memoirs of a Girlhood among Ghosts*. New York: Vintage, 1975.

Klaver, Elizabeth, ed. *Images of the Corpse: From the Renaissance to Cyberspace*. Madison, WI: Popular Press, 2004.

Kneale, Douglas. "Romantic Aversions: Apostrophe Reconsidered." *ELH* 58, no. 1 (1991): 141–65.

Konstan, David. *Before Forgiveness: The Origins of a Moral Idea*. New York: Cambridge University Press, 2010.

Kowalski, Robin M. *Complaining, Teasing, and Other Annoying Behaviors*. New Haven, CT: Yale University Press, 2003.

Kristeva, Julia. *Powers of Horror: An Essay on Abjection*. Translated by Leon S. Roudie. New York: Columbia University Press, 1982.

Krumholz, Linda. "The Ghosts of Slavery: Historical Recovery in Toni Morrison's *Beloved*." In Andrews and McKay, *Toni Morrison's "Beloved,"* 107–26.

Kushner, Tony. *Angels in America*. 1995. Reprint, New York: Theater Communications Groups, 2003.

———. *Thinking about the Longstanding Problems of Virtue and Happiness: Essays, a Play, Two Poems and a Prayer*. New York: Theater Communications Group, 1995.

Lacan, Jacques. "L'Éclat d'Antigone." 1960. Vol. 7, *La Séminaire de Jacques Lacan*, 285–331. Paris: Sevil, 1986.

Lanza, Carmela Delia. "Hearing Voices: Women and Home in Ana Castillo's *So Far from God*." *MELUS* 23, no. 1 (1998): 65–79.

Larsen, Nella. *Passing*. 1929. Reprinted in *Quicksand and Passing*, 143–242. New Brunswick, NJ: Rutgers University Press, 1986.

Lazare, Aaron. *On Apology*. New York: Oxford University Press, 2004.

Lee, Ken-fang. "Cultural Translation and the Exorcist: A Reading of Kingston's and Tan's Ghost Stories." *MELUS* 29, no. 2 (2004): 105–27.

Levine, Robert. *Dislocating Race and Nation: Episodes in Nineteenth-Century American Literary Nationalism*. Chapel Hill: University of North Carolina Press, 2008.

Lewis, Leslie. *Telling Narratives: Secrets in African American Literature*. Urbana: University of Illinois Press, 2007.

Lim, Jeehyum. "Cutting the Tongue: Language and the Body in Kingston's *The Woman Warrior*." *MELUS* 31, no. 3 (2006): 49–65.

Lim, Shirley Geok-lin, ed. *Approaches to Teaching Kingston's "The Woman Warrior."* New York: MLA, 1991.

Liman, James. "Addie in No-Man's-Land." In *Faulkner and War: Faulkner and Yoknapatawpha, 2001*, edited by Noel Polk and Ann J. Abadie, 36–54. Jackson: University of Mississippi Press, 2004.

Linafelt, Tod. "The Undecidability of Barak in the Prologue to Job and Beyond." *Biblical Interpretation* 4, no. 2 (1996): 154–72.

Lioi, Anthony. "An End to Cosmic Loneliness: Alice Walker's Essays as Abolitionist Enchantment." *ISLE* 15, no. 1 (2008): 11–37.

Loeffelholz, Mary. "Poetry, Slavery, and Personification: Mary Lowell's 'Africa.'" *Studies in Romanticism* 38, no. 2 (1999): 171–202.

Lopate. Philip. *The Art of the Personal Essay*. New York: Doubleday, 1994.

Lorde, Audre. "The Transformation of Silence into Language and Action." 1978. In *Sister Outsider*, 40–44. Berkeley, CA: Crossing Press, 1984.

Lubiano, Wahneema, ed. *The House That Race Built: Black Americans, U.S. Terrain*. New York: Pantheon, 1997.

Luck, Georg. *Arcana Mundi: Magic and the Occult in the Greek and Roman Worlds*. 2nd ed. Baltimore: Johns Hopkins University Press, 2006.

Lustig, T. J. *Henry James and the Ghostly*. Cambridge: Cambridge University Press, 1994.

Lutz, Gretchen Kay. "Save Me from the Fall, Mythic Mother: The Curse Motif in Four Traditional Medieval Ballads." *Mid-America Folklore* 18, no. 1 (1990): 27–33.

Lynch, Eve M. "Spectral Politics: The Victorian Ghost Story and the Domestic Servant." In Brown and Burdett, *Victorian Supernatural*, 67–86.

Madoff, Ray D. *Immortality and the Law: The Rising Power of the American Dead*. New Haven, CT: Yale University Press, 2010.

Martin, Philip. "Imagination." In *The Handbook of the Gothic*, 2nd ed., edited by Marie Mulvey-Roberts, 193–97. New York: New York University Press, 2009.

Matthews, John T. Preface. *Faulkner and Death*. Special Issue, *Faulkner Journal* 24, no. 2 (2009): 3–6.

Mbembé, Achille. "Necropolitics." Translated by Libby Meintjes. *Public Culture* 15, no. 1 (2003): 11–40.

McCoy, Sheila Smith. "Rescuing the Black Homosexual Lambs: Randall Kenan and the Reconstruction of Southern Gay Masculinity." In *Contemporary Black Men's Fiction and Drama*, edited by Keith Clark, 15–36. Urbana: University of Illinois Press; 2001.

McDowell, Deborah. Introduction to *Passing and Quicksand*, by Nella Larsen, ix–xxxv. New Brunswick, NJ: Rutgers University Press, 1986.

McGill, Meredith. *American Literature and the Culture of Reprinting, 1834–1853*. Philadelphia: University of Pennsylvania Press, 2003.

McMillan, Laurie. "Telling a Critical Story: Alice Walker's *In Search of Our Mothers' Gardens*." *Journal of Modern Literature* 28, no. 1 (2004): 107–23.

McRuer, Robert. "Queer Locations, Queer Transformations: Randall Kenan's *A Visitation of Spirits*." In *South to a New Place: Region, Literature, Culture*, edited by Suzanne W. Jones and Sharon Monteith, 184–95. Baton Rouge: Louisiana State University Press, 2002.

———. "A Visitation of Difference: Randall Kenan and Black Queer Theory." In *Critical Essays: Gay and Lesbian Writers of Color*, edited by Emmanuel S. Nelson, 221–32. New York: Haworth, 1993.

Meeropol, Michael, ed. *The Rosenberg Letters: A Complete Edition of the Prison Correspondence of Julius and Ethel Rosenberg*. New York: Garland, 1994.

Metress, Christopher. "'No Justice, No Peace': The Figure of Emmett Till in African American Literature." *MELUS* 28, no. 1 (2003): 87–103.

Michael, Magali Cornier. *New Visions of Community in Contemporary American Fiction: Tan, Kingsolver, Castillo, Morrison*. Iowa City: University of Iowa Press, 2006.

Michasiw, Kim Ian. "Some Stations of Suburban Gothic." In *American Gothic: New Interventions in a National Narrative*, edited by Robert K. Martin and Eric Savoy, 237–58. Iowa City: University of Iowa Press, 1998.

Millard, Kenneth. *Coming of Age in Contemporary American Fiction*. Edinburgh: Edinburgh University Press, 2007.

Miller, Perry. *Errand into the Wilderness*. Cambridge, MA: Harvard University Press, 1956.

Mittlefehldt, Pamela Kiss. "'A Weaponry of Choice': Black American Women Writers and the Essay." In *The Politics of the Essay: Feminist Perspectives*, edited by Ruth-Ellen Boetcher Joeres and Elizabeth Mittman, 196–208. Bloomington: Indiana University Press, 1993.

Morante, Linda. "From Silence to Song: The Triumph of Maxine Hong Kingston." *Frontiers* 9, no. 2 (1987): 78–82.

Morrison, Toni. *Beloved*. 1987. Reprint, New York: Vintage, 2004.

———. *Playing in the Dark: Whiteness and the Literary Imagination*. Cambridge, MA: Harvard University Press, 1992.

Morrow, Collette. "Queering Chicano/a Narratives: The Lesbian as Healer, Saint, and Warrior in Ana Castillo's *So Far from God*." *Journal of the Midwest Modern Language Association* 30, nos. 1–2 (1997): 63–80.

Muñoz, José Esteban. *Cruising Utopia: The Then and There of Queer Futurity*. New York: New York University Press, 2009.

Murphy, Michael. "Vows, Boast, and Taunts, and the Role of Women in Some Medieval Literature." *English Studies* 2 (1985): 105–12.

Nagel, James. *The Contemporary American Short Story Cycle*. Baton Rouge: Louisiana State University Press, 2001.

Nair, Supriya. *Caliban's Curse: George Lamming and the Revisioning of History*. Ann Arbor: University of Michigan Press, 1996.

Neville, John F. *The Press, the Rosenbergs, and the Cold War*. Westport, CT: Praeger, 1995.

Newton, Judith, and Judith Stacey. "Learning Not to Curse, or, Feminist Predicaments in Cultural Criticism by Men: Our Movie Date with James Clifford and Stephen Greenblatt." *Cultural Critique* 23 (1992): 51–82.

Ngai, Mae. *Impossible Subjects: Illegal Aliens and the Making of Modern America*. Princeton, NJ: Princeton University Press, 2005.

Ngai, Sianne. *Ugly Feelings*. Cambdrige, MA: Harvard University Press, 2005.

Norman, Brian. *The American Protest Essay and National Belonging: Addressing Division*. Albany: SUNY Press, 2007.

———. "The Historical Uncanny: Segregation Signs in *Getting Mother's Body*, a Post–Civil Rights American Novel." *African American Review* 43, nos. 2–3 (2009): 443–56.

———. *Neo-Segregation Narratives: Jim Crow in Post–Civil Rights American Literature*. Athens: University of Georgia Press, 2010.

Nussbaum, Martha. *From Disgust to Humanity: Sexual Orientation and Constitutional Law*. New York: Oxford University Press, 2010.

Ogden, Daniel. "Binding Spells: Curse Tablets and Voodoo Dolls in the Greek and Roman Worlds." In *Witchcraft and Magic in Europe: Ancient Greece and Rome*, edited by Bengt Ankarloo and Stuart Clark, 1–90. Philadelphia: University of Pennsylvania Press, 1999.

———. *Magic, Witchcraft, and Ghosts in the Greek and Roman Worlds*. 2nd ed. New York: Oxford University Press, 2009.

Ong, Walter J. *Orality and Literacy*. 2nd ed. New York: Routledge, 1992.

Palca, Joe, and Flora Lichtman. *Annoying: The Science of What Bugs Us*. Hoboken, NJ: John Wiley and Sons, 2011.

Parks, Suzan-Lori. *Getting Mother's Body*. New York: Random House, 2003.

Patterson, Orlando. *Slavery and Social Death*. Cambridge, MA: Harvard University Press, 1982.

Peeples, Scott. "Poe's 'Constructiveness' and 'The Fall of the House of Usher.'" In Hayes, *Cambridge Companion to Edgar Allan Poe*, 178–90.

Perdigao, Lisa. *From Modernist Entombment to Postmodernist Exhumation: Dead Bodies in Twentieth-Century American Fiction*. Hampshire, UK: Ashgate, 2010.

Perdigao, Lisa, and Mark Pizzato, eds. *Death in American Texts and Performances: Ghosts, Corpses, and the Reanimated Dead*. Hampshire, UK: Ashgate, 2010.

Pérez, Gail. "Ana Castillo as Santera: Reconstructing Popular Religious Praxis." In *A Reader in Latina Feminist Theology: Religion and Justice*, edited by María Aquino, Daisy L. Machado, and Jeanette Rodríguez, 53–79. Austin: University of Texas Press, 2002.

Pfeiffer, Kathleen. *Racepassing and American Individualism*. Amherst: University of Massachusetts Press, 2003.

Phillips, Bob, and Kimberly Alyn. *How to Deal with Annoying People: What to Do When You Can't Avoid Them*. Eugene, OR: Harvest House, 2005.

Pile, Judith. "Poe and the Revenge of the Exquisite Corpse." *Studies in American Fiction* 26, no. 2 (1998): 171–92.

Piper, Karen. "The Signifying Corpse: Re-reading Kristeva on Marguerite Duras." *Cultural Critique* 31, no. 1 (1995): 159–77.

Plasa, Carl. *Columbia Critical Guides: Toni Morrison,* Beloved. New York: Columbia University Press, 1998.

Platt, Kamala. "Ecocritical Chicana Literature: Castillo's 'Virtual Realism.'" *ISLE* 3, no. 1 (1996): 67–96.

Pocock, J. G. A. "The Ideal of Citizenship since Classical Times." In *The Citizenship Debates: A Reader*, edited by Gershon Shafir, 31–42. Minneapolis: University of Minnesota Press, 1998.

Poe, Edgar Allan. *Collected Works*, edited by Thomas Olive Mabbott, 3 vols. Cambridge, MA: Harvard University Press, 1969.

———. "The Fall of the House of Usher." 1839. Reprinted in *Poetry and Tales*, 317–36. New York: Modern Library, 1984.

Pollack, Harriet, and Christopher Metress, eds. *Emmett Till in Literary Memory and Imagination*. Baton Rouge: Louisiana State University Press, 2008.

Poole, Ralph J. "Body/Rituals: The (Homo)Erotics of Death in Elizabeth Stuart Phelps, Rose Terry Cooke, and Edgar Allan Poe." In *Soft Canons: American Women Writers and Masculine Tradition*, edited by Karen L. Kilcup, 239–61. Iowa City: University of Iowa Press, 1999.

Posnock, Ross. "Roy Cohn in America." *Raritan* 13, no. 3 (1994): 64–77.

Presner, Todd Samuel. "'The Fabrication of Corpses': Heidegger, Arendt, and the Modernity of Mass Death." *Telos* 135 (2006): 84–108.

Puig, Claudia. "Between Book and Film, 'Bones' Breaks." *USA Today*, December 11, 2009, 2D.

Rabinowitz, Paula. "Eccentric Memories: A Conversation with Maxine Hong Kingston." 1987. Reprinted in Skenazy and Martin, *Conversations with Maxine Hong Kingston*, 67–76.

Raymond, Claire. *The Posthumous Voice in Women's Writing from Mary Shelley to Sylvia Plath*. Hampshire, UK: Ashgate, 2006.

Raynaud, Claudine. "*Beloved* or the Shifting Shapes of Memory." In *The Cambridge Companion to Toni Morrison*, edited by Justine Tally, 43–58. Cambridge: Cambridge University Press, 2007.

Reddy, Maureen T. "Race and American Crime Fiction." In *The Cambridge Companion to American Crime Fiction*, edited by Catherine Ross Nickerson, 135–47. Cambridge: Cambridge University Press, 2010.

Reinhardt, Mark. "Who Speaks for Margaret Garner? Slavery, Silence, and the Politics of Ventriloquism." *Critical Inquiry* 29, no. 1 (2002): 81–119.

———. *Who Speaks for Margaret Garner? The True Story That Inspired Toni Morrison's "Beloved."* Minneapolis: University of Minnesota Press, 2010.

Rich, Adrienne. *Poems: Selected and New, 1950–1974*. New York: W. W. Norton, 1975.

———. "When We Dead Awaken: Writing as Re-vision." 1971. Reprinted in *On Lies,*

Secrets, and Silence: Selected Prose, 1966–1978, 33–50. New York: W. W. Norton, 1995.

Ripstein, Arthur. "Philosophy of Tort Law." In *The Oxford Handbook of Jurisprudence and Philosophy of Law*, edited by Jules Coleman and Scott Shapiro, 656–86. New York: Oxford University Press, 2004.

Rishoi, Christy. *From Girl to Woman: American Women's Coming-of-Age Narratives*. Albany: SUNY Press, 2003.

Rivkin, Julie. *False Positions: The Representational Logics of Henry James's Fiction*. Stanford, CA: Stanford University Press, 1996.

Roach, Joseph. *Cities of the Dead: Circum-Atlantic Performance*. New York: Columbia University Press, 1995.

Roach, Mary. *Stiff: The Curious Lives of Human Cadavers*. New York: W. W. Norton, 2003.

Robben, Antonius C. G. M., ed. *Death, Mourning, and Burial: A Cross-Cultural Reader*. Malden, MA: Blackwell, 2004.

Robbins, Bruce. *The Servant's Hand: English Fiction from Below*. Durham, NC: Duke University Press, 1993.

———. "'They Don't Much Count, Do They?': The Unfinished History of *The Turn of the Screw*." In *Case Studies in Contemporary Criticism: The Turn of the Screw*, 3rd ed., edited by Peter G. Beidler, 376–89. Boston: Bedford / St. Martin's, 2010.

Robinson, E. Arthur. "Order and Sentience in 'The Fall of the House of Usher.'" *PMLA* 76, no. 1 (1961): 68–81.

Rodriguez, Ralph. "Chicana/o Fiction from Resistance to Contestation: The Role of Creation in Ana Castillo's *So Far from God*." *MELUS* 25, no. 2 (2000): 63–82.

Rosenheim, Shawn, and Stephen Rachman, eds. *The American Face of Edgar Allan Poe*. Baltimore: Johns Hopkins University Press, 1995.

Ross, Marlon B. "Beyond the Closet as Raceless Paradigm." In *Black Queer Studies*, edited by E. Patrick Johnson and Mae G. Henderson, 161–89. Durham, NC: Duke University Press, 2005.

———. *Manning the Race: Reforming Black Men in the Jim Crow Era*. New York: New York University Press, 2004.

Ross, Stephen M. Reply to Shari Benstock. *PMLA* 94, no. 5 (1979): 958–59.

Rowe, John Carlos. *The Other Henry James*. Durham, NC: Duke University Press, 1998.

Royle, Nicolas. *The Uncanny*. New York: Routledge, 2003.

Rushdy, Ashraf. "Daughters Signifyin(g) History: The Example of Toni Morrison's *Beloved*." In Andrews and McKay, *Toni Morrison's "Beloved,"* 37–66.

———. *Remembering Generations: Race and Family in Contemporary African American Fiction*. Chapel Hill: University of North Carolina Press, 2001.

Saeta, Elsa. "A *MELUS* Interview: Ana Castillo." *MELUS* 22, no. 3 (1997): 133–49.

Sato, Gayle K. Fujita. "*The Woman Warrior* as a Search for Ghosts." In S. Lim, *Approaches to Teaching*, 138–45.

Savoye, Jeffrey. "Sinking under Iniquity." *Edgar Allan Poe Review* 8, no. 1 (2007): 70–74.

Scarry, Elaine. *On Beauty and Being Just*. Princeton, NJ: Princeton University Press, 1999.

Schneir, Walter, and Miriam Schneir. *Invitation to an Inquest*. London: W. H. Allen, 1966.

Schwab, Gabrielle. "The Multiple Lives of Addie Bundren's Dead Body: On William Faulkner's *As I Lay Dying*." In *The Other Perspective in Gender and Culture: Rewriting Women and the Symbolic*, edited by Juliet Flower MacCannell, 209–41. New York: Columbia University Press, 1990.

Schweik, Susan. *The Ugly Laws: Disability in Public*. New York: New York University Press, 2009.

Schwenger, Peter. "Corpsing the Image." *Critical Inquiry* 26, no. 3 (2000): 395–413.

Seale, Clive. *Constructing Death: The Sociology of Dying and Bereavement*. Cambridge: Cambridge University Press, 1998.

Sebold, Alice. *The Lovely Bones*. New York: Little, Brown, 2002.

———. "The Oddity of Suburbia." In "A Reading Group Guide," *The Lovely Bones*, 2–3. New York: Little, Brown, 2004.

Selley, April Rose. "Satisfied Shivering: Emily Dickinson's Deceased Speakers." *ESQ* 37, nos. 2–3 (1991): 215–33.

Shewey, Don. "Tony Kushner's Sexy Ethics." *Village Voice*, April 20, 1993, 29–32, 36.

Shockley, Evie. "Buried Alive: Gothic Homelessness, Black Women's Sexuality, and (Living) Death in Ann Petry's *The Street*." *African American Review* 40, no. 3 (2006): 439–60.

Skenazy, Paul, and Tera Martin, eds. *Conversations with Maxine Hong Kingston*. Jackson: University of Mississippi Press, 1998.

Skloot, Rebecca. *The Immortal Life of Henrietta Lacks*. New York: Crown, 2010.

Slankard, Tamara. "'No Such Thing as Was': The Fetishized Corpse, Modernism, and *As I Lay Dying*." *Faulkner Journal* 24, no. 2 (2009): 7–28.

Smajic, Srdjan. "The Trouble with Ghost-Seeing: Vision, Ideology, and Genre in the Victorian Ghost Story." *ELH* 70, no. 4 (2003): 1107–35.

Smith, Suzanne E. *To Serve the Living: Funeral Directors and the African American Way of Death*. Cambridge, MA: Harvard University Press, 2010.

Socarides, Alexandra. "The Poetics of Interruption: Dickinson, Death, and the Fascicles." In *A Companion to Emily Dickinson*, edited by Mary Loeffelholtz and Martha Nell Smith, 309–33. Hoboken, NJ: Blackwell, 2008.

Solomon, Alisa. "Wrestling with *Angels*: A Jewish Fantasia." In *Approaching the Millennium: Essays on "Angels in America,"* edited by Deborah R. Geis and Steven F. Kruger, 118–33. Ann Arbor: University of Michigan Press, 1998.

Somerville, Siobhan. *Queering the Color Line: Race and the Invention of Homosexuality in American Culture*. Durham, NC: Duke University Press, 2000.

Sperling, Daniel. *Posthumous Interests: Legal and Ethical Perspectives*. Cambridge: Cambridge University Press, 2011.

Spillers, Hortense. "'All the Things That You Could Be by Now, If Sigmund Freud's Wife Was Your Mother': Psychoanalysis and Race." In *Female Subjects in Black and*

White: Race, Psychoanalysis, Feminism, edited by Elizabeth Abel, Barbara Christian, and Helene Moglen, 135–58. Berkeley: University of California Press, 1997.

Stanford, Ann Fallwell. *Bodies in a Broken World: Women Novelists of Color and the Politics of Medicine*. Chapel Hill: University of North Carolina Press, 2003.

Stockton, Kathryn Bond. "Erotic Corpse: Homosexual Miscegenation and the Decomposition of Attraction." Chap. 4 in *Beautiful Bottom, Beautiful Shame: Where "Black" Meets "Queer."* Durham, NC: Duke University Press, 2006.

———. *The Queer Child, or Growing Sideways in the Twentieth Century*. Durham, NC: Duke University Press, 2009.

Stowe, Harriet Beecher. *Uncle Tom's Cabin; or, Life among the Lowly*. New York: Modern Library, 2001.

Su, John J. "Ghosts of Essentialism: Racial Memory as Epistemological Claim." *American Literature* 81, no. 2 (2009): 361–86.

Tambling, Jeffrey. *Becoming Posthumous: Life and Death in Literary and Cultural Studies*. Edinburgh: Edinburgh University Press, 2001.

Tanner, Laura E. *Lost Bodies: Inhabiting the Borders of Life and Death*. Ithaca, NY: Cornell University Press, 2006.

Tate, Claudia. *Psychoanalysis and Black Novels: Desire and the Protocols of Race*. New York: Oxford University Press, 1998.

Tettenborn, Éva. "'But What If I Can't Change?': Desire, Denial, and Melancholia in Randall Kenan's *A Visitation of Spirits*." *Southern Literary Journal* 40, no. 2 (2008): 249–66.

Thiselton, Anthony. "The Supposed Power of Words in Biblical Writings." *Journal of Theological Studies* 25 (1974): 283–99.

Thorburn, David. "The Rosenberg Letters." In Garber and Walkowitz, *Secret Agents*, 171–82.

Torres, Hector. *Conversations with Contemporary Chicana and Chicano Writers*. Albuquerque: University of New Mexico Press, 2007.

Tucker, Lindsey. "Gay Identity, Conjure, and the Uses of Postmodern Ethnography in the Fictions of Randall Kenan." *Modern Fiction Studies* 49, no. 2 (2003): 306–31.

United States Justice Department. "September 11th Victim Compensation Fund of 2001." www.justice.gov/archive/victimcompensation. Accessed August 20, 2010.

Urbrock, William. "Blessing and Curse." In *Anchor Bible Dictionary*, vol. 1, 755–61. New York: Doubleday, 1992.

Vendler, Helen. *Dickinson: Selected Poems and Commentaries*. Cambridge, MA: Harvard University Press, 2010.

Verdery, Katherine. *The Political Lives of Dead Bodies: Reburial and Postsocialist Change*. New York: Columbia University Press, 1999.

Vorlicky, Robert, ed. *Tony Kushner in Conversation*. Ann Arbor: University of Michigan Press, 1998.

Walker, Alice. *In Love and Trouble*. 1973. Reprint, New York: Mariner, 2003.

———. *In Search of Our Mother's Gardens*. San Diego: Harcourt, Brace, 1983.

Walker, Melissa. *Down from the Mountaintop: Black Women's Novels in the Wake of the Civil Rights Movement, 1966–1989*. New Haven, CT: Yale University Press, 1991.

Wall, Cheryl. "On Freedom and the Will to Adorn: Debating Aesthetics and/as Ideology." In *Aesthetics and Ideology*, edited by George Levine, 283–303. New Brunswick, NJ: Rutgers University Press, 1994.

———. *Worrying the Line: Black Women Writers, Lineage, and Literary Tradition*. Chapel Hill: University of North Carolina Press, 2005.

Walton, Priscilla, and Manina Jones. *Detective Agency: Women Rewriting the Hard-Boiled Tradition*. Berkeley: University of California Press, 1999.

Wardi, Anissa. *Death and the Arc of Mourning in African American Literature*. Gainesville: University Press of Florida, 2003.

Warner, Michael. *Publics and Counterpublics*. New York: Zone Books, 2002.

Washington, Theresa. *Our Mothers, Our Powers, Our Texts: Manifestations of Àjẹ̀ in Africana Literature*. Indianapolis: Indiana University Press, 2005.

Weekes, Karen. "Poe's Feminine Ideal." In Hayes, *Cambridge Companion to Edgar Allan Poe*, 148–62.

Wester, Maisha. "Haunting and Haunted Queerness: Randall Kenan's Re-inscription of Difference in *A Visitation of Spirits*." *Callaloo* 30, no. 4 (2007): 1035–53.

Whalen, Terence. *Edgar Allan Poe and the Masses: The Political Economy of Literature in Antebellum America*. Princeton, NJ: Princeton University Press, 1999.

Worthington, Marjorie. "Posthumous Posturing: The Subversive Power of Death in Contemporary Women's Fiction." *Studies in the Novel* 32, no. 2 (2000): 243–63.

Young, Elizabeth. *Black Frankenstein: The Making of an American Metaphor*. New York: New York University Press, 2008.

Zamora, Lois Parkinson, and Wendy B. Faris, eds. *Magical Realism: Theory, History, Community*. Durham, NC: Duke University Press, 1995.

Zeitlin, Judith T. *The Phantom Heroine: Ghosts and Gender in Seventeenth-Century Chinese Literature*. Honolulu: University of Hawaii Press, 2007.

Zimmerman, Susan. "Psychoanalysis and the Corpse." *Shakespeare Studies* 33 (2005): 101–8.

INDEX